THE COMPLETE GUIDE TO
Crafts

THE COMPLETE GUIDE TO

Crafts

Oceana

AN OCEANA BOOK

This book is produced by
Quantum Publishing Ltd
6 Blundell Street
London N7 9BH

ISBN 1-84573-158-1

QUMCGT5

Manufactured in Singapore by
Pica Digital Pte. Ltd

Printed in Singapore by
Star Standard Industries Pte. Ltd

CONTENTS

DECORATIVE TILING

Tiles are attractive to look at, permanent, easy to maintain and extraordinarily versatile. They are also one of the oldest forms of decorative surface, whether it is from illustrations of ancient Babylonian gateways or from Victorian public houses. Although they are usually seen on large, flat surfaces, especially on walls in kitchens and bathrooms, there is no reason why they should not be used in other areas of the home or to produce decorative objects in their own right. They have been widely used for years in warm countries, especially those around the Mediterranean. The ideas in this chapter have been desi designed to show how tiles can be used relatively easily to produce a variety of ornamental objects. Once you have mastered the techniques, you will be able to use the ideas here to inspire you to try tiles

in other, more adventurous and imaginative ways. And, despite what you might think, tiles are actually a remarkably easy material to work with, and the results can look stunning. From simple abstract patterns to more elaborate decorative creations, there is no limit to what can be achieved.

MATERIALS AND EQUIPMENT

Ceramic tiles are widely available from countless suppliers in an enormous range of styles and sizes. In fact, choosing tiles can be quite a daunting experience. Once you have made your selection, however, the skills needed are straightforward and easy to learn, and you are likely already to have most of the tools you will need in your standard household tool kit.

If there is one near to you where you live, it is probably worth visiting a specialist tile shop. Not only will you be able to look at a vast range of tiles, but you will also be able to ask for advice about using them in the best possible ways.

TIP
■ Check carefully whether the tiles you are using are sized in metric or imperial units. Sometimes the slight difference is unimportant, but it could ruin a project. Measure before you begin—it is easy to adjust measurements before cutting, impossible afterwards.

Below: It is worth investing in a tile cutter for accuracy and convenience.

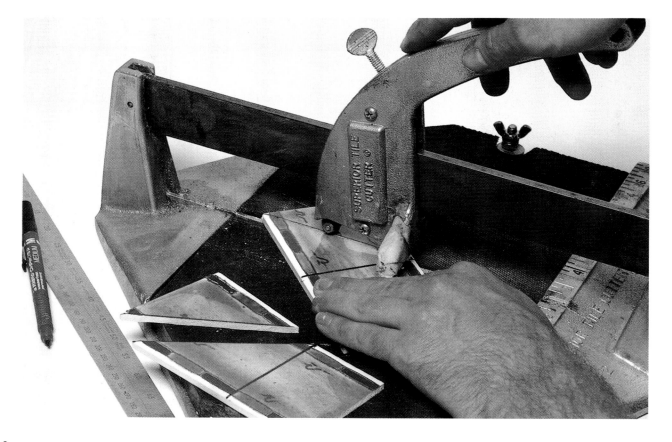

TILES

At their most basic, ceramic tiles are flat slabs of fired clay, usually covered with a glaze to protect the surface or with a decoration of some kind. They are hard and brittle, but extremely durable. They range in size from mosaic pieces about ¾ in. (15 mm) square to floor tiles that are 12 in. (30 cm) square; floor tiles are often, but not always, larger than wall tiles. Rectangular tiles are becoming increasingly popular, although they have always been successfully used in public areas such as underground railway stations. Interlocking shapes are also sometimes used for floors. Tiles may be plain-colored, screen-printed, hand-painted, or decorated by a combination of techniques. Raised images are sometimes incorporated, especially to give a period or traditional appearance to an area.

WALL TILES

There are practically no limits to the size, colors and designs of wall tiles, but they are most often about 4 in. (10 cm) or about 6 in. (15 cm) square, with the 6 in. (15 cm) squares being most widely used. You will, therefore, find the greatest range of designs and colors in this size.

TIP
- All the quantities and dimensions are given in both metric and imperial units. The measurements are not interchangeable, however, and you should keep to one system or the other.

MOSAIC TILES

Small tiles are generally known as mosaics, and they were used in the past for large, decorative panels in churches and other public buildings. Although they may be made of ceramic, they are often made of glass, and they are usually sold in sheets of a single color. Most are square, although interlocking shapes are also available. Ceramic mosaics are hard-wearing and can be used for floors in entrance halls, where they can be arranged to create images or even names. Glass mosaics are more often used on walls or in swimming pools, and they are not available in such a wide range of colors as the ceramic equivalents.

BORDER TILES

There are few better ways of enlivening a room than by introducing some of these brightly colored strips, which are enjoying something of a revival. They are usually available in lengths of 6 in. (15 cm) or 8 in. (20 cm), in almost every possible width, and they can be used to edge any other size of tile.

EMBOSSED OR RAISED TILES

Although these tend to be slightly more expensive than plain tiles, they are widely available and they are worth using to give an extra special finish.

TIP
- Cut tiles have surprisingly sharp edges, so take care that you do not nick your fingers as you handle them. Clear away any broken pieces immediately to avoid accidents.

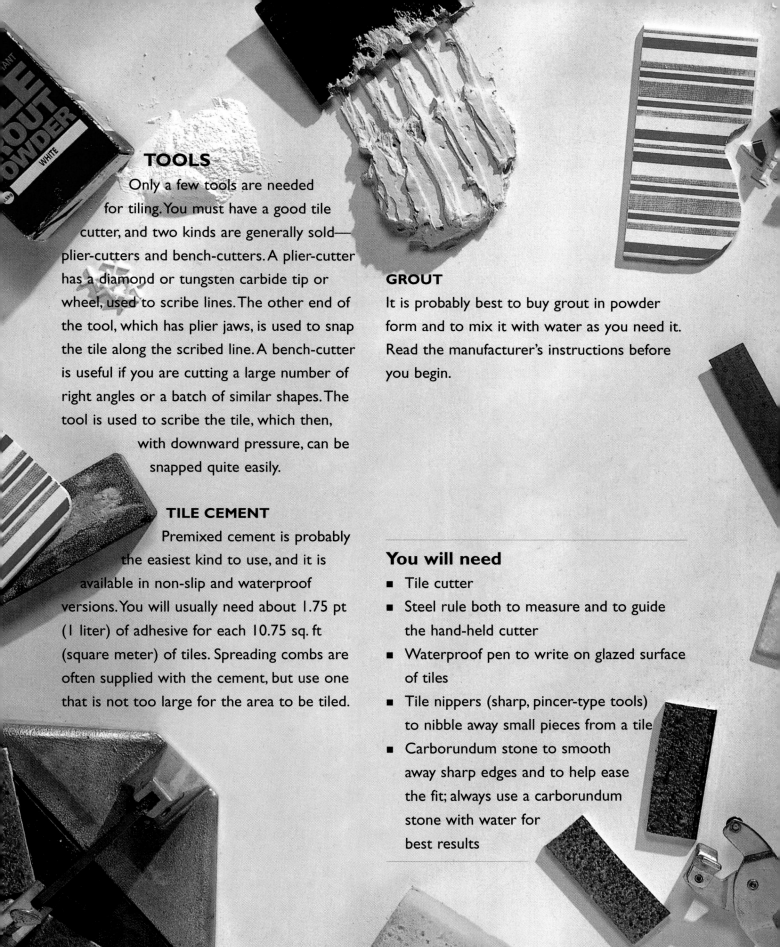

TOOLS

Only a few tools are needed for tiling. You must have a good tile cutter, and two kinds are generally sold—plier-cutters and bench-cutters. A plier-cutter has a diamond or tungsten carbide tip or wheel, used to scribe lines. The other end of the tool, which has plier jaws, is used to snap the tile along the scribed line. A bench-cutter is useful if you are cutting a large number of right angles or a batch of similar shapes. The tool is used to scribe the tile, which then, with downward pressure, can be snapped quite easily.

TILE CEMENT

Premixed cement is probably the easiest kind to use, and it is available in non-slip and waterproof versions. You will usually need about 1.75 pt (1 liter) of adhesive for each 10.75 sq. ft (square meter) of tiles. Spreading combs are often supplied with the cement, but use one that is not too large for the area to be tiled.

GROUT

It is probably best to buy grout in powder form and to mix it with water as you need it. Read the manufacturer's instructions before you begin.

You will need

- Tile cutter
- Steel rule both to measure and to guide the hand-held cutter
- Waterproof pen to write on glazed surface of tiles
- Tile nippers (sharp, pincer-type tools) to nibble away small pieces from a tile
- Carborundum stone to smooth away sharp edges and to help ease the fit; always use a carborundum stone with water for best results

TILE SPACERS

Small plastic crosses are the most popular kind of tile spacer, which are used to make sure that all the tiles are evenly spaced, and they are left between the tiles and grouted over. You can use matchsticks instead.

OTHER EQUIPMENT

The projects in this book also require the use of some other tools. Even if you do not already have them in your existing tool kit, you will find them in all DIY stores and general hardware shops.

TIP
■ Some people are sensitive to certain kinds of cement and adhesives, so it is a sensible precaution to use a barrier cream and to wear rubber gloves. Always apply cements and adhesives in well-ventilated rooms and avoid inhaling the fumes, and remember to wash your hands after using them.

TIP
■ When wood is included in the lists of materials, the lengths quoted are usually slightly more than is actually required to allow for cutting.

You will need

- Small hammer
- Selection of panel pins, both sunk-head copper pins and fine steel frame pins
- Hand or power drill with a selection of bits suitable for wood
- PVA-based wood glue—choose a quick-drying kind if you can
- Sandpaper of various grades
- Paint and paintbrushes; both oil- and water-based paints are used in different projects
- Steel rule and pencil for measuring and marking wooden frames and battens
- Spirit level; essential for fixing the batten for the first row of tiles but useful in other projects, too
- Fine tenon saw and miter box to give frames true right-angled corners
- Small frame clamps (cramps)

BASIC WALL TILING

It is not the purpose of this book to explain all about wall tiling—there are plenty of good do-it-yourself guides available—but here are the key points.

You will need

- Spirit level
- Pencil
- Batten
- Ruler or measuring tape
- Hammer and pins
- Tiles
- Tile cement and comb
- Spacers
- Grout

TIP
- Always make sure that the surface to be tiled is sound because tiles are considerably heavier than most other forms of wall covering. Wash the surface with warm water and detergent before you begin to tile.

1 Use a spirit level to establish a horizontal line and fix a batten on the wall at the level of the first full row of tiles. This might not be the base of the wall but, because it is better to finish with a complete, uncut row of tiles, do some preparatory measuring.

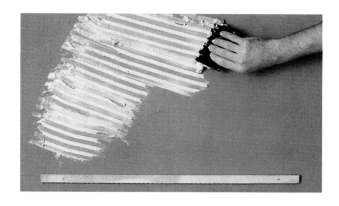

2 Spread tile cement over the wall with a notched comb. Do not cover more than 5 sq. ft (0.5 sq. m).

3 Press each tile firmly to the cement with a slight twisting action to make sure that there is full contact between the tile, the cement and the wall.

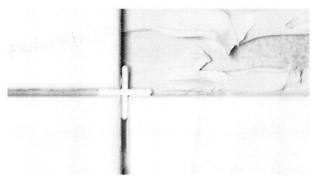

4 Place spacers at each corner to make sure that the grout lines are even, pressing the spacers firmly against the wall because they will be left in place and grouted over.

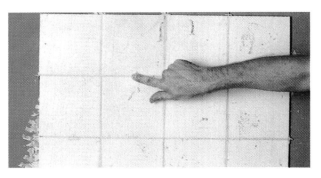

5 *Continue to fix tiles in place, cleaning off any cement that is left on the front of the tiles before it dries and becomes hard to remove.*

7 *Smooth the joins with a finger and add more grout if necessary.*

TIP
- If you have to cut tiles, try to make sure that the cut pieces are as large as possible and fit them into the least noticeable positions.

6 *Leave the cement to dry, preferably overnight, then spread grout into the gaps between the tiles.*

8 *When the grout is set, polish the tiles with a clean, dry cloth.*

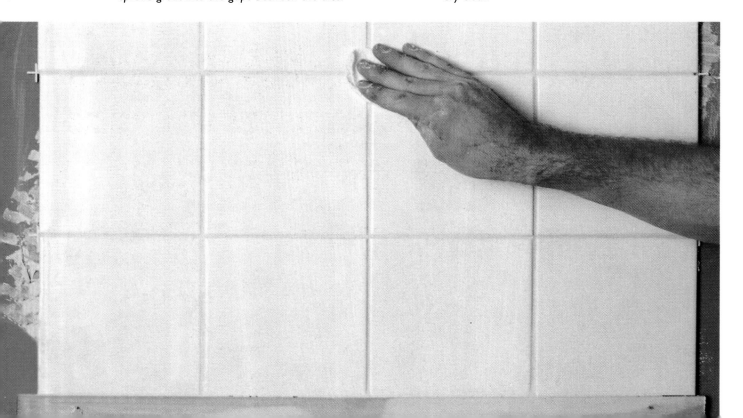

STENCILED FLOWERS

If you feel like a change of decor but don't have sufficient funds to allow you to re-tile a whole wall with patterned tiles, a semi-permanent solution is to use enamel paints to decorate some plain tiles or even to give existing tiles a new lease of life.

You will need

- Plain tiles
- Stencils
- Masking tape
- White tiles for mixing colors
- Cold ceramic paints—red, yellow, and green
- Stencil brushes
- Craft knife
- Tile cement and comb
- Border tiles
- Grout

TIP

- A range of cold enamel paints has been specially produced for use on ceramics, but although the paints will last for several years if treated with care and cleaned gently, they are not permanent. You can clean them off completely with a solvent and paint on new decorations if you wish. They are not suitable for use on tiles in places where they are likely to become wet—in showers, for example—although you can use them in other areas of the bathroom that do not become wet.

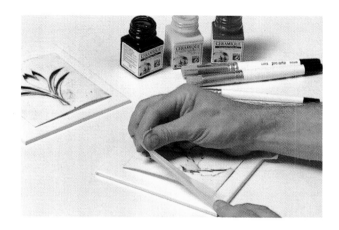

I Use masking tape to hold the stencil in position on a tile.

2 Mix a range of greens from the yellow and green on a spare white tile. The different shades will enhance the overall appearance of the motifs.

3 Carefully apply the green paint with an upright stencil brush. Use only a little paint at a time. If you overload the brush, the paint will smudge around the edges.

4 Mix red and green to make brown for the stem and apply as before.

7 Use a notched comb to spread tile cement over the area to be tiled.

5 Leave the paint to dry for a few moments before lifting the stencil.

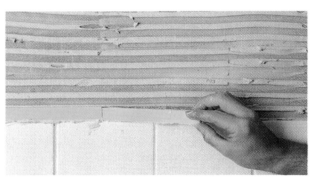

8 Fix the border tiles to the wall. Stagger the joins for best results.

6 Use the other designs to decorate as many tiles as you need. You can remove any smudges of paint with a craft knife before the paint is set, then leave overnight for the paint to dry completely.

TIP
■ Do not mix too much of any one color at a time because the paint dries quickly.

9   *Add the decorated tiles above the row of border tiles, making sure that they are pressed firmly against the wall. Add another row of border tiles before fixing any additional plain tiles that are required. Leave the tile cement to set overnight.*

10   *Spread grout into the spaces between the tiles, trying to avoid getting grout on the decorated areas. Make sure that the joints are completely filled, adding more grout if necessary.*

11   *Leave the grout to dry, then polish with a clean, dry cloth.*

DECORATING A TILED WALL
■ You can work directly onto an already tiled wall. Make sure that the surface is completely clean, and just before you begin stenciling, wipe it over with methylated spirits to remove any traces of grease. Take great care when you apply the colors not to overload your brushes, and leave each color to dry before you apply a new shade to avoid smudging.

TRADITIONAL HALL PANEL

Many Victorian and Edwardian houses in Britain have decorative tiled panels on each side of the front door. There is no reason these panels should be confined to porches, however—they would be ideal in a conservatory or a bathroom, or even set into a tiled wall as a special feature.

You will need

- 2 sets of decorative picture tiles—i.e., ten 6 x 6 in. (15 x 15 cm) tiles
- Additional tiles and border strips to complement the picture tiles
- Tile cutter
- Spirit level
- Batten, hammer and pins
- Tile cement and comb
- Sponges
- Grout

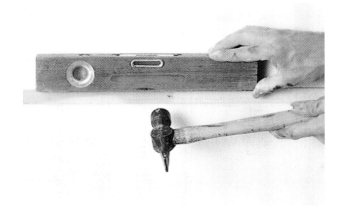

2 Use a spirit level to establish a horizontal line and fix a batten to the wall.

1 Measure the area to be tiled and lay out the various tiles on a large flat area so that you can double-check the measurements. Cut tiles to size if necessary.

3 Spread tile cement over the area to be tiled with a notched comb.

4 *Beginning with the bottom tiles, press each tile firmly to the cement with a slight twisting action.*

TIP
- If the panel is going to be fixed outdoors, make sure that you use a waterproof tile cement that is recommended for outside use.

6 *As you apply each picture tile, check that it is the right way up. It is all too easy to position tiles the wrong way round and not to notice until it is too late!*

5 *Work upwards in horizontal rows to ensure that the joins are even. It is more difficult to make fine adjustments if you apply the tiles in vertical rows.*

7 *Continue to position the tiles, using a sponge to remove any cement from the front of the tiles before it sets.*

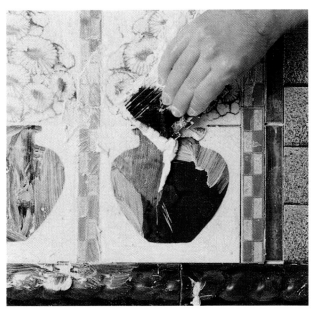

8 When the tile cement is dry, remove the batten and make good the surface. Spread grout over the entire pattern and wipe off the surplus with a damp sponge.

9 Leave the grout to dry, then polish the surface with a clean, dry cloth to remove any remaining traces.

TABLE STAND

Tiles are often used because they are durable, but they are also heat-resistant, which makes them ideal for use as stands for hot pans and teapots.

You will need

- 1½ x 1½ in. (38 x 38 mm) wooden molding, 5 ft. (1.5 m) long
- Saw
- PVA wood adhesive
- Clamps
- 1 decorative tile, 8 x 8 in. (20 x 20 cm)
- ¼ x ⅞ in. (4 x 20 mm) wooden strip, 32 in. (80 cm) long
- Hammer and pins
- Base color paint and picture frame rubbing gold
- Paintbrush
- Silicone sealant

1 Cut the molding into four pieces with mitered corners so that each has an internal length of slightly more than 8 in. (20 cm) to make fitting the tile easier.

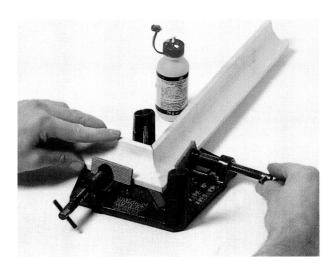

2 Glue a corner and hold the frame pieces together with clamps, using small off-cuts of wood to prevent the clamps from marking the frame.

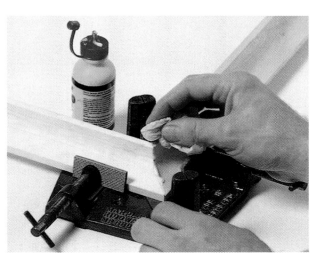

3 Use a damp cloth to wipe off any surplus adhesive and leave to dry.

4 *Repeat steps 2 and 3 on the other three corners.*

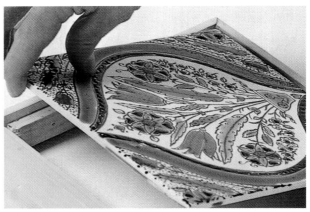

7 *Check that the tile rests firmly on the supports.*

5 *Place the tile on a flat surface and turn the frame upside down over the tile. Mark the tile level on the frame.*

8 *Remove the tile and paint the frame with the base color of your choice. Allow to dry.*

6 *Cut the wooden strip into four lengths. Pin these to the frame so the upper edges are flush with the marked line.*

9 *Use your fingers to apply an even coat of frame rubbing gold to the external sides of the frame.*

Pipe a line of silicone sealant along the top edge of the support.

Insert the tile into the frame, pressing it down firmly onto the sealant. Leave to dry.

Leave the rubbing gold to dry, then carefully rub it back with a dry sponge to reveal traces of the base coat.

SUN AND MOON PANEL

Tiled rooms can sometimes appear very plain, especially if a limited budget has meant that you have used tiles of a single color for quite a large area. This project, which would be ideal for a kitchen or bathroom, uses just a few colored tiles to create an eye-catching feature. The quantities quoted are for one sun and one moon, but you could use several motifs in the same room.

You will need

- 8 white tiles, each 6 x 6 in. (15 x 15 cm)
- 3 yellow tiles, each 6 x 6 in. (15 x 15 cm)
- 1 orange tile, 6 x 6 in. (15 x 15 cm)
- Pair of compasses and felt-tipped pen
- Tile cutter
- Tile nippers
- Carborundum stone
- Cold ceramic paint—brown
- Stencil brush
- Tile cement and comb
- Grout

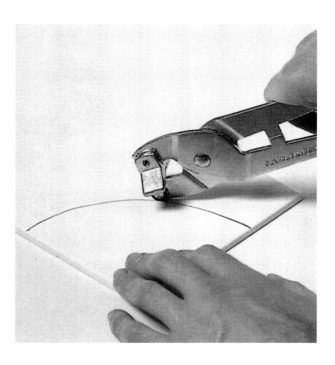

1 Lay four tiles in a square and, using the center point, draw a circle with a radius of 2 in. (6.5 cm) so that each tile has a quadrant of the circle marked on it. Scribe the line on each tile, pushing the cutter away from you so that you can see clearly the line you are following. Turn over the tile and tap it roughly along the line you have scribed. This will help the tile snap along the line.

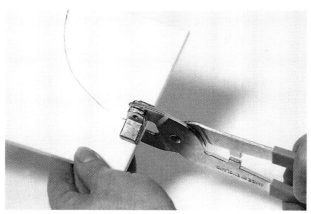

2 Gently squeeze the tile cutter to crack the tile. You can often hear the sound of the tile beginning to crack.

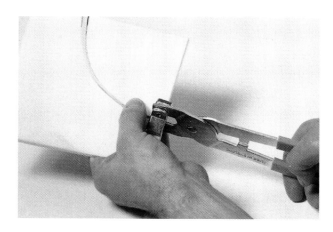

3 Snap a tile along a curved line. Repeat on all four tiles, but with a 2½ in. (6.5 cm) radius for the moon.

6 Smooth the edge with a carborundum stone. Make a second yellow circle for the moon.

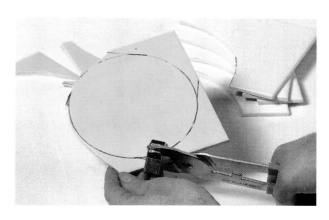

4 Trace a circle on a yellow tile. Scribe the outline of the circle and cut away the pieces from the edge.

7 Cut strips 1 x ⅜ in. (2.5 x 1 cm) from orange and yellow tiles.

5 Use tile nippers to snap off the protruding edges to give a neat outline.

8 Using cold ceramic paint, stencil the moon's face on to a yellow circle and the sun's face on to the other circle.

9   *Lay out the pieces of the design on a flat surface to make sure that all the elements fit together. If necessary, trim the strips cut in step 8 so that they fit neatly around the sun's face.*

10   *Fix the white tiles with the cutout sections to the wall, making sure that they form even circles.*

11   *Position the sun in the center. Place alternate strips of orange and yellow around the sun's face.*

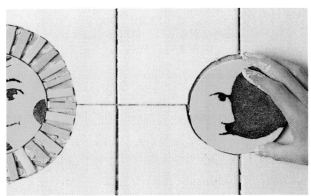

12   *Fit the moon's face into the other space.*

13   *Use grout to fill the spaces between the sun's rays and also other exposed joins. Apply it with a sponge.*

Mirror Frame

Few of us would admit to being vain, but there is no doubt that an extra mirror is always useful. This one, with its border of dolphins, would be perfect for a bathroom, but if you visit a specialist tile shop you are almost certain to find tiles that would suit nearly any room.

You will need

- Approximately 2 x ¼ in. (50 x 5 mm) wooden strip, 6 ft. 6 in. (2 m) long
- Saw and miter box
- 1 piece of ¼ in. (6 mm) plywood, 18 x 18 in. (45 x 45 cm)
- 1 square mirror glass, 14 x 14 in. (36 x 26 cm)
- Ruler and pencil
- Bradawl
- 4 mirror corners and screws
- Screwdriver
- Silicone sealant
- PVA wood adhesive
- Hammer and pins
- 12 border tiles, each 6 x 3 in. (15 x 7.5 cm)
- Carborundum stone
- Grout
- 2 screw eyes

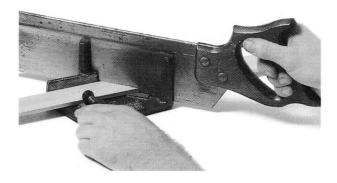

1 Cut four pieces of wooden strip with mitered corners so that they fit the edges of the plywood square.

2 Lay the strips along the edges of the base square and the mirror tile in the center. Mark the positions.

3 Use a bradawl to mark the positions for the screws for the mirror corners.

4 With the mirror in place, screw the mirror corners to the base board.

5 Fill the mirror corners with small amounts of silicone sealant to cushion the mirror. This protects the corners.

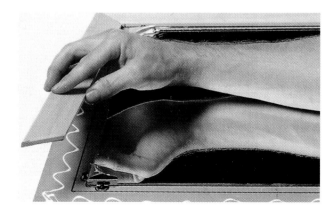

6 Fix wooden strips around the mirror with wood adhesive. Align the edges with the outside edges of the base.

7 Tap in a few pins to make sure that the strips are firmly attached to the base board.

8 Use a tile cutter to cut four right-handed miter angles and four left-handed miter angles. Smooth the cut edges with a carborundum stone to make sure that they fit neatly together.

9 *Cover the wooden edging strip with silicone sealant and position the tiles. Adjust the tiles so that they are evenly spaced, then leave to dry overnight.*

10 *Apply grout to the tiles, also covering the sides that lie against the mirror. Remove any grout trace with a sponge. Fix two screw eyes to the back for hanging.*

ART DECO FISH

Simple designs can be cut from tiles of
contrasting colors to form interesting panels
or borders. The process is time-consuming,
although it is much less expensive than buying
specially decorated border tiles. Large and
small geometric patterns can look extremely
effective, but we have used a fish, which would
be ideal in a bathroom.

You will need

- Tracing paper and pencil
- Cardboard
- Felt-tipped pen
- 2 white tiles, each 6 x 6 in. (15 x 15 cm)
- 2 black tiles, each 6 x 6 in. (15 x 15 cm)
- Tile cutter
- Tile nippers
- Carborundum stone
- Tile cement and comb
- Narrow border tiles
- Grout

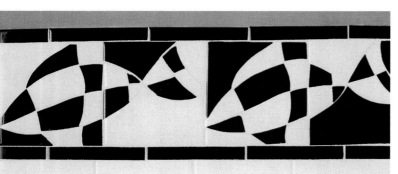

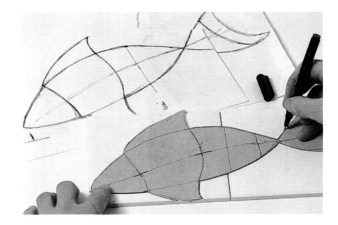

1 Transfer the fish pattern to a piece of cardboard and use it to transfer the outline to the white tiles.

2 Join up the register marks by hand.

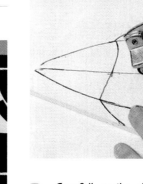

3 Carefully scribe along the marked lines, beginning with the longest cuts. Try to cut in one smooth action.

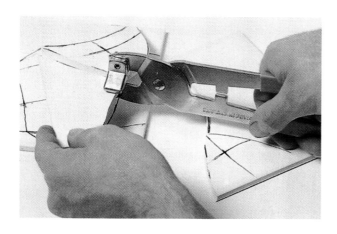

4 Tap the underside of the tiles and break along the scribed lines.

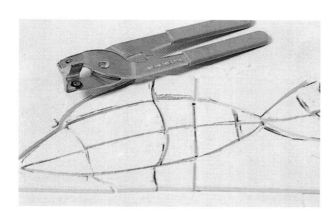

5 Lay out the pieces on top of the tracing to avoid confusion later on.

6 Repeat steps 1-5 inclusive with the black tiles.

7 Re-arrange the black and white pieces to create a checkered design.

8 Use your tile nippers to remove any protruding pieces of tile.

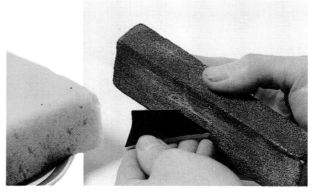

9 Smooth the edges with a carborundum stone. Use water with the carborundum to stop the edges from chipping.

TIP

■ When you use border strips above plain tiles, try to stagger the vertical lines of the joins.

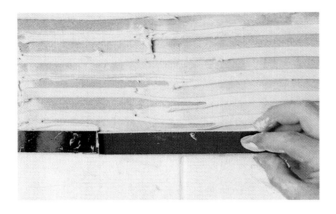

10 Apply tile cement to a small area of the wall with a toothed scraper or comb, then start to position the tiles, beginning with the bottom row of border tiles.

11 Working from the left-hand side, start positioning the mosaic pieces.

TIP

■ When you are applying grout between cutout pieces of tile, use a sponge. It is very easy to cut your fingers on the sharp edges.

12 Continue to fix tile pieces, building up the motifs from left to right.

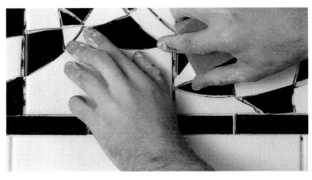

13 Finish off with another row of border tiles, making sure all the surfaces are flat. Check that all the pieces are pressed to the cement and that the spaces between them are even. Leave overnight to dry.

14 Use a sponge to apply the grout. Remove surplus grout from the tile surface before it dries, making sure that all the joins are completely and neatly filled. When the grout is dry, clean with a slightly damp sponge.

WINDOW BOX

A window box is a wonderful way of brightening up a dull windowsill, and this planter could be used indoors or out. We have used tiles with a fairly traditional floral pattern, but it would look equally stunning with geometric or abstract patterns. Although it is rather time-consuming, this project is well worth the effort.

You will need

- Saw and miter box
- 1 x 1 in. (2.5 x 2.5 cm) wooden strip, 15 ft (4.5 m) long
- PVA wood adhesive
- Hammer and panel pins
- Clamps
- 1 piece of ¼ in. (6 mm) plywood, 5 ft 6 in. x 10 in. (165 x 25 cm)
- Hockey stick molding, 3 ft (1 m) long
- 2 x ⅜ in. (50 x 12 mm) wooden strip, 15 ft (4.5 m) long
- Drill
- 8 small wooden knobs
- ¾ x ¼ in. (18 x 4 mm) wooden strip, 6 ft (2 m) long
- Sandpaper
- Oil-based paint for exterior use
- Silicone sealant
- Grout

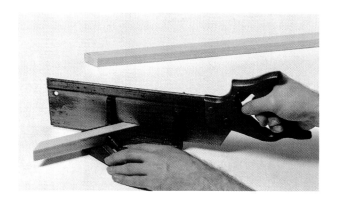

1 With the saw and miter box cut the wooden strip into two, each with an inside length of just over 24 in. (60 cm), and two more with a just over 6 in. (15 cm) inside length each.

2 Check that the angles at each end of each piece run in opposite directions, then glue one short piece to one long piece with wood adhesive.

3 Clamp them together until the adhesive is dry. Insert pins diagonally across the corners for extra strength. Repeat steps 2 and 3 until the frame is complete.

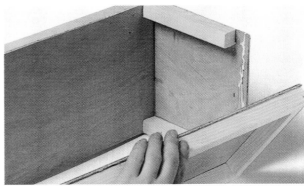

4 Cut a plywood piece to the frame's dimensions. Glue and pin it to the frame. Make a second frame with a plywood cover. These are the two long sides of the window box.

7 Glue and pin the second long side to the short sides to create a box. Leave to dry.

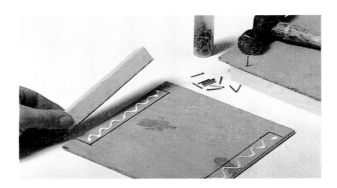

5 Cut two squares from the left plywood, each 8 x 8 in. (20 x 20 cm). From the 1 x 1 in. (2.5 x 2.5 cm) wooden strip cut four lengths, each 6 in. (15 cm) long. Pin a strip along two opposite sides of the plywood squares, in the center of the edges. These form the two short sides.

8 Cut four pieces of hockey stick molding, each 8 in. (20 cm) long. Pin these to each vertical corner edge.

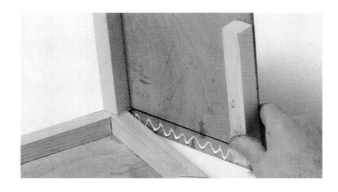

6 Glue and pin both short sides to a long side. Leave to dry.

9 Cut the 2 x ⅜ in. (50 x 12 mm) strip in two pieces, each with an inside length of just over 24 in. (60 cm), and two pieces, each with a just over 6 in. (15 cm) inside length. Making sure that the inside edge is flush with the inside of the box, pin the pieces along the top edge and the foot.

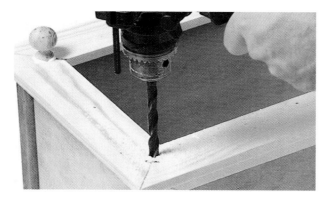

10 Drill through the top ledge corners to make seating holes for the knobs. Repeat at the bottom corners.

13 Apply silicone sealant to one long side and position four tiles. Once dry, repeat on the other long side.

11 From the ¾ x ⅙ in. 18 x 4 mm strip cut two lengths, each 65 cm (26 in.) long. Pin the strips to the inside bottom ledge to provide supports for the pots.

14 Spread grout along the joins between and around the tiles, cleaning off any surplus. Leave to dry, then use a dry cloth to remove the final traces of grout.

TIP
- The materials quoted here are for a window box with four 6 x 6 in. (15 x 15 cm) tiles along each of the long sides. Larger or smaller versions can be made in the same way, however, by increasing or reducing the dimensions of the basic frame.

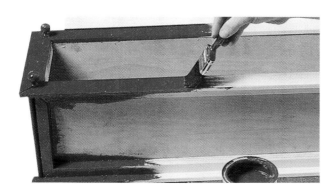

12 Smooth any rough surfaces with sandpaper and paint the box, inside and out, with coats of an oil-based paint. This will protect the box when outdoors.

DECORATIVE PAINTING

Paint is an exciting medium with much potential, and it can be used to transform rather plain or battered items into unusual, pretty things. Once you know what paint is appropriate, you will be able to experiment and transform practically every room in your home. Familiar items will become unrecognizable, and junk-shop finds will become heirlooms. Do not waste time trying to transform an object that you will never want to have in a room with you. On the other hand, pieces of furniture that are just a bit tattered or rusty—but are elegant— are well worth rejuvenating. This chapter explains how to prepare a variety of surfaces so that they will accept decorative paint, as well as how different techniques and finishes can be applied.

MATERIALS AND TECHNIQUES

PAINTS

ARTISTS' ACRYLIC PAINTS, which come in tubes, are available in a range of colors. The colors can be mixed, and because acrylics are water-based, they can be dissolved in water. When they are dry they are waterproof and can only be removed with methylated spirits (de-natured alcohol).

ARTISTS' OIL PAINTS, which are also available in tubes, look much like acrylic paints. They contain linseed oil, however, and are, therefore, classified as oil-based. They can be dissolved with turpentine or white (mineral) spirit.

EMULSION PAINT (LATEX) is water-based, and perhaps most associated with home decorating. It needs a porous surface to adhere to, though it will also cover spirit-

Emulsion (latex)

Enamels

Ceramic paint

Water-based acrylic varnish

Casein paint

Shellac

Metal paint

based paints and varnishes.

ACRYLIC PRIMER/UNDERCOAT is similar to emulsion paint but has an acrylic binder, which makes it stronger.

CASEIN OR BUTTERMILK PAINT, made from a by-product of cheese-making, is a water-based paint but remains water-soluble when dry. It can be polished by burnishing to give a smooth finish.

METAL PAINTS are very hard-wearing and adhere to most surfaces. Some types can be used to isolate rust, while others should be applied only when the rust has been treated and isolated.

ENAMEL PAINTS are oil-based and can be used on metal, glass, ceramics, plastics and wood. Dilute the paint with turpentine or white (mineral) spirit.

Artists' acrylic and oil paints

ACRYLIC VARNISH is water-based. It is quick-drying and non-yellowing. The varnish can be tinted with artists' acrylics, gouache and universal stainers, which need to be diluted with water before they are added to the varnish.

SHELLAC comes in a variety of grades and stages of refinement, all of which are quick drying, and it is also obtainable in flakes, which can be dissolved in methylated spirits (de-natured alcohol) even when they are dry. Shellac will adhere to most surfaces. It is often used to form an isolating layer between incompatible paints.

WHITE POLISH, a more refined form of shellac, gives a transparent finish. It dissolves in methylated spirits (de-natured alcohol), even when it is dry.

OIL-BASED VARNISH contains resins and oils that often cause it to yellow as it ages. It adheres to most surfaces, and can be tinted with artists' oil paints, which should be diluted with white spirit before being added to the varnish.

CRACKLE VARNISH is a two-part product. The first, slow-drying coat continues to dry under the second, fast-drying coat, causing the top coat to crack. The varnish has to be patinated with artists' oil tube paints or

powders to reveal the cracks to best effect.

WAX is useful for antiquing surfaces, and can also be tinted with artists' oil paints or with shoe polish. Wax should always be the final finish: do not attempt to varnish over it.

ANTIQUING FLUID can be bought readymade, or you can mix your own with artists' oil paints and white spirit. The consistency can range from thick cream to a runny liquid. Earth colors—raw umber and Payne's gray, for example—are usually used.

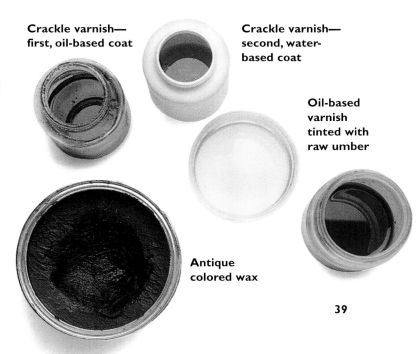

Crackle varnish—first, oil-based coat

Crackle varnish—second, water-based coat

Oil-based varnish tinted with raw umber

Antique colored wax

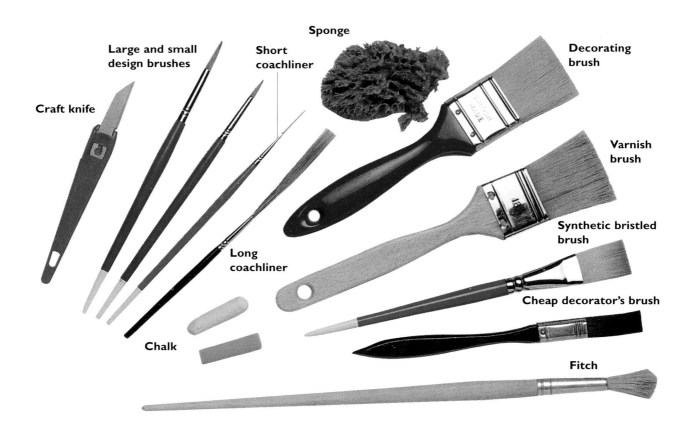

Craft knife

Large and small design brushes

Short coachliner

Sponge

Decorating brush

Varnish brush

Synthetic bristled brush

Long coachliner

Chalk

Cheap decorator's brush

Fitch

BRUSHES

VARNISH BRUSHES are flat and are available in a variety of widths and kinds, ranging from pure bristle to synthetic fibers. When applying water-based paints and varnishes, synthetic brushes are generally better because they give a better flow. In general it is best to keep separate brushes for paint and for varnish, and for oil- and water-based products.

DECORATOR'S BRUSHES have much thicker heads than varnish brushes. When you are applying paint, use the largest brush you can, simply because it will give you quicker coverage.

FITCHES are used for oil painting. They usually have long handles and short, stiff bristles. They are useful for spattering and for mixing paints and varnishes.

Design brushes are available in a range of sizes and different kinds of hair. Brushes known as coachliners are used for painting free-hand lines. They have long hairs that are tear-shaped, so that the line is the same width throughout.

OTHER EQUIPMENT

- Natural marine sponge
- Craft knife
- Wire wool
- Sandpaper
- Chalk
- Graphite tracing-down paper
- Tracing paper
- Drawing pens

PREPARING SURFACES

BARE WOOD

Bare wood must be sealed, usually with an oil- or water-based priming paint or with shellac/sanding sealer. There are practically no limitations to the paints or varnishes that can be used.

VARNISHED WOOD

Before applying emulsion (latex) paint, sand down with medium to coarse sandpaper to create a key to which the paint can adhere. If the sanding exposes a lot of bare wood, apply a coat of acrylic primer/undercoat or a coat of shellac/sanding sealer.

The surface must be sound before a coat of oil-based paint or varnish is applied. Flaking or loose varnish must be removed.

PAINTED WOOD

If something is already painted with a water-based finish, as long as the finish is sound you can paint over it with any kind of paint. If the existing paint is oil-based, it may still be possible to use a water-based paint, especially if the existing surface was applied some time ago, because the water-resistant oils will have tended to dry out.

An alternative is to sand the surface lightly and apply an isolating coat of shellac, which is compatible with both oil- and water-based paints.

MEDIUM DENSITY FIBERBOARD (MDF)

You should treat this as you would ordinary wood.

METAL

Use a wire brush to remove any loose rust, and a rust remover to stop the metal from corroding further. Apply a coat of metal primer before giving a top coat of metal or oil-based paint.

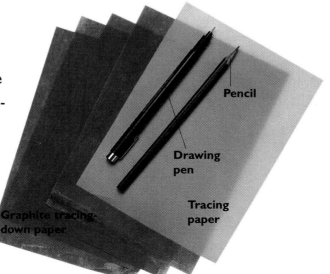

Pencil

Drawing pen

Tracing paper

Graphite tracing-down paper

BRUSH STROKES

FREE-HAND LINING

Use a coachliner or a sword liner because the length of the hairs will help you get a straight line that is the same width along its length. Load the whole brush, drawing it through the paint without twisting the hairs. Place the length of the brush down, just keeping the metal ferule clear of the surface. Draw the brush towards you because your arm will naturally move in an arc if you paint from side to side. If you are painting close to an edge, place your little finger on the edge to support your hand. Always have a straight edge—a ruler, for example—about 1 in. (2.5 cm) from the line you are drawing so your eye can use it as a guide. Small wobbles and uneven lines can be rectified by going over the line once it is dry. As you near the end of the line, begin to lift the brush.

ROSES

Complete each rose before moving on to the next because the paint must be kept wet to blend the colors. Mix a light, mid- and dark tone of the same color on your palette before starting. When you are painting anything that is to look three-dimensional, you must decide on the position of an imaginary light source and then be consistent in the placing of highlights and shadows.

CURVES AND PETALS

Use a round-ended design brush and press the brush down firmly, twisting it anticlockwise as you slide it sideways (A). Gradually lift the brush as you draw the arc, still twisting the hairs to give a clean point.

To paint a tear-shaped petal (B) use a round-ended design brush and push the brush down. Then lift while turning the handle anticlockwise to bring the hairs to a fine point.

Use a pointed design brush to paint a curved line (C). Place the tip of the brush on the surface, gradually pressing it down as you move the brush to increase the width of the stroke. Twist the handle anticlockwise while drawing it up again to make a point.

Paint a leaf with two strokes of the brush (D). Make a gentle S-shape.

A. Curve

B. Tear-shaped petal

D. Leaf

C. Curved line

TRAY

Naive art has a wonderfully refreshing simplicity. The style was originally used to record events and objects that were important in everyday life, and because the paintings were not executed by great artists, they have a beguiling and often humorous charm. Prize livestock was a popular subject and is appropriate for a kitchen tray. We chose a sheep and finished off the design with some free-hand lines.

You will need

- Tray (ours was wooden)
- Shellac and brush
- Fine sandpaper
- Emulsion paint—dark blue-green
- Tracing paper
- Pencil
- Masking tape
- Graphite tracing-down paper
- Artists' acrylic paints—white, raw umber, and black
- Design brushes—no. 8 or 9 and no. 4
- Saucer or plate (for mixing paint)
- Short coachliner
- Varnish and varnish brush

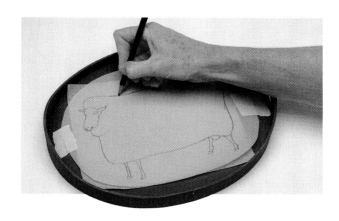

1 *Seal the tray with a coat of shellac. Sand it lightly to smooth the surface before applying a coat of blue-green emulsion. Transfer the design to tracing paper, hold it in position with masking tape, and use tracing-down paper to transfer the outline to the tray.*

2 *Mix white acrylic paint with a little raw umber in a saucer or plate to create an off-white color and use it to block in the sheep's body. Because the background is dark, you will probably not achieve a perfect cover with one coat.*

3 When the first coat of paint is dry, use the same off-white to stipple on a second coat very thickly to give the texture and impression of the fleece.

5 Use raw umber mixed with a little white to paint the details of the face—eyes, nose and ears—and to add more shadow under the chin. Use black acrylic for the pupils of the eyes and for the legs.

4 Add more raw umber to the original color and shade the sheep's body, adding shadow to the belly, along the back and around the neck to create a three-dimensional effect.

6 Add a sparkle to the eyes and highlights to the hooves with white acrylic paint.

8 *Use a fine design brush to paint the top edge of the tray. Hold the brush so that its side is flat on the top edge and simply run it along the edge to give a good, clean line. Finish off the tray with a coat of varnish.*

7 *Hold the tray on its side so that one end is towards you, and, using a short coachliner and white or off-white paint, draw a line around the outside edge of the tray, close to the top edge.*

TIP
- Keep a damp cloth handy when you are doing free-hand lines. You can remove mistakes as long as you act quickly, before the paint has a chance to dry.

TIP
- There is a wide range of varnishes. When you are selecting one, bear in mind the end use of the article. A tray, for example, is likely to be used for hot cups, and so you should choose a varnish that will be durable enough to withstand high temperatures or your handiwork may be ruined.

CHAIR

Most of us have pieces of furniture
that have seen better days, but that we would
be sad to part with. As long as the underlying
shape is attractive, there are all kinds of ways
in which we can turn these battered items
into beautiful objects. The finish described
here would suit a period setting and would
blend in well with other antiques.

You will need

- Chair
- Coarse sandpaper
- Acrylic primer/undercoat
- Decorator's brush—1-1½ in. (2.5-4 cm)
- Emulsion (latex) paint—white and dark
  blue-green
- Methylated spirits (de-natured alcohol)
- Kitchen paper or old cloth
- Chalk
- Tracing paper
- Pencil
- Graphite tracing-down paper
- Masking tape
- Artists' acrylic paints—Hooker's green,
  phthalocyanine blue, and white
- Saucer or plate (for mixing paint)
- Design brush—no. 4
- Varnish and varnish brush

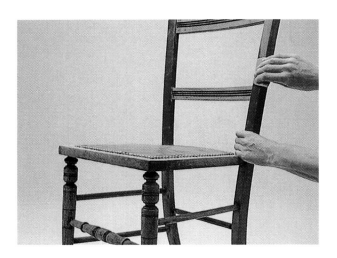

1 *This worn and scuffed chair still had the remains of its original varnish, which, because of the chair's age, would probably have been shellac. Since the chair will receive several coats of paint, use coarse sandpaper to remove the old finish. Work outside if possible because this is a messy job; if you have to work indoors wear a face mask and make sure that your working area is well ventilated.*

2 *When the chair is back to the bare wood, seal it with acrylic primer or undercoat. Begin by painting the legs and support rails, then paint around the turned rails. If the legs are not turned, follow the grain of the wood and paint up and down. The chair can then be turned the right way up and the top half painted.*

3 Apply three coats of white emulsion, allowing each coat to dry completely before adding the next. Paint as neatly as you can because the brush marks will show when the chair is finished. When the white emulsion is dry, apply a coat of dark blue-green emulsion diluted in the proportions of 1 part paint to 5 parts water. Leave to dry.

5 On turned areas and moldings, rub across indentations so the blue-green is intact and the crevices stay quite dark. On raised areas, remove more of the blue-green so they seem lighter than the main body of the chair.

TIP
- If you inadvertently remove too much paint with the methylated spirits, apply more blue-green emulsion and allow it to dry before proceeding.

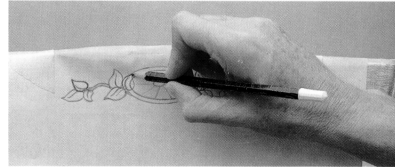

4 Wet a kitchen towel with methylated spirits and rub over the chair, one section at a time. Methylated spirits is a solvent for dry emulsion paint, so it may remove not only the blue-green but also enough white to reveal the wood beneath. You want a grainy look with the blue-green sitting in the brush marks and the white coming through.

6 Use chalk to mark the center of the back rail. Transfer the design to tracing paper and place it centrally on the back rail, holding it in place with masking tape. Use tracing-down paper and a sharp pencil to transfer the design to chair.

7 Mix the green and blue acrylic paints with a little white and use it to block in the central oval. To give the design depth, it needs to be shaded and highlighted. Decide on an imaginary source of light and use darker green to add shade. We assumed that light was coming from the top left, and added shade under the oval, on the right-hand side of the curve and the top left-hand side of the inner curve, where the imagined roundness of the outside molding of the oval would have cast a shadow. Paint dark lines radiating from the center to the inner edge. Mix more white into the original color and highlight the facets that are towards the light source—in our case this was the top left-hand side, the bottom-right inner edge of the oval and the left-hand side of the central oval.

8 Use a slightly greener shade to block in the stems and leaves at the sides of the oval. With a still darker green, shade the leaves, observing the same imagined light source as in step 7. Also add shade to the underside of the stem by painting in a fine dark-green line. Add a highlight to the opposite side.

9 When the paint is completely dry, apply the varnish. Since chairs are usually subjected to a good deal of wear and tear, you should apply two or three coats, allowing each coat to dry before applying the next.

COMMEMORATIVE PLATE

A hand-painted plate to mark a special occasion is a wonderfully personal way to show that you have thought about the event. You could use the same basic idea to make a house-warming gift, when you might replace the child's name with the new address. We have used an inexpensive enamel plate and based the design on traditional barge-ware. The same technique could be used on other enamel items.

You will need

- White enamel plate
- Colored chalk
- Enamel craft paints—red, white, light green, and dark green
- Design brush—no. 4
- White (mineral) spirit (for cleaning brush)

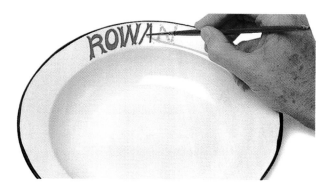

Use chalk to indicate the position of the letters of the name, making sure they are evenly spaced. Paint the name in light green paint.

2 *Shade the letters with dark green, remembering that you must determine your imaginary light source. In our example the light source was from the top left-hand side, and the shading was, therefore, applied to the right-hand side and the bottom of the letters.*

3 *Sketch the central motif with chalk, indicating the positions of the leaves and main branch. If you want to use traditional roses, see Brush Strokes (page 42). Use light green to block in the leaves.*

TIP
■ Enamel items decorated in this way will withstand occasional gentle washing, but they are not suitable for everyday use.

5 *Load the brush with red and drop paint onto the plate to form round blobs to represent the berries. Take care not to overload your brush and test the amount of paint you need on the side of the plate. You can wipe it off with kitchen towel soaked in white spirit before it dries.*

4 *Shade the leaves to give a three-dimensional appearance, again bearing the imaginary light source in mind as you work. Mix a little red with the green to create a brown for the branch.*

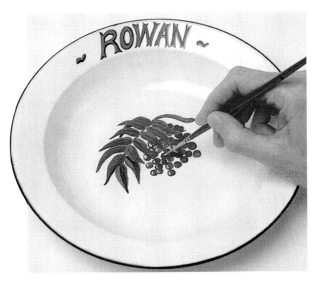

6 *Allow the berries to dry a little, then paint in the highlights with white paint to make them look round and shiny.*

7 Hold the plate so that the name is at the top and find the center of the bottom. Allow sufficient room for the word and date, chalking the characters in so that they are evenly and symmetrically placed. Paint in the letters and numbers.

8 Paint a line around the border in red. Most enamel plates already have a blue edge, and you can paint over this. Leave the paint to dry for about 24 hours, although it will be dry to the touch after about 6 hours.

CLOCK FACE

A piece of medium density fiberboard (MDF) was used for the face, and battery-operated hands are widely available in various styles. Although it looks complicated, the ship design is traced and the central compass is drawn with ruler and compasses. Perhaps the most difficult feature are the free-hand lines, and you should practise these on scrap paper before you begin. The face has been given an "antique" finish by a final coat of two-stage crackle varnish.

You will need

- Clockface and hands and movement
- Acrylic primer/undercoat
- Sandpaper
- Brushes for base coat and varnish— 1-1½ in. (2.5-4 cm)
- Emulsion (latex) paint—yellow
- Square of card, 10 x 10 in. (25 x 25 cm)
- Pair of compasses
- Ruler and pencil
- Protractor
- Scissors
- Artists' acrylic paint—Payne's gray, raw sienna, Venetian red, and white
- Design brush—no. 4
- Short coachliner—no. 1
- Tracing paper
- Masking tape
- Graphite tracing-down paper
- Crackle varnish (optional)
- Oil-based varnish
- Artists' oil paint—raw umber
- White (mineral) spirit

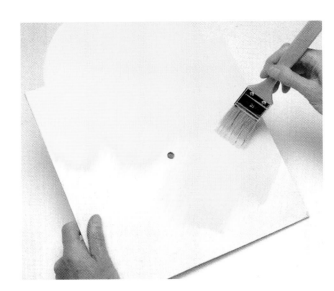

1 Seal the MDF with a coat of acrylic primer/undercoat and, when dry, sand it lightly. Apply a coat of yellow emulsion paint.

2 Draw a circle, 10 in. (25 cm) in diameter, on the card. Draw a line through the center of the circle, and mark off sections every 30 degrees with a protractor. Join the marks to give 12 sections. Subdivide sections by marking off 6 degrees to give the minutes. Cut out the card.

3 Mark the central points of each side of the clock face. Position the card dial centrally, aligning the 3, 6, 9 and 12 o'clock points. Draw around the card and transfer the hour and minute measurements to the clock face.

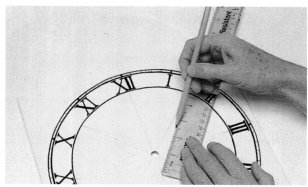

6 Draw a pencil line from 9 to 3 and a vertical line from 12 to 6. Place your protractor at the intersection and mark off 45 degrees between each line. Join these points through the center. Find a point about 1 in. (2.5 cm) from the center on each line and join this point to the top of the adjacent lines to form an eight-pointed star.

4 Use Payne's gray and a coachliner to paint in the circle. Paint a second circle, ⅛ in. (3 mm), outside the first, and between the two paint in the minute and hour marks.

7 Use raw sienna to paint in the star compass, remembering to identify the imaginary light source before you do so.

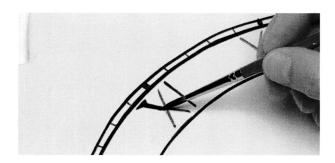

5 Draw in the numerals with pencil before painting them in. Make the line starting at the top left of the Xs and Vs as thick as the upright line of the Is.

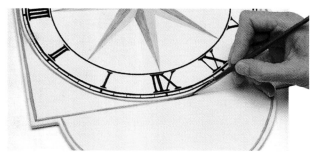

8 With a coachliner and raw sienna, paint a circle outside the dial. Outline the whole clock face, following the arc at the top and joining the lines between the top corners.

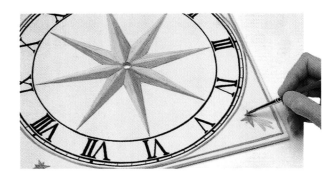

9 Trace the ship and shooting star motifs and use tracing-down paper to transfer them to the clock face. Paint in the shooting stars in each corner, making the stars darker than the tails.

10 Use diluted raw sienna to paint in the ship, moon and sun. Paint the sails in white and add shadows with a little Payne's gray.

11 Mix some Venetian red into the raw sienna and make the paint a little thicker to add more shadows to the ship. Leave the paint to dry.

12 If you use crackle varnish, apply the first, oil-based coat. Use the varnish sparingly, spreading it out from the center before reloading your brush. Leave to become tacky, which can take from 1 to 4 hours.

13 Press the varnish lightly with your fingers. It should feel almost dry but your fingers will feel a slight tackiness. Apply the second, water-based coat over the whole surface. While this coat is wet, massage it lightly to have it adhere to the first coat. Stop when the varnish begins to pull against your fingers and feels almost dry.

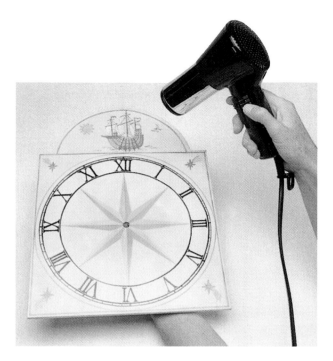

14 *Leave to dry for at least 30 minutes, but preferably overnight. Take care that the second coat does not come into contact with water. Apply gentle heat to encourage the varnish to crack.*

16 *Different pigments in oil paints dry at different rates. Raw umber dries in about 24 hours, but some colors take longer. When you are sure the paint is dry, seal the surface with an oil-based varnish.*

TIP
■ If the crackle varnish does not turn out as you hoped, remove the top, water-based coat by washing it off. You can then start again with the first coat of varnish without damaging the underlying painting.

15 *To patinate the clock face squeeze about ½ in. (10 mm) of oil paint onto the surface. Do not use acrylic paint, which will remove the finish. Dampen a piece of kitchen towel with white spirit and use a circular motion to spread the paint over the whole clock face. Use kitchen towel to wipe off any excess.*

GAMES BOARD

This could be the ideal present for someone who has everything. The board was cut from a piece of medium density fiberboard (MDF), although the same idea could be used to decorate a table-top.

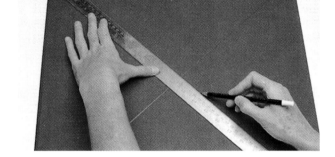

1 Seal the board with a coat of shellac. When dry, sand it and apply a coat of dark red emulsion. Leave to dry. Find the center of the board by drawing two diagonal lines.

You will need

- Square of MDF, 18 x 18 in. (46 x 46 cm), or a suitable table
- Shellac and brush
- Methylated spirits (de-natured alcohol) (to clean brush)
- Sandpaper
- Emulsion (latex) paint—dark red
- Decorator's brush
- Long ruler and pencil
- Artists' acrylic paints—black, gold, burnt umber, and raw sienna
- Design brush—no. 8 or 9
- Coachliner
- Chalk
- Varnish and varnish brush
- Black felt and all-purpose adhesive to back board
- Craft knife

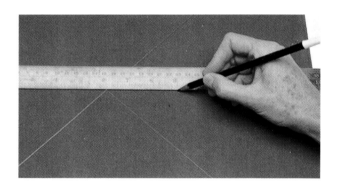

2 Measure from the intersection of the two diagonals the eight by eight squares needed for the standard games board.

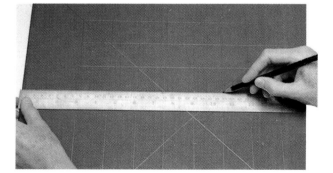

3 Mark the positions for the 64 squares. Our squares measured 3.75 cm (1½ in.), giving an overall area of 30 x 30 cm (12 x 12 in.).

TIP
- The project requires some skill with the paintbrush, and you should practise the brush strokes on scrap paper before you begin.

4 *Check that the width of the outside border is the same on all sides before drawing in the squares.*

5 *Color alternate squares with black acrylic paint. Begin with your brush inside the line, move it up to the line, and draw it in again before you lift it from the surface.*

6 *Use a coachliner and black acrylic to paint a line around the squares and just inside the edge of the board.*

7 *Draw a chalk line about ½ in. (10 mm) in from the outer border and, working from the center, draw in symmetrical wavy lines, using the chalk line as a guide for the base of the wavy lines.*

TIP
- If you have difficulty finding shellac, use two coats of emulsion paint, sanding the surface lightly between coats.

8 *Use a fine design brush or short coachliner to paint over the wavy chalk lines with raw sienna. When the paint is dry, wipe away the straight chalk lines with a damp cloth.*

9   *Use a single stroke to chalk in the leaves, positioning them so they grow from the center towards the corners. Paint the leaves in raw sienna with a single stroke.*

11   *Use burnt umber to shade the design, making the shadows consistent with an imagined light source. When dry, apply two or three coats of varnish.*

10   *Go over the design painted in raw sienna in gold acrylic paint, using single strokes for the leaves.*

12   *Coat the underside of the board with an even layer of adhesive, and place the felt over it, smoothing it down.*

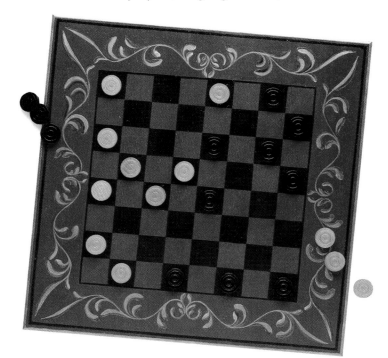

13   *Turn over the board and use a craft knife to trim away the excess felt.*

CHEST OF DRAWERS

This miniature chest of drawers has been prettily decorated so that it is perfect for storing jewelry or all the other odds and ends that gather on a dressing table. The design can be scaled up for a larger piece of furniture too.

You will need

- Miniature chest of drawers
- Acrylic primer/undercoat
- Decorator's brush
- Sandpaper
- Emulsion (latex) paint—turquoise
- Chalk
- Artists' acrylic paints—Hooker's green, cadmium red, cadmium yellow, and white
- Design brush—no. 4
- Antiquing fluid (use raw umber artists' oil paint mixed with white [mineral] spirit to give a runny consistency)
- Oil-based varnish and varnish brush

1 *Seal the chest of drawers with acrylic primer/undercoat and sand lightly when it is dry. Apply a coat of turquoise emulsion. So that the drawers do not stick, do not paint the inside, but take the paint just around the top and sides of the drawers and just inside the drawer openings.*

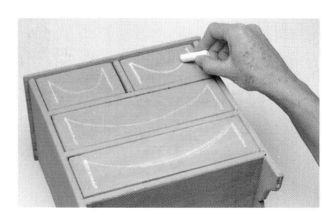

2 *Replace the drawers and mark the design in chalk on the front, aligning the drops of the garlands on each drawer. Indicate the positions of the roses by drawing circles. Do not worry about the leaves at this stage.*

3 *Paint in the roses one by one. Mix three shades of coral pink with the red, yellow and white. Remember to apply shadow consistently.*

4 *Paint in the buds by making a small oval with coral paint. Use green to paint the sepals. Starting at the stem end, push the brush down and then up to form the sepals.*

5 *Paint in the leaves so that they just peep from behind the roses. Shade them on one side, using the same imagined light source as for the roses.*

6 *Paint in the stems for the garland and drops with green. Paint the garland from a point just above the center—so that it looks as if it is supporting the roses.*

7 *Paint in the leaves along the garland, making them look as if they are growing from the center outwards. The leaves on the drops point down and end in a single leaf.*

8 *Add darker green to the leaves in the garlands, keeping the shadows consistent with the shading added around the roses.*

9 Chalk in an oval on each side and on the top of the chest, drawing around an oval plate if you have one that is a suitable size. Paint the leaves on the sides so that they appear to grow from the bottom, up each side, and meet at the top.

11 Use clean, dry kitchen towel to wipe off the excess antiquing fluid. How much you remove is a matter of choice, but it is a good idea to wipe off more around the main design while leaving the edges slightly dirtier. Leave to dry for 24 hours before sealing with oil-based varnish.

10 Paint over the whole chest and drawers with antiquing fluid. Do not worry if you do not like the effect because it can be removed with white spirit without harming the underlying paint.

STENCILING

Astencil is simply a design shape cut out of a piece of wax card, thin metal, or plastic film.
When paint is applied through the cutout, the shape is reproduced on the surface below.
Stenciling has been used for centuries as a means of decorating fabrics, books, pottery
and, of course, the home itself. Early examples can still be seen in homes and museums all over
the world. In recent years, as people have looked for new and aesthetic ways to bring
individuality to their homes, stenciling has come back into fashion.

The projects in this chapter explore the versatility of the craft. They range from a very
simple yet effective gift tag, through more complicated items to the challenge of designing your
own stencil. The projects have been planned to
allow you to develop your knowledge and
skills of stenciling in a gradual way.

MATERIALS AND EQUIPMENT

PAINTING KIT

Readymade Stencils

There is a wide choice available, but do consider the size, shape and intricacy of a design when you are deciding what would be most appropriate.

Stencil Brushes

Thick bristled brushes are used to apply paint through the stencil. A good range to start would be sizes 4, 8, 12 and 16.

Low-tack Masking Tape

You must ensure that the stencil lies flat in place for painting, and low-tack tape reduces the risk of damaging your work surface. Spray adhesive is an alternative for fixing your stencil temporarily in place.

Stencil Paints

Artists' acrylics can be applied to most surfaces. Special paints are available for ceramics and glass. Use fast-drying paints to avoid smudging problems during layering. Water-based paints are easier to clean up.

Bowls

Old, small china bowls are useful for mixing colors.

Paper Kitchen Towel

This is for general cleaning up and for removing excess paint from the brush.

Scrap Paper

Have plenty of scrap paper handy so that you can practice.

Ruler

Always have a ruler for measuring and placing your stencils.

Right *Painting materials.*

Scissors

Apart from trimming some of the papery projects, you will need a pair of scissors for dozens of other uses.

Pencil, Sharpener and Rubber Eraser

Finally, make sure your pencil is sharp so that you cut along a clean line.

CUTTING KIT

Polyester Drafting Film

This is excellent material for making your own stencils. The frosted transparent film is easy to draw on and perfect for lining up extra layers. It is also hard-wearing and can be used repeatedly. Thick, waxed paper is another option.

Cutting Knife

You will need a scalpel knife with extra blades to cut your own stencil designs because a very sharp blade is necessary. A blade set at an angle is ideal for cutting arcs and circles.

> **TIP**
> ■ After every project, clean up when you have finished and wash out your brushes and stencils made of polyester with soap and warm water.

Cutting Mat

A "self-healing" mat, obtainable from most artist's materials suppliers, is recommended for cutting out your stencil designs because it will not disintegrate or blunt your blade as quickly as a cutting board would.

Tracing Paper and Graph Paper

You will find that both of these items are extremely useful for copying and reproducing balanced designs.

Now that you have all the materials and equipment you will need, let's start with the first project.

Below *Cutting materials.*

Fun Gift Tag

This is a great project to introduce you to the art of stenciling because it is simple yet effective. Enhance your gifts with a specially stenciled gift tag and delight everyone.

You will need

- Painting kit with acrylics
- Pad of colored paper
- Hole punch
- Curling ribbon

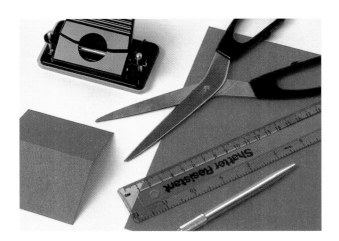

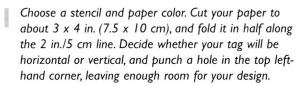

1   *Choose a stencil and paper color. Cut your paper to about 3 x 4 in. (7.5 x 10 cm), and fold it in half along the 2 in./5 cm line. Decide whether your tag will be horizontal or vertical, and punch a hole in the top left-hand corner, leaving enough room for your design.*

2   *For our practice session we chose to stencil a red heart onto white scrap paper. Put a small amount of paint into a bowl. Dip the bristles of a medium-sized brush into the paint and rub off any excess paint on kitchen towel. Your brush should be very dry.*

3 *Place your stencil design over a scrap paper and hold it with one hand. Hold your stencil brush upright and press it through the cutout, in a circular motion around the inside edge of the stencil. Build up the color by moving the brush around the edges. Try some 10 turns, but do not let the color build up in the middle of the cutout.*

5 *You can now apply the same principle to your pre-cut tag. Use a clean, dry brush. Put a little of your paint color into a clean, dry bowl. Dip the brush in the paint and wipe off the excess. Position the stencil over the tag, hold both in place, and build up the color in a circular motion around the edge of the cutout.*

Finally, twirl a good length of ribbon and feed it through the hole. Just look at the wonderful gift tags you can easily and so simply make yourself. You may then also want to impress your friends further by stenciling the wrapping paper to match!

4 *Practice, practice, practice! If your brush is too wet with paint, it may give a flat, filled-in stencil shape that bleeds around the edges. The brush has to be very dry. The heart at the bottom of the photograph, with the shaded edges and light area in the middle, is perfect.*

TIP
- When you are cutting out your tag, placing your cutting knife along the edge of a ruler offers a more accurate line than cutting with scissors. Use a metal ruler and hold the ruler and paper firmly in place, taking care to keep your fingers out of the way!

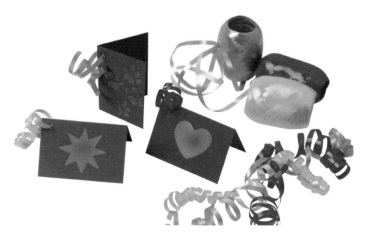

MERRY MUGS

Stenciled mugs will brighten any kitchen and they also make great gifts. In this project we made a set of three.

You will need

- Painting kit with ceramic paints
- 3 matching mugs in a plain color

1 Decide on a design that will suit the shape and size of your mugs. We chose stars.

3 Holding your stencil with masking tape on the curved surface will make stenciling easier.

2 Experiment with colors on a scrap piece of colored paper. Silver and gold are ideal for stars, and they work well on a blue background.

4 Stencil your first image in the usual way. You may need to stipple the edges to deepen the color on this dark, non-absorbent surface.

5 *Continue to apply the first image to all three mugs. By the time you have stenciled the third mug, the first mug should be dry enough for you to apply the next image.*

6 *We chose smaller silver stars for the next image. Using a freer approach, build up the stars into a pattern.*

7 *Put some silver paint on your brush, then pull back the bristles so they are a little way from the mug, and let them flick onto the mug so that small flecks of paint are deposited. But first, protect anything you do not wish to spatter, including the insides of the mug.*

8 *Finish off the other mugs also using the spattering technique. It works especially well with the star stencil design, giving the impression of distant galaxies!*

TIP
- Personalise a mug with a stenciled name to make the perfect gift.

Here is your new set of mugs. Treat a friend or yourself!

69

TERRIFIC T-SHIRT

For your introduction to fabric stenciling, choose a fun stencil and make your own designer T-shirt. Our cat's paw stencil went for a walk all over this one.

You will need

- Painting kit with fabric paints
- Clean, dry T-shirt in a plain color

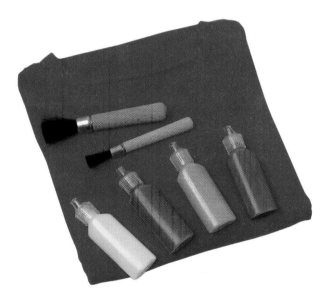

Choose a design and a set of colors that will complement your T-shirt.

2 *Tape a spare piece of fabric to a smooth surface and practice your stenciling technique on this surface.*

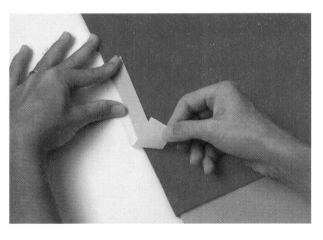

3 *Once you are happy with your efforts, place some scrap paper inside the T-shirt to stop any paint soaking through to the reverse side. Smooth out any creases and tape the T-shirt to a flat surface.*

TIP
- Follow the manufacturer's instructions for your chosen fabric paints; you may need to iron over the paints to fix the colors.
- Use a gentle stenciling technique to avoid stretching the fabric.

4 *Move your stencil design along the front of the T-shirt, around the side, and over the back.*

5 *To give it a sparkle, go over the stencil again with some glitter fabric paint, using the stipple technique.*

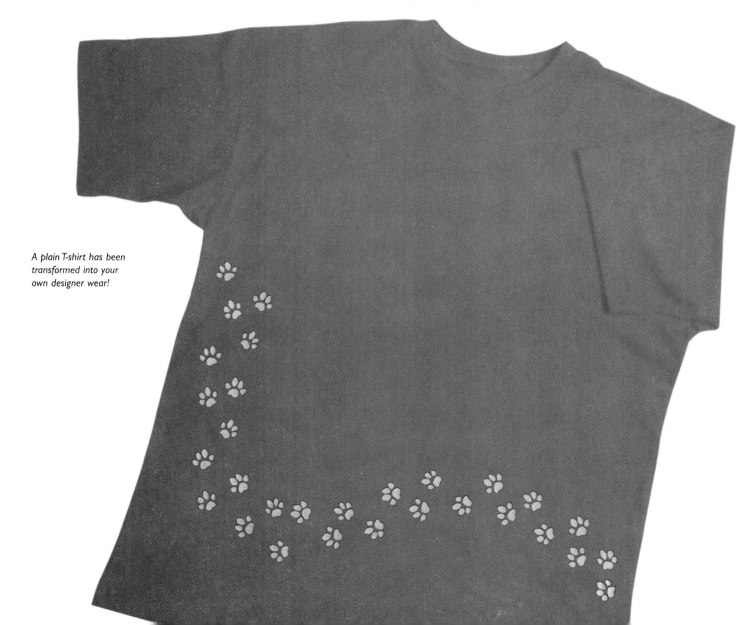

A plain T-shirt has been transformed into your own designer wear!

CHILD'S CHEERFUL CHAIR

This is your first attempt at decorating a piece of furniture. A plain child's stool can be made to look extra special with a stenciled seat and is certain to be a hit!

You will need

- Painting kit with acrylics
- A new, wooden child's stool, untreated (i.e., not varnished or waxed)
- Pair of compasses
- Fine-grade sandpaper
- Tin of polishing wax

1 Select an appropriate stencil design and a suitable color scheme. Give the stool a light rub-down with fine sandpaper.

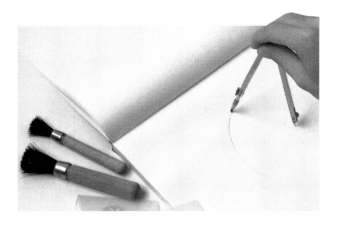

2 *We decided to stencil our floral design in a circular layout. Start by drawing your circle with the compass on rough paper. Placing an edge of your image on the pencil mark and following the line of the circle will enable you to calculate how close the repeats should be to complete the circle.*

3 *Apply the first color. Since you are being creative with this approach, you will be unable to rely on the stencil for exact spacing of images, so line them up by eye as well.*

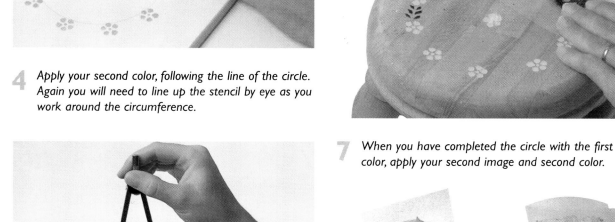

4 Apply your second color, following the line of the circle. Again you will need to line up the stencil by eye as you work around the circumference.

7 When you have completed the circle with the first color, apply your second image and second color.

5 Use your compass to mark a light circle on the seat of the stool. Allow enough room between the line and the edge of the stool for your design.

6 Roughly calculate the position of the design and apply your first color, following the line of the circle.

8 Add any finishing touches to suit the piece.

TIP
- When you are working out how to place your design, it may be helpful to mark key points. You must continue to check the placement as you work.
- Remember that these small designs need a lot of paint to build up the color.

9 *Seal your design by applying a coat of wax polish. Buff it up to obtain a deep luster.*

This chair will cheer up any child's day!

A New Lease Of Life

You can give any old piece of furniture a new lease of life by adding a stenciled decoration. Resurrect something from your attic and bring it back into your home. We have given an old school desk a pretty, rustic feel.

You will need

- Painting kit with acrylics
- Paint and varnish stripper
- Fine-grade sandpaper
- Small tin of emulsion paint
- Old piece of furniture
- Small tin of varnish

2 *Consider your stencil design and color scheme, and gather the materials you will need.*

3 *The old varnish on this desk must be removed. Apply the varnish remover and scrape it off. Take care with these materials; always follow the manufacturer's instructions and wear protective clothing.*

1 *Almost any old piece of furniture can be used as long as it is in good repair and is well prepared. You will need to remove old paint and varnish.*

4 *When it is dry, rub down the surface with fine sandpaper to give a smooth, clean surface. Dust off with a brush or cloth.*

5 Apply a coat of slightly thinned emulsion paint in your chosen background color. Allow to dry.

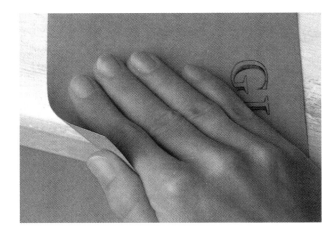

6 Rub down the emulsion coat with fine sandpaper to highlight the grain.

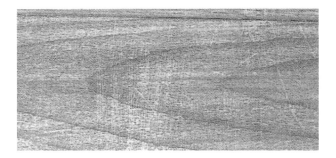

7 The combination of the beech wood grain and emulsion give the desired rustic effect.

8 We have chosen a border design for the desk lid. Measure and mark a light guideline so that you can position the stencil correctly.

9 Make sure that the stencil is applied in the correct place and fix it with masking tape.

10 Apply the first color over the whole area.

11 Line up your second stencil and apply all of the second color.

12 Continue with a third color.

13 A close-up of the completed design reveals that the yellow and green are a little bright for the overall rustic feel of the desk.

14 We stenciled the edges of the design with a little burnt sienna to tone down and add depth to the flowers and leaves.

TIP
- If your piece of furniture needs only a good clean, use sugar soap.
- When you apply the coat of emulsion, paint your strokes in the same direction as the grain.
- To give an even more rustic look, lightly sand over your finished design.

| 5 | *The result is an "older" and much more interesting design.* |
| 6 | *Add some finishing touches to suit the piece.* |

| 7 | *Seal in the effect and design with two coats of varnish.* |

A total transformation—the desk is worthy of pride of place!

FINISHING TOUCHES

Stenciling on a wall can bring a room to life. A design above a picture or a plain window can provide the perfect finishing touch, and this project provides an opportunity to coordinate colors with the rest of the room.

You will need

- Painting kit with acrylics
- Clean, dry wall
- Tape measure
- Step ladder

1 The space above this picture is the perfect place for a ribbon stencil.

2 With the picture in place, measure and mark the center point above it.

3 Center the stencil above the picture, making certain it is straight, and mark the key points.

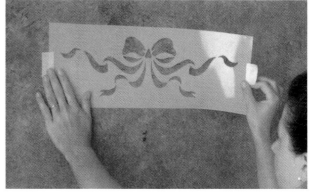

4 Remove the picture. Line up your stencil on the key points and fix it on the wall with masking tape.

5 We chose iridescent gold to complement the gold highlights in the picture frame. Stencil in the usual way.

8 Now that's more like it!

6 A peek at our efforts shows that we need to build up this transparent medium on such a dark background.

9 Hang your picture back up and admire your handiwork. Does it need anything else?

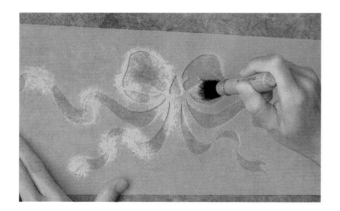

7 Heavy stippling is required on key edges of the design.

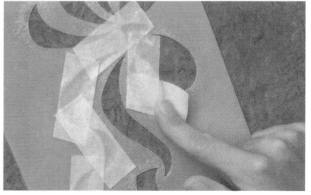

10 Add a finishing touch by selecting a bit of the design. Tape off the specific areas you want to use.

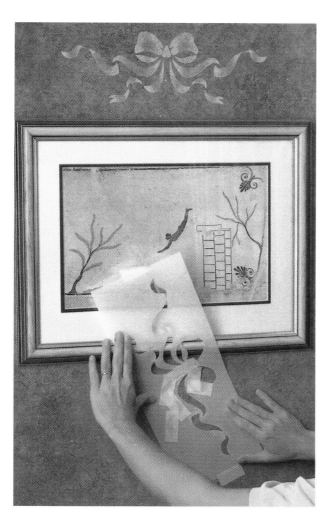

▌▐ Measure and mark the center and key points again. Stencil as before.

The stencil has provided an elegant finishing touch for this study.

TIP

■ When you tape off part of your stencil, be sure to add tape to both sides so that the sticky side of the tape does not damage your earlier work.

DESIGNER'S DELIGHT

The aim of this project is to design, cut and apply your own border stencil. Your inspiration should come from your own surroundings. We have chosen some lobelia flowers and used them to create a glorious border for a living room.

You will need

- Cutting kit
- Painting kit with acrylics
- Appropriate wall space to decorate
- Reference material
- Colored pencils
- Permanent felt-tip pen

2 Choose simple objects and practice simplifying the shapes. Break down your chosen object into sections.

3 Trace your design and hold it in place over graph paper with masking tape. Choose a simple shape from the design to build the outside border.

1 Look around for inspiration for a design for your own border stencil.

4 Experiment with ways of developing your design and also with colors. Keep your design straight by using masking tape to attach your tracing paper to graph paper.

5 *Transfer your design to clear polyester drafting film—one film for each color. Place your film with the frosted side up and trace a straight line from the graph paper. Trace all the design shapes of the first color in a line.*

8 *With a cutting mat and a sharp blade, begin cutting your stencil. Turn the stencil when you come to a corner, rather than turning your blade.*

6 *Trace the rest of the design in dotted lines with a permanent felt-tip pen.*

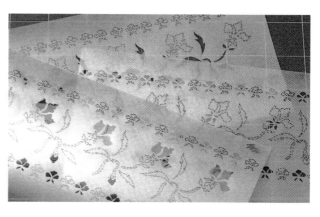

9 *Cut out the shapes of the continuous line from each piece of film. Do not cut any dotted lines.*

7 *Repeat for your second-color and third-color images.*

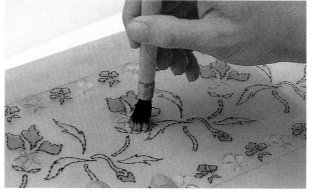

10 *As a trial run on rough paper, stencil the first color, align and stencil the second, and repeat with the third.*

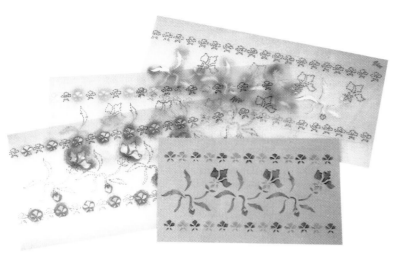

11   *Now you are ready to move to your chosen wall.*

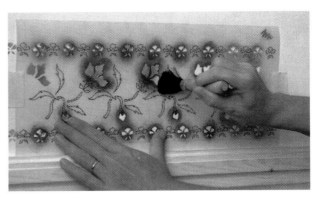

13   *Start your first stencil in a relatively inconspicuous place because you will gain on confidence as you proceed and your technique will improve. After using your first stencil once, move it along and position the repeat by laying the first cutout over the last image.*

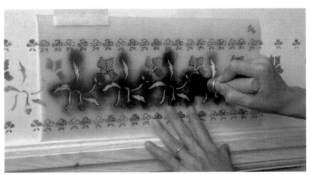

14   *Once you have completed all of the chosen area with the first color, proceed with the second color. Your dotted lines will make alignment simple.*

12   *This pretty room needs a little something to finish it off.*

15   *Complete the design with the third color.*

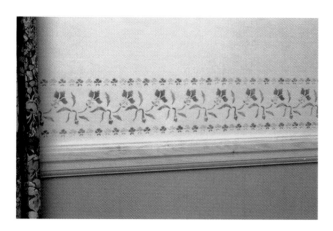

TIP
- The more of your repeat you can fit on to your stencil, the more images you will be able to color in one go. Remember, though, that the cutting time will be increased.
- When you align your repeat by laying a cutout over a stenciled image, as in Step 13, do not worry if alignment is not exact. You have cut this by hand, so it is bound to be a little different.
- Do not use more than three colors.
- If your design cuts or tears, it can be easily mended; apply tape on both sides of the tear and trim the excess tape with a blade.

16 *Put your room back together.*

Congratulations! A work of art and a cause for celebration.

DECOUPAGE

The fascination of decoupage lies in its ability to transform old items of battered furniture or household articles into eye-catching pieces. Once you appreciate the potential of the technique, you will want to try it on almost everything. Every junk shop, charity shop, jumble sale and car-boot sale will seem like an Aladdin's cave, brimming with articles ready for you to practice your skill.

Provided that the surfaces are correctly prepared, decoupage can be used on metal, wood, terracotta and pottery, glass, plastic and cardboard. As you experiment you will find that different approaches and techniques can be applied to achieve a variety of results.

Always make sure that something is worth rejuvenating before you begin. Decoupage can give worn and rusty pieces a new lease of life, but if you do not like the underlying proportions of an item, no amount of hard work will change these—or create an attractive object from something that is inherently unappealing.

MATERIALS AND EQUIPMENT

MOTIFS AND PICTURES

As your skill and interest in decoupage grows, you will begin to regard all kinds of printed material in a new light.

The recent revival in interest in the craft has meant that there are several books available that reprint interesting and amusing Victorian illustrations, which can be photocopied and colored. You will also find that gift-wrapping paper is a wonderful source of motifs, as are greetings cards. You can photocopy photographs, old prints, sheet music, letters and stamps, which can be made to look as if they are antique by a simple ageing process. Even magazines and newspapers contain illustrations that can be used—look out for fashion and computer magazines, which often contain stunning and colorful pictures. Old books can be an unexpected source—old history books, for example, often contain interesting maps.

If you are using modern magazines or greetings cards you can, of course, simply cut out the motifs. It is, however, better to photocopy illustrations from books, and most libraries and many stationery shops now have photocopiers, many with enlargement and reduction facilities. The great advantage of photocopying is that you can repeat a motif as often as you wish. Although there may be occasions when you prefer a colored copy, it

is less expensive and more satisfying to hand-tint a black-and-white copy.

CUTTING EQUIPMENT

You will need a large pair of scissors for general cutting out, a smaller pair for cutting out motifs from gift-wrapping paper or magazines, and a pair of nail scissors for cutting out intricate shapes. A craft knife or scalpel can be useful, more so if you have to cut out especially delicate shapes. Remember to rest your work on a cutting mat.

SEALANTS

Paper must be sealed before it can be used for decoupage in order to prevent it from absorbing paint or varnish, to stop discoloration, and to inhibit colors from running. In addition, when a water-based adhesive such as PVA is used with paper, the paper tends to stretch when it is applied to a surface, causing wrinkles and air bubbles.

Many prefer to use a sanding sealer or button polish, which you apply to both sides of the image. This gives the paper a slightly crisp feel, and it makes intricate cutting out easier.

ADHESIVES

The projects illustrated in this book were decorated with motifs glued with PVA (polyvinyl acetate) adhesive. This water-based adhesive is white when it is wet and transparent when dry. It can be thinned with water and used as a varnish. When you use it to apply individual motifs, wipe away any excess from around the edge of the design with a damp cloth.

PAINTS

Water-based emulsion (latex) and acrylic paints dry reasonably quickly. Artists' paints can be used to color or decorate objects. Acrylic paints cannot be used to bring out the cracks in a crackle varnish, however, because they are water-based and the paint will adhere to the second coat of crackle varnish, which is also water-based, and will smudge when you try to wipe it off. You can use artists' acrylic paints to tint white emulsion (latex) paint both to create a background color or add lines and details to finished objects.

Artists' oil paints are used in an antique glaze or to bring out the cracks when crackle varnish is used. The paint is applied by dampening a cloth with white spirit, squeezing a small amount onto the cloth and rubbing it over the surface of the decoupaged item once the second-stage varnish is dry and the cracks have appeared. Raw umber can enhance the cracks after the second stage of crackle varnish, while burnt umber creates reddish-brown cracks.

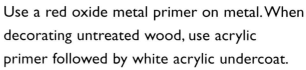

PRIMERS AND UNDERCOATS

Use a red oxide metal primer on metal. When decorating untreated wood, use acrylic primer followed by white acrylic undercoat.

VARNISHES AND FINISHES

Once you have stuck down the motifs and the adhesive is absolutely dry, apply several layers of varnish. The aim is to "lose" the edges of the motifs. However many coats you apply, leave each one to dry thoroughly, then rub it down very lightly with the finest grade

sandpaper before applying the next. Do not sand the final coat.

ACRYLIC VARNISH

This water-based varnish is especially easy to use. You can wash your brushes in water, it does not have a strong, pungent smell, it dries fairly quickly, and it does not yellow with age.

WATER-BASED VARNISH

A water-based varnish takes only 10-15 minutes to dry, making it especially useful when you are trying to build up several layers to blur the edges of your cutout motifs as quickly as possible.

POLYURETHANE VARNISH

Polyurethane wood varnish tend to yellow slightly with age, and so it can provide an "aged" effect to your work.

SHELLAC

You can use shellac to seal most surfaces, but it is not heat-resistant and you must apply a coat of varnish to finish off. Shellac is honey-colored and is often used to "age" pieces. It is also useful as an insulating layer between two incompatible paints or varnishes.

WHITE POLISH

White polish gives a transparent finish that dissolves in methylated spirits. Use it when you do not want an antique effect.

CRACKLE VARNISH

Also known as cracklure, crackle varnish is sold in a two-stage pack from good art shops. The first coat is oil-based, and it continues to dry under the second, water-based layer, which causes the top coat to crack. The results here are always unpredictable. When dry, the cracked varnish can be aged with artists' oil paints to reveal the cracks to best effect.

CRACKLE GLAZE

Use it between two different colors of emulsion (latex) paint to produce a cracked second color, through which the underlying color is visible.

WAX

Ordinary furniture wax can be used to give a polished sheen to an object that has been finished with matt varnish.

ANTIQUING GLAZE

Use this when you want to produce really beautiful objects. Mix them to a creamy consistency in a small glass jar and apply the glaze with a soft cloth to give a soft "aged" appearance.

SANDING

Not only must you prepare the surface of the object to be decorated, but finishing the decoupaged article with very fine sandpaper gives a smooth, professional-looking finish.

BRUSHES

You will need a selection of brushes. After applying emulsion (latex) paint, wash your brushes in water and detergent. It is best to have separate brushes for oil paints and varnishes.

ADDITIONAL EQUIPMENT

SPONGES

Natural sponges produce the best and softest effects when you are sponging on paints. If you use a synthetic sponge, tear rather than cut off small pieces so that they have slightly rough edges.

ROLLER

A small rubber or plastic roller is useful for pressing over glued images to remove air bubbles and to ensure even adhesion.

Craft knife

Design brushes

Decorating brush

Sponge

Varnish brush

Synthetic bristled brush

House-painter's brush

TECHNIQUES

PREPARING SURFACES

NEW WOOD

Seal new wood with an acrylic primer/undercoat or with a shellac sanding sealer. Then apply a coat of emulsion (latex) or oil-based paint.

VARNISHED WOOD

Use medium-grade sandpaper to rub down the surface to provide a key to which the paint can adhere.

PAINTED WOOD

If an article has been previously painted with a water-based paint, it can usually be painted over with either oil- or water-based paint. If you are re-painting wood previously painted with oil-based paint, it may have dried out sufficiently for you simply to apply emulsion (latex) paint after rubbing it down lightly.

MEDIUM DENSITY FIBERBOARD (MDF)

Treat it as you would untreated wood.

METAL

Use a wire brush to remove loose rust. Apply a base coat of metal primer.

CERAMICS

Apply acrylic primer/undercoat after lightly sanding the surface.

SEPARATING PICTURES

The images on greetings cards are sometimes printed on thick card, and in decoupage the picture needs to be separated from the card backing.

Paint the picture side of the card with a coat of shellac. Carefully insert a craft knife between the picture and the card. Use a paintbrush or ruler to hold the card as you gently lift the picture from its backing. After separating the picture, apply a coat of shellac to the back of the image to thicken it.

PLACE MATS

These mats illustrate the different kinds of crackle varnish that can be applied and the results that can be achieved.

You will need

- Pieces of MDF, each 12 x 10 in. (30 x 25 cm)
- Acrylic primer/undercoat
- Fine sandpaper
- Emulsion (latex) paint (we used cream for the backgound and maroon for the edging line)
- Decorating brush
- Flat-edged, stiff-bristled paintbrush
- Photocopied motifs
- Watercolor paints (light brown, maroon, and green for color-washing the motifs)
- Watercolor brush
- Hair-drier
- Shellac
- Nail scissors
- Craft knife or scalpel
- PVA adhesive
- Sponge or roller
- Crackle varnish (see below)
- Artists' oil paint (raw umber)
- Oil-based varnish (gloss or satin finish)

1 *Seal the MDF with acrylic primer/undercoat. When the primer is dry, apply two coats of cream-colored emulsion (latex) paint, allowing the first coat to dry and sanding lightly before applying the second coat.*

2 *Use the flat-edged paintbrush to paint a maroon line around the edge of each mat. Leave to dry.*

3 *Age the photocopied motifs by covering the whole image with watered-down dark gold or light brown. Do not allow the motif to become too wet and mop up any excess liquid with kitchen towel.*

4 *When the background is dry, color the knights' cloaks (we used red but you could use green), but do not use too strong a color or you will not get the "aged" effect. Use a hair-drier to speed up the drying process.*

5 *When the paint is dry, apply a coat of shellac or white button polish to the back and front of the paper. Use a hair-drier for speed.*

6 *When the shellac is completely dry, cut neatly around the image with sharp nail scissors.*

7 *Use a craft knife or scalpel to cut out the intricate shapes, then place the motif on the mat, lightly marking the position with a pencil.*

8 *Apply a fine layer of PVA adhesive to the back of the motif, working from the center outwards to cover the shape evenly.*

9 *Place the motif on the mat, positioning it correctly, and press it down firmly with a damp sponge or roller.*

10 *Once dry, check for air bubbles and lifting edges. Air bubbles can be pierced with the point of a craft knife, which can then be used to insert a tiny amount of adhesive. Use the point of the craft knife to add minute amounts of adhesive under any lifting edges.*

APPLYING CRACKLE VARNISH

This kind of varnish is used to give an "antique" effect. The cracks are rarely consistent, and this unpredictability helps to give a feeling of authenticity to objects. We have used the place mats to illustrate the differences between oil-based and water-based crackle varnishes.

You will need

- Two-stage oil-based or water-based crackle varnish
- Varnishing brushes
- Hair-drier (optional)
- Artists' oil paint (raw umber)
- White spirit
- Varnish
- Fine sandpaper

> ### TIP
> - Hold the items you are varnishing up to the light to check that you have completely covered the surface and have not missed any small patches. Holding the object to the light will also help you see the crackles, which can be difficult to detect until you have worked over the surface with artists' oil paint.

WATER-BASED VARNISH

OIL-BASED VARNISH

OIL-BASED CRACKLE VARNISH

This varnish is affected by the atmosphere because the second coat is water-based and therefore absorbs moisture. If the second-stage crackle effect is not to your liking, you can simply wash it off and start again without any damage done.

1 *Use a flat varnishing brush to apply the first, oil-based crackle. Apply the varnish from the center outwards.*

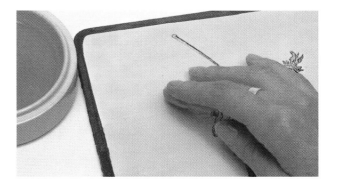

2 *Leave the varnish to dry. When the varnish is ready for the second stage it feels smooth and dry when stroked, but tacky when gently touched with the finger tips.*

95

3 Use a well-cleaned brush or a different one to apply the second coat of water-based varnish. Make sure you cover the entire surface and brush it in so that it adheres well to the first coat. Leave to dry for at least 1-4 hours, but preferably overnight. The cracks will begin to appear as soon as the varnish begins to dry, but they will not be visible unless you hold it to the light. Using a hair-drier, set on medium and held at a distance from the surface of the varnish, will encourage cracks to appear.

4 Squeeze about ³/4 in. (2 cm) of artists' oil paint into a dish and add a small amount of white spirit to soften the paint. Use a soft cloth or piece of kitchen towel to spread paint all over the surface of the varnish. Wipe off the excess paint with a clean cloth, leaving the crackle-effect enhanced by the darker oil paint.

5 Leave to dry for about 24 hours, then apply three to four coats of varnish, allowing the varnish to dry between coats and sanding each coat gently. Gloss varnish is hard-wearing and effective for table mats.

WATER-BASED CRACKLE VARNISH

If you buy this two-stage varnish from a good art shop, you will be able to choose between large or small cracks. Although the cracks tend to look fairly predictable, you can achieve a good ageing effect by rubbing artists' oil paint over the surface.

1 The first stage is a milky white fluid and it takes about 20 minutes to dry, when it becomes clear. If you want small cracks, apply a second coat of the stage-one fluid, which should be left to dry for a further 20 minutes.

2 When the stage-one varnish is dry, apply the second stage. Make sure that the base coat is completely covered by holding your work up to the light. Leave to dry for 20 minutes. Cracks will have appeared over the whole surface.

3   Use a soft cloth, dampened with white spirit, to rub artists' oil paint over the surface of the varnish. Leave this to dry, which can take up to 24 hours.

4   Apply four coats of gloss, heat-proof polyurethane varnish, sanding with fine sandpaper between each coat.

CERAMIC LAMP

The base of this lamp was bought in a car-boot sale, but you can find similar, plain bases in most do-it-yourself and home furnishing stores. This kind of lamp is suitable for Victorian animal illustrations—we used lizards, which we enlarged on a photocopier and color-washed.

You will need

- Ceramic lamp base
- Medium and fine sandpaper
- Emulsion (latex) paint (yellow)
- Decorating brushes for emulsion (latex) paint and varnish
- Photocopied motifs
- Watercolor paint (olive-green)
- Scissors and craft knife
- PVA adhesive
- Sponge
- Oil-based crackle varnish
- Hair-drier (optional)
- Artists' oil paint (raw umber)
- White spirit
- Polyurethane varnish (satin finish)

TIP
- When you have used oil-based crackle varnish, you must finish off with oil-based varnish. Alternatively, use a layer of shellac between the crackle varnish and the acrylic varnish.

1 *Rub over the lamp base gently with sandpaper, then apply two coats of emulsion (latex) paint.*

2 *While the paint is drying, apply olive-green watercolor to the lizards. Use the paint thinly for an aged look. When dry, apply shellac to both sides of the motifs and let dry.*

3 *Use PVA adhesive to stick the cutout lizards to the base of the lamp. Press the motifs down firmly and evenly on the surface and wipe away the excess glue.*

4 When the adhesive is dry, apply the first stage of the crackle varnish. Leave it to dry until it feels smooth when stroked—though still sticky to the touch.

TIP
- Always clean away any glue from around the motifs because the adhesive will show up as lighter patches on the finished object if you apply crackle varnish over it.

6 The drying process will depend on the temperature and humidity of the room, but after a couple of hours you can use a hair-drier to push the crackles to form.

5 Apply the second stage of the crackle varnish, making sure that the whole surface is covered.

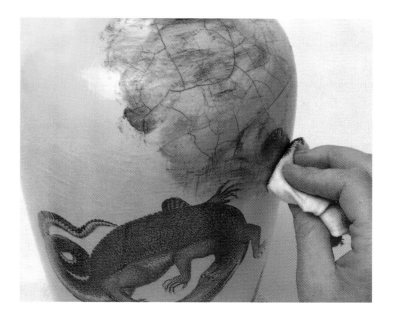

7 Mix some artists' oil paint with white spirit and apply it to the surface of the lamp with a cloth.

8 Rub the mixture into the cracks with a circular movement and remove the excess with a clean cloth. Leave to dry for about 2 hours.

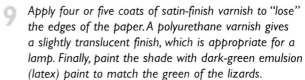

9 Apply four or five coats of satin-finish varnish to "lose" the edges of the paper. A polyurethane varnish gives a slightly translucent finish, which is appropriate for a lamp. Finally, paint the shade with dark-green emulsion (latex) paint to match the green of the lizards.

FABRIC LAMPSHADE

Lampshades are available in a range of styles, sizes and shapes. We used an old one, but a new, fabric-covered shade would do just as well. You can use any kind of motif—teddy bears for a child's room, for example—and this was so easy to do that we decorated an old tray to match.

You will need

- Lampshade
- PVA adhesive
- 1 in. (2.5 cm) decorating brush
- Emulsion (latex) paint (midnight-blue)
- Brushes for applying emulsion (latex), watercolor, and acrylic paints and varnish
- Photocopied motifs
- Watercolor paint (pink)
- Artists' acrylic paint (gold)
- Scissors and craft knife
- Varnish

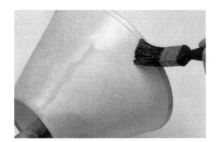

If you are using a fabric lampshade, apply a coat of PVA adhesive, diluted to the consistency of paint, to bond the material and give a smooth surface to work on. PVA glue will not be affected by the heat of a 60 w light bulb.

2 *When the PVA adhesive is dry, apply two coats of emulsion (latex) paint.*

3 *Paint the angels with watered-down pink watercolor.*

4 *Use a fine brush to add highlights to the angels with gold acrylic paint.*

5 *When the angels are quite dry, apply a coat of shellac to both sides of each one.*

6 *Cut out and stick the angels in position around the lampshade.*

7 *Add the edging to the top and bottom of the shade, snipping at 1 in. (3 cm) intervals to ensure it lies flat. When the adhesive is dry, apply at least five coats of varnish so that the edges of the paper are "lost".*

TIP
■ When sticking motifs to curved surfaces, make small snips around the edges at intervals of about 1 in. (2.5 cm) to ensure that the motifs lie flat.

TRAY

An old tray was given an undercoat of acrylic paint followed by two coats of midnight-blue emulsion (latex) paint. When the paint was dry, cherubs like those used on the lampshade, were stuck down with PVA adhesive. When the adhesive was dry, a coat of matt varnish was applied.

A water-based crackle varnish was then used to create small cracks over the surface of the tray (see page 96). After painting on the first stage and allowing 20 minutes' drying time, the second-stage coat was added. The cracks began to show after about 20 minutes, when the tray was held to the light. A little raw umber artists' oil paint was rubbed in, and the tray was left to dry overnight; then four coats of gloss polyurethane varnish were applied.

LETTER RACK

This MDF letter rack was bought in a furniture warehouse and it was decorated to be given as a wedding present. The motifs were photocopied from a log of the tour of the British Empire made by King George V and Queen Mary in 1901. The design was finished off with some stamps from the same period.

You will need

- Letter rack
- Shellac
- Brush for shellac
- Emulsion (latex) paint (petrol-blue)
- 1 in. (2.5 cm) decorating brush
- Photocopied motifs, stamps, and letters
- Watercolor paint
- Scissors and craft knife
- PVA adhesive
- Sponge and roller
- Watercolor brush
- Acrylic paint (gold)
- Polyurethane varnish (satin finish)
- Fine sandpaper
- Fine wire wool

1 Seal the letter rack with shellac and, when it is dry, apply two coats of emulsion (latex) paint.

2 While the paint is drying, color-wash the photocopies with light-brown watercolor to get an aged effect. Make sure the paper does not get too wet. Leave to dry.

3 Paint both sides of the motifs with shellac. Cut out the motifs and stick to the letter rack with PVA adhesive.

4 Use a fine paintbrush to apply gold acrylic paint to the edges of the letter rack.

6 Apply four coats of satin-finish polyurethane varnish, sanding lightly between each coat.

TIP

- Make a pencil holder for your desk from a cylindrical cardboard container or even an old tin can. This is an ideal way of using up those greetings cards that you don't want to throw away because you will need only one or two images. See page 92 for advice on separating the picture from thick card.

5 When the gold paint is dry, rub the corners with fine wire wool to achieve an aged effect.

METAL TRUNK

This old metal trunk had been stored in a garage for years. It was used by an aunt to ship her possessions back and forth to Africa. There was a small area of rust, which was easily removed, then turning the trunk into a useful storage space that does double-duty as a coffee table was a straightforward matter.

You will need

- Metal trunk
- Medium and fine sandpaper
- Rust remover
- Inexpensive brushes for rust remover, iron oxide paint, and shellac
- Iron oxide, rust-resistant paint
- White spirit
- Primer/undercoat
- Emulsion (latex) paints
- Decorating brushes for paint and varnish
- Gift-wrapping paper with appropriate motifs
- Shellac
- Methylated spirits
- Scissors and craft knife
- Masking tape
- PVA adhesive
- Sponge or roller
- Polyurethane varnish (matt)
- Artists' oil paint (raw umber)
- Wax polish

1 *Wash the trunk to remove all dirt and grease, then dry carefully. Rub away any loose paint or rust with medium sandpaper, brushing away all dust with a soft, dry brush. Apply rust remover to any areas affected by rust, remembering to treat the inside of the trunk as well. As you apply the rust remover, white appears on the affected areas. Apply further coats until no more white appears.*

2 *Paint the trunk, inside and out, with red oxide rust-resistant paint. Clean your brush thoroughly in white spirit.*

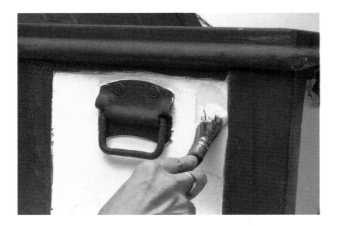

3 *Paint the trunk with primer/undercoat. When the primer is dry, apply two coats of emulsion (latex) paint. Apply the coats in opposite directions—crosshatching—to give a surface that has an old, rough appearance, rather like linen.*

4 *Use a narrower brush to pick out the handles and edging strips in a contrasting color.*

5 *Apply shellac to both sides of the gift-wrapping paper and clean your brush in methylated spirits. When the shellac is dry, carefully cut out the motifs you want.*

6 Arrange the motifs on the trunk, using masking tape to hold them in place until you are satisfied with their position. Mark the positions lightly with pencil. Remove the tape and apply an even coat of PVA adhesive to the back of the motifs, pressing them down with a sponge or roller. When the adhesive is dry, apply a coat of matt polyurethane varnish to prevent too much oil paint accumulating around the edges of the decoupage.

7 Use a soft cloth to apply a mixture of artists' oil paint and white spirit unevenly over the surface of the trunk. For example, we made the edges and corners darker and applied more oil paint around the locks and other areas where a well-traveled trunk would be expected to gather dust. Leave to dry overnight before applying three or four further coats of varnish, leaving each coat to dry and rubbing it down lightly with fine sandpaper between coats. Finally, build up several layers of wax polish to create a deep, lustrous sheen.

KEY BOX

This unpainted key box was found, almost by accident, in a furniture shop. It is worth looking in large do-it-yourself stores, which often stock a range of inexpensive, unpainted shelves and small cupboards that are ideal subjects for decoupage.

4 *Give the front panel two coats of cream-colored emulsion (latex) paint. Making the first coat slightly darker than the second and allowing it to show through streaks in the second coat will help give depth to a flat surface. Leave the paint to dry.*

1 *Gently rub down the surface of the box with fine sandpaper.*

You will need

- Unpainted wooden key box
- Fine sandpaper
- White spirit
- Shellac or acrylic primer/undercoat
- Brushes for shellac, varnish (you will need two), and emulsion (latex) and watercolor paints
- Emulsion (latex) paint (rust, blue, and two shades of cream)
- Wax candle
- Photocopied coat of arms and keys
- Watercolor paints
- Hair-drier (optional)
- Scissors and craft knife
- PVA adhesive
- Sponge or roller
- Fine wire wool
- Water-based crackle varnish
- Artists' oil paint (raw umber)
- White spirit
- Oil-based varnish (matt)

2 *Use white spirit on a clean cloth to remove any dust and grease from the surface of the wood, then seal the box. We used shellac sanding sealer rather than white primer so that the grain of the wood showed through when the box was rubbed down to give a distressed effect.*

3 *Paint the outer panels, the top and bottom and inside the box with two coats of rust or brick-red emulsion (latex) paint.*

5 Rub the areas you would like to look distressed with a wax candle—usual places are near the knob and on the edges of the door. The wax makes it easier to remove the contrasting color with wire wool.

8 When the motifs are dry, cut them out and apply shellac to the front and back.

6 Paint the door surround with blue emulsion (latex) paint.

9 Apply PVA adhesive to the back of the motifs and place them on the front of the central panel, carefully pressing them down with a damp sponge or roller.

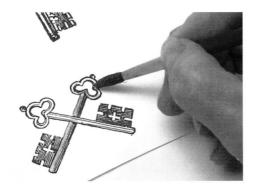

7 While the paint dries, color the motifs. Use a hair-drier to speed up the drying process if you wish.

10 When the adhesive is dry, use fine wire wool to distress the areas you have previously rubbed with the candle wax. Remove all traces of dust with a dry paint brush.

11   *Apply the first stage of the crackle varnish and leave to dry for about 20 minutes.*

14   *Leave overnight for the paint to dry, then apply two or three coats of matt varnish.*

12   *Apply the second stage of the crackle varnish, then leave it to dry thoroughly.*

13   *Rub artists' oil paint into the cracks with a soft cloth dampened with white spirit. Wipe away excess paint.*

WOODEN BOX

These round wooden boxes are sold in some large do-it-yourself stores, and are sometimes sold through mail order. They are available in a range of sizes, and are ideal as a personalized gift.

You will need

- Wooden box
- Shellac
- Emulsion (latex) paint (black)
- Brushes for applying shellac, emulsion (latex), and watercolor paints and varnish
- Photocopied motifs
- Watercolor paint
- Masking tape
- PVA adhesive
- Gift-wrapping tape (optional)
- Acrylic varnish

2 *While the box dries, paint the photocopied motifs with watercolors. We used lions from an old history book and painted them yellow. When the paint is dry, apply shellac to both sides of each motif.*

I *Seal the surface of the box with a coat of shellac. When it is dry, apply a coat of black emulsion (latex) paint, which will dry to charcoal gray.*

3 *Arrange the motifs around the box, holding them in place with masking tape. When you are done, remove the tape and glue the motifs with PVA adhesive.*

4 *If you wish, decorate the rim of the box lid with a strip of narrow gift-wrapping tape.*

5 *When the adhesive is dry, apply at least five coats of quick-drying acrylic varnish.*

WATERING CAN

These watering cans are sold in hardware stores and garden centers. If you are careful, you can use the can after you have decorated it. You must protect the decoupage with many coats of varnish, and take care when you fill the can that you do not knock it against the tap and chip the varnish.

You will need

- Galvanized iron watering can
- Vinegar
- Iron oxide, rust-resistant paint
- Inexpensive decorating brushes for rust-resistant paint and shellac
- Emulsion (latex) paint (pale-blue)
- Decorating brush
- Gift-wrapping paper or suitable motifs
- Shellac
- Scissors and craft knife
- Masking tape
- PVA adhesive
- Sponge or roller
- Watercolor brush
- Acrylic paints
- Artists' oil paint (raw umber)
- White spirit
- Quick-drying varnish
- Polyurethane (gloss)

1 *Carefully wipe the metal with a solution of one-part vinegar to one-part water to remove all traces of grease. If your watering can is an old one, clean it as shown for the the trunk (see page 105).*

2 *Apply a coat of red oxide, rust-resistant paint to the watering can. Use an inexpensive brush.*

3 *When the rust-resistant paint is dry, apply two coats of emulsion (latex) paint. Leave to dry.*

4 While the paint dries, prepare the motifs by applying shellac to both sides. When the shellac is dry, carefully cut out the motifs.

TIP
■ You will find a small number of acrylic paints useful because you can mix the colors with white emulsion (latex) paint to make a range of colors that can be used for touching up images, highlighting edges, or painting lines.

5 Arrange the motifs on the watering can, holding them in place with small pieces of masking tape until you are satisfied with their position. Draw in their positions lightly with a pencil. Remove the tape and glue the motifs in position with PVA adhesive. Press them down carefully and evenly with a damp sponge or small roller.

6 While the adhesive is drying, use a watercolor brush to paint the edges of the can. Use tubes of artists' acrylic paint, which are ideal for small areas such as this.

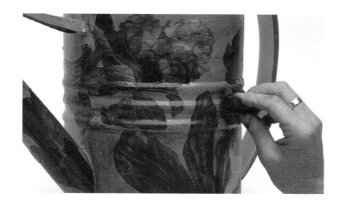

7 *When the adhesive and paint are completely dry, mix a small amount of raw umber with white spirit and use a clean cloth to rub it over the surface of the can to "age" the surface. Add extra antique glaze to areas that you would expect to accumulate dirt over the years.*

8 *Apply at least four coats of a quick-drying varnish to "lose" the edges of the motifs. Give a final coat of hard-gloss polyurethane. If you want to use the can, you will need to apply at least five coats of varnish to seal and protect it. Handle the finished can carefully so that no water gets under the surface of the varnish.*

PAINTED TABLE WITH CRACKLE EFFECT

Once you have started to use decoupage to transform old furniture, nothing will escape your attention. This old table had stood outside for many years, but it needed only sanding to remove the surface and remains of the old varnish and to provide a key for the undercoat before it was ready to be decorated for its new life.

You will need

- Small wooden table
- Medium and fine sandpaper
- Acrylic primer/undercoat
- Decorating brushes for primer/undercoat, crackle glaze, and emulsion (latex) paint
- Emulsion (latex) paint (mauve and yellow)
- Crackle glaze
- Flat-edged brush
- Gift-wrapping paper or suitable motifs
- Shellac
- Scissors and craft knife
- Masking tape
- PVA adhesive
- Sponge or roller
- Quick-drying acrylic varnish

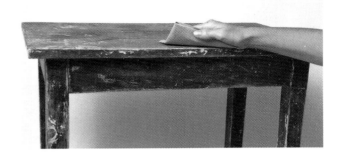

1 *Prepare the surface of the table by rubbing it down with medium, then fine, sandpaper. Brush away any dust and apply a coat of acrylic primer.*

2 *Paint the surface of the table with emulsion (latex) paint. Choose a color that you want to show through the cracks in the glaze. When the paint is dry, apply a coat of crackle glaze.*

3 *When the glaze is dry—after about 30 minutes— apply the second coat of emulsion (latex) paint. Load your brush well and cover the surface of the table in one movement. If you apply two coats, the crackle effect will not work. As the paint dries, you will see the cracks appearing.*

4   *Use a flat-edged brush to highlight the edges of the table with the first color of emulsion (latex) paint.*

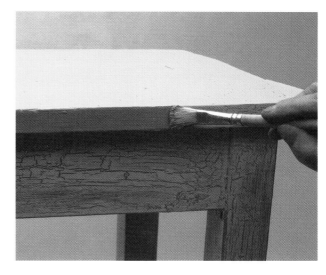

TIP

■ Apply as many coats of varnish as necessary to "sink" the edges of the motifs. When it is completely dry, it can be finished with a coat of oil-based satin varnish.

5   *While the paint is drying, apply shellac to both sides of the motifs and, when it is dry, carefully cut out the motifs. Arrange the motifs over the table, holding them in place with masking tape until you are happy with the arrangement.*

6   *Use PVA adhesive to glue the motifs in place, pressing them in place with a damp sponge or roller. On a large area such as a table, you could even use a rolling pin.*

7 *Use a damp sponge to press the motifs into awkward corners.*

8 *When the adhesive is completely dry, apply four or five coats of a quick-drying acrylic varnish.*

GALVANIZED IRON BUCKET

This old galvanized iron bucket was found in a skip, but it was such an unusual shape that we decided to give it a new life as a container for dried flowers. It needed a lot of work to remove patches of rust and to clean it up before it could be decorated.

Remove as much dirt as you can with a stiff brush, then use medium sandpaper to remove patches of rust. Paint rust remover on all affected areas, continuing to apply until it stops turning white. Paint the bucket inside and out with rust-resistant paint.

2 Since we wanted the color of the red oxide paint to show through the cracks, we left this as the base coat. You can also apply a coat of primer in any color. When the base coat is dry, apply a coat of crackle glaze, completely covering the surface of the bucket.

You will need

- Iron bucket
- Medium and fine sandpaper
- Rust remover
- Inexpensive brushes for rust remover and iron oxide paint
- Iron oxide, rust-resistant paint
- Primer/undercoat (optional)
- Crackle glaze
- 1 1/4 in. (3 cm) decorating brushes for glaze and paint
- Emulsion (latex) paints (sea-green and dark-blue)
- Gift-wrapping paper or suitable motifs
- Shellac
- Scissors and craft knife
- Adhesive tak (optional)
- PVA adhesive
- Sponge or roller
- Artists' oil paint (raw umber)
- White spirit
- Quick-drying varnish (matt)
- Soil-based varnish (matt)
- Wax polish

3 When the glaze is dry, apply a coat of emulsion (latex) paint. Use a well-loaded brush, but do not go over areas that have already been painted because this will prevent the cracking effect. As the second coat begins to dry, cracks will appear. Leave until it is quite dry.

5 Cut out the motifs when the shellac is dry and use PVA adhesive to stick them to the sides of the bucket, using a damp sponge or roller to press them down evenly.

4 Apply shellac to both sides of the motifs or gift-wrapping paper. The honey-colored shellac will have a slightly ageing effect on the motifs.

6 Use the point of your craft knife to check that all the edges are firmly stuck down, adding tiny amounts of adhesive if necessary. Remove air bubbles by making a small slit in the paper and inserting a little adhesive on your craft knife.

7 *Soften a small amount of artists' oil paint in a little white spirit to make an antique glaze. Use a soft cloth to apply it all over the surface of the bucket.*

9 *Apply five coats of a quick-drying varnish to "lose" the edges of the motifs. It is milky white when it is wet, but it dries clear.*

8 *Use a paintbrush to apply extra antique glaze in the areas you expect dirt to accumulate. Dip your cloth in the glaze, adding extra to the corners and edges.*

10 *Now you can stand back to assess your handiwork before applying the final coats of varnish. We decided to add contrasting blue to the lid handle.*

11 *Apply a final coat of oil-based satin-finish varnish and, when it is dry, polish with wax to give a warm sheen to the finished bucket.*

TIP
■ Because there are so many different varnishes on the market, always read the manufacturer's instructions before you begin.

PAPER RACK

This old paper rack was transformed into a gift for a friend who was going to live in Paris. The antique-looking "French newspapers" were, in fact, photocopied from a decoupage source book—it is amazing just how many different kinds of image are being reproduced these days.

You will need

- Paper rack
- Fine and medium sandpaper
- White spirit
- Brushes for primer, shellac and gloss, and watercolor paints
- Acrylic primer/undercoat
- Gloss paint (black)
- Photocopied newspapers
- Scissors
- Watercolor paints
- Paintbrushes
- Shellac
- Masking tape
- PVA adhesive
- Gloss varnish

1 Use medium sandpaper to rub down the rack and clean it with white spirit. Apply primer/undercoat and, when dry, apply a coat of black gloss paint. Leave to dry overnight.

2 Cut out the newspaper photocopies and apply a wash of watercolor to age them.

3 When the paint is dry, apply shellac to both sides of each piece.

4 *Arrange the motifs on the paper rack, holding them in position with small pieces of masking tape so that you can assess their positions. Remove the tape and glue the motifs in place with PVA adhesive.*

5 *Leave the adhesive to dry before varnishing. You should apply at least five coats, rubbing down each coat lightly with fine sandpaper before applying the next.*

TIP

■ When you want a good black background, use black gloss paint. Black emulsion (latex) paint tends to dry to charcoal gray.

SMALL BUREAU

This pretty little bureau was found in a charity shop. It had been left out in the rain, which had lifted the veneer from the surface, revealing the underlying pine. It was such a perfect size and such a useful piece that it was impossible to resist decorating it.

You will need

- Medium sandpaper
- White spirit
- Acrylic primer/undercoat
- Decorating brushes for primer/undercoat, crackle glaze, and emulsion (latex) paint (wide and narrow)
- Gift-wrapping paper or suitable motifs
- Shellac
- Emulsion (latex) paint (cream, petrol-blue, and sand)
- Natural sponge
- Scissors and craft knife
- Masking tape
- PVA adhesive
- Sponge or roller
- Acrylic varnish
- Oil-based crackle varnish (optional)
- Oil-based varnish (satin finish)
- Wax polish

1 Remove all old varnish and polish by rubbing down with medium sandpaper and wiping with white spirit.

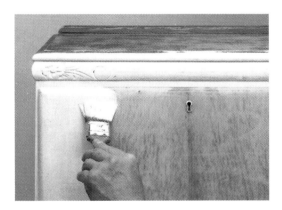

2 Apply a coat of acrylic primer/undercoat. While it is drying, apply shellac to both sides of the motifs.

3 When the primer/undercoat is dry, paint the desk with the first coat of cream-colored emulsion (latex) paint.

4 Leave the paint to dry, then use the natural sponge to dab the blue and sand-colored paint over the cream undercoat. Turn your wrist slightly to vary the pattern of sponging. If you do not like the result, you can wash off the paint before it dries.

5 Use a narrow brush to pick out the edges of the desk with blue emulsion (latex) paint.

6 While the paint dries, cut out the motifs from the gift-wrapping paper and arrange them over the surface of the desk, holding them in place with masking tape until you are satisfied. Glue the motifs with PVA adhesive, using a sponge or roller to press down evenly.

7 Use a craft knife to check that the edges are held down by adhesive. Slit any air bubbles with your craft knife. Insert tiny amounts of adhesive before pressing down the paper again.

8 Apply 4-5 coats of acrylic varnish to "lose" the edges of the motifs. When dry, apply a coat of oil-based crackle varnish. Conclude with satin-finish varnish and wax polish.

TIP

- Before sticking a large motif to a surface, prepare it thoroughly with shellac. Not only will this help prevent it from stretching as you glue it in place, the shellac will also help overcome the problem of air bubbles and creases.

WASTEPAPER BIN

This bin has been decorated with a collage of illustrations cut from comics and computer magazines. It was going to be placed in a boy's room.

You will need

- Metal wastepaper bin
- Acrylic primer/undercoat
- Emulsion (latex) paint (red)
- Paint and varnishes brushes
- Comics and magazines
- Scissors and craft knife
- Shellac
- PVA adhesive
- Quick-drying acrylic varnish
- Acrylic varnish (gloss)

2 While the paint is drying, cut out the images from the magazines. Coat both sides of each one with shellac. You may find it easier to do this before cutting the shapes from the magazines.

3 Beginning with the large background pictures, use PVA adhesive to stick the images over the surface of the bin.

4 When the adhesive is completely dry, apply five coats of acrylic varnish, then finish with a coat of gloss varnish.

1 Paint the inside and outside of the bin with acrylic primer, then apply two coats of emulsion (latex) paint so that a bright color will be visible if there are any gaps in the collage.

TOLEWARE

The name "toleware" originates from the French *la tole peinte* ("painted tin") and it was the French who developed sophisticated toleware or "japanning" to imitate the exquisite lacquerware being imported in the late 17th and early 18th centuries from Japan. Beautiful pieces were made, culminating in Chippendale and lace-edged trays, painted in floral designs or decorated with gold leaf.

It was the early settlers in the United States who first produced household tinware. This tinware was undecorated, and it was not until the late 18th century that American tinware was being japanned in the manner of the European ware.

Soon, rural tinsmiths also began to produce a type of simple painted tin, decorating their tin with brushstroke painting. The painted objects were various: trays, pitchers, coffee pots and trinket boxes. Today, we can recapture the pleasure of those early artists by creating colorful and personal accessories to grace our own homes.

EQUIPMENT AND MATERIALS

PAINTS

Water-based acrylic paints and primers have been used for all the projects in this book because of their ease of application, quick-drying properties, and absence of toxic substances.

Until recently, it was felt preferable to use oil-based products on tinware because of the non-absorbency of the surface and because painted surfaces on tin tend to chip more easily. However, the phasing out of oil- or solvent-based products has brought water-based versions to the fore.

PRIMERS

There are two types of primer, one for galvanized or zinc-plated tin, and one for non-ferrous metals (brass and copper, etc). The majority of tin items fall in the galvanized category.

BASE COATS

Acrylic paints in large containers can be bought from art shops and suppliers.

Emulsion paints, which can be used as base coats for wooden items, are not suitable for painting on to tinware. These paints adhere to surfaces by sinking into them, which they cannot do with metal.

Oil-based base coats can be used but they must be applied on top of an oil-based primer.

Enamel paints can be used on metal and give a glossy, lacquer-like finish that is similar to "japanned" articles. These paints are oil-based, so once again a coat of shellac or sanding sealer will be needed to isolate the base coat from your acrylic designs. Finally, cellulose metal paints and **car spray paints** can be used. They are compatible with acrylics and the design can be painted directly on to the finishes.

OTHER MATERIALS

RUST INHIBITOR

A proprietary "paint" that contains chemicals to seal in and prevent further rusting. You will need this if you are preparing old, rusty tinware.

SHELLAC, SANDING SEALER AND WHITE POLISH

These products seal and protect. They are solvent-based, quick-drying, and are compatible with both oil-based and water-based preparations.

METHYLATED SPIRIT

Apart from cleaning brushes, methylated spirit can remove acrylic and water-based paints from surfaces—either where paint has been spilt, or where the intention is to remove paint as an antiquing or distressing device.

GOLD LEAF

Gold leaf can be real gold (very expensive), or Dutch metal leaf—which is more economical. It is available as loose leaf or transfer leaf. The transfer leaf is the easiest to handle as it is on a backing paper. Try not to touch the metal leaf more than you need to, because it can be marked very easily. Unlike real gold leaf, Dutch metal leaf will tarnish and needs to be varnished or lacquered to prevent this.

BRONZE POWDERS

These are fine metallic powders made from copper, silver, aluminum or alloys. They too need to be protected with varnish or lacquer.

GOLD SIZE

Gold size is used in gilding to adhere the metal leaf to the surface and is available in many different drying times ranging from 30 minutes to 24 hours.

VARNISHES

Oil-based varnishes take a long time to dry, 24 hours or longer, and can "yellow" your colors because of the linseed oil content. Water-based varnishes dry very quickly, which means that you can apply several coats in a day. As they contain no oil, they will not yellow with age.

BRUSHES AND APPLICATORS

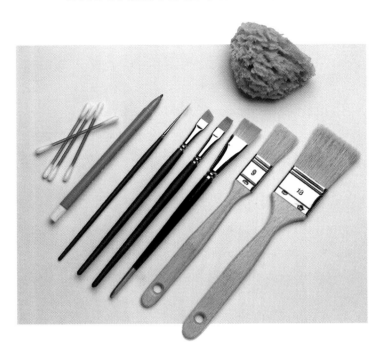

For decorative painting, brushes fall into two types: base-coating or varnishing brushes and design brushes.

VARNISH BRUSHES

Varnish brushes are flat and can be bought in a variety of sizes. The 1 in. (2 cm) and 1½ in. (4 cm) sizes are most useful for small items and can be used for primers, base coats and varnishes.

DESIGN BRUSHES

Design brushes come under the heading of artists' brushes. A liner or script brush is useful for fine lines or tendrils, and a flat brush or angled shader for heavier borders.

STYLUS

This multi-purpose tool is used when tracing designs on to objects, and it can be used for adding dots of paint.

OTHER EQUIPMENT

SANDPAPER

The coarser grades of sandpaper are needed to sand down enamel-painted items before priming. The finer grades can be used between coats of varnish.

PAPERS

Tracing paper is used for tracing designs and patterns. To transfer the designs you will need tracing-down paper. This wax-free carbon-paper comes in a variety of colors. It is used in conjunction with tracing paper to transfer the design.

MASKING TAPE

Used for either holding the tracing and transfer papers when applying a design, or for isolating adjoining areas when painting, the masking tape needs to be "low-tack". If the adhesive on the tape is too sticky it may pull off the paint when removed.

TECHNIQUES

PRIMING

The items for decorating will fall into one of three categories: new tinware, old tinware and enameled tinware (the last includes previously painted tinware).

The first step is a good wash. If the tinware is old, it is probably dusty. If it is new galvanized tin, it will probably have an oily coating that will need removing. Once the item has been washed, it will need drying thoroughly. A small item could be put in the oven at a low temperature for a while. Otherwise, stand the item in a warm place for a day or two.

Once the new metal is clean, the item will be ready for priming. If old metal, examine the item for any rust patches or spots. Remove any loose rust by brushing with a wire brush or very coarse sandpaper. Then treat with rust inhibitor. If the item is enameled or painted, give it a sand-down with coarse sandpaper to form a key to which the paint can adhere.

The primer can be applied now. Check that you have the correct primer for the type of metal you are painting. Once the primer is dry, you can carry on with your base-coating.

BRUSHSTROKES

Decorative and folk art painting are based on brushstrokes, of which the most common are the comma and "S" strokes.

For the comma stroke, hold a round brush perpendicular to the paper. Gently put the whole length of the brush down on to the paper, then apply a little pressure so that the brush hairs flare out forming the rounded head

Comma

of the comma. Pull the brush slowly back towards you, releasing the pressure on the brush and letting the hairs return to a point. Keep pulling back towards you and lifting the brush until you come to a fine point. Stop and then lift off.

To get the "S" stroke, begin on the tip of the brush. Pull the brush towards you,

"S" stroke

gradually increasing pressure. Change direction, until you are halfway through the "S". Start to decrease pressure while still pulling back towards you. Change direction

back to the original, and carry on lifting pressure until you are back on the tip of the brush. Stop, then lift off.

The stylus, or the end of the brush, can be used to put dots. If you want the dots to be consistent, dip the stylus in the paint each time.

CRACKLE GLAZE

This is applied between two layers of paint. The base coat is applied and, when dry, the crackle glaze is applied. This is allowed to dry and then the top coat is put on. The glaze will promptly start "working" and cracking the paint. The base coat and topcoat need to be contrasting colors for the coat underneath to show through.

CRACKLE VARNISH

Crackle varnish works when two layers of special varnish are applied at the end of painting. After the design work is completed, an oil-based coat of varnish is applied. This is left until nearly dry and then the second water-based coat is applied. This is left until dry and then heat is applied, and the top coat of the varnish will crack. Finish off with a coat of oil-based varnish.

WATERING CAN

A second-hand discovery, a little tender care, and one of my favorite designs made this watering can both useful and decorative. The background foliage is simply sponged on. Don't be daunted by painting all the flowers: with a little practice, they'll flow happily from your brush.

You will need

- Watering can (primed and painted with dark-green base coat)
- Tracing paper
- Transfer paper
- Masking tape
- Stylus
- Sponge
- Kitchen paper towel
- Nos. 2 and 4 round artists' brushes
- No. 5/0 script artists' brush
- Palette or plate for paint
- Acrylic paints in Fawn, Antique White, Raw Umber, Hooker's Green, Ocean Green, Leaf Green, and Yellow Oxide
- Varnish
- Varnish brush

1 Trace the daisy design on to tracing paper and attach to the side of the watering can using masking tape. Slide transfer paper underneath the tracing paper. Trace only the dotted line on to the can.

TIP

- When decorating old, secondhand tinware, use a stiff wire brush to remove as much flaking metal or rust as possible. A proprietary rust inhibitor will prevent any further deterioration before painting.

2 Dampen with the sponge. For the foliage, fill in the space below the traced-on dotted line with the three greens. Sponge on the darkest green at the bottom, to a height of 1½ in. (4 cm). Blot excess paint on to kitchen paper.

3 The mid-green is sponged on next and the lightest green is applied last, letting this color run up to the dotted line. Take care not to leave a line between each color; merge them to make the foliage look natural.

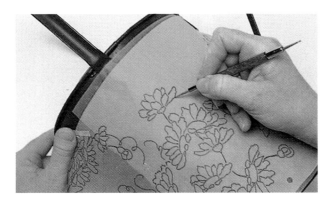

4 When the paint is dry, replace the traced design, hold in place with masking tape and slide the transfer paper underneath. Now trace down the whole of the design, using the stylus, and repeat for the smaller design on the top of the can.

5 Using the Fawn paint, and a No. 4 brush, base-coat in the daisy petals.

6 Take the Raw Umber and the No. 2 brush and base-coat in the centers of the daisies.

7 Now finish the daisy petals with the Antique White applied with the No. 4 brush.

8 Complete the centers of the daisies by adding highlights. Use Yellow Oxide and the No. 2 brush and pat in some color on the part of the Raw Umber centers where the light would catch them.

9 Finish off the centers with a few random, white dots applied with the stylus.

10 Use the very palest green to paint in the tendrils, stalks and sepals.

Lantern

The Turkish-style lantern begged a decoration that hinted of the exotic. I felt that a midnight-blue background studded with gold and silver stars was the best way to enhance it.

You will need

- Lantern (primed and painted with blue base coat)
- Sponge
- Kitchen paper towel
- Palette or plate for paint
- Acrylic paints in gold, silver, and Yellow Oxide
- Tracing paper
- Transfer paper
- Masking tape
- Stylus
- No. 2 round artists' brush
- Varnish

1 Dampen the sponge and dip it into the gold paint. Pat off excess paint on to paper towel and then sponge the gold on to the lantern with light, "pouncing" movements.

> **TIP**
> - Synthetic brushes are perfectly acceptable to use with acrylic paints for toleware. Do not feel you must buy expensive sable or real hair paintbrushes.

2 Trace the design on to tracing paper. Holding the tracing with masking tape, slide the transfer paper beneath. Transfer the design on to the lantern, using the stylus.

3 With the artists' brush, paint in the silver, six-pointed stars.

4 To create a sparkling shooting star trail, use the stylus and the silver paint to add a sweeping curve of dots for each silver star.

5 *For the golden, four-pointed stars, base-coat in the shapes with the Yellow Oxide and the No. 2 brush. Leave to dry.*

6 *Rinse out the brush and, with the gold paint, paint over the Yellow Oxide to complete the four-pointed stars. Make sure the paint is completely dry before applying a coat of varnish.*

Set of Pitchers

A favorite design of mine, and one that is based on an early 19th century French pattern. The design is modified for the different sizes of the pitchers and is painted over a basecoat, devised specially to create an old, aged appearance.

You will need

- Set of pitchers (primed, ready for base coats)
- Base coats in Deep Orange and Brown Umber
- Brush to apply base coats
- Tracing paper
- Transfer paper
- Masking tape
- Stylus
- No. 5/0 script artists' brush
- Nos. 2 and 4 round artists' brushes
- No. 4 flat brush
- Palette or plate for paint
- Acrylic paints in Burnt Umber, Leaf Green, Antique Gold, Bonnie Blue, Persimmon, Antique White, and Hooker's Green
- Varnish
- Varnish brush

TIP
- Do not skimp with preparation: apply two base coats to the metal before decoration, allowing the first coat adequate time to dry before applying the second.

1 Before beginning the design, paint the pitchers with a Deep Orange base coat and then apply a Brown Umber wash (50:50 paint:water) over the top. Leave to dry.

2 Trace the designs on to tracing paper and, selecting the appropriate design for the size of your pitcher, attach it to the side with masking tape. Slide the transfer paper underneath the tracing paper and transfer the design with the stylus.

3 Using the script brush, paint in the stalks in Burnt Umber.

4 *Thoroughly rinse the script brush, and paint in the rosebud stalks with Hooker's Green.*

5 *Paint in the leaves using the Leaf Green and the No. 2 brush.*

6 *Rinse the No. 2 brush and paint in the petals on the pinwheel daisies with Bonnie Blue.*

7 *Using the No. 4 brush and the Persimmon, paint in the base petals of the rose, the heart of the rose, and the rosebuds.*

8 *Take the Burnt Umber and with the No. 2 brush paint in the center of the rose as also of the pinwheel daisies.*

9 Put some Persimmon paint in your palette and add some white to create a paler red. Use this color and the No. 4 brush to paint in the bowl of the rose.

10 Complete the design by adding highlights to the daisy centers, the rose and the rosebuds, using Antique White and the No. 2 brush.

11 These pitchers are offset by a burnished-style golden rim. Use the No. 4 flat brush and the Antique Gold to paint the top and bottom of the pitcher, and to rim the edges of the handle. When the paint is completely dry, apply a coat of varnish.

Water Fountain

This novel fountain is designed for washing soiled and muddy hands in the garden or outhouse. I pictured it in an old country-style garden, so decided to give it a crackled-painted effect for an aged and well-worn look. The trailing, overgrown ivy complements the garden theme.

You will need

- Water fountain (primed and painted with pink base coat)
- Chalk
- Crackle glaze
- Brush to apply glaze
- Contrasting topcoat—we have used cream
- Brush for applying the top coat
- Tracing paper
- Transfer paper
- Stylus
- No. 5/0 script artists' brush
- Nos. 2 and 4 artists' brushes
- Palette or plate for paint
- Acrylic paints in Hooker's Green, Ocean Green, Salem Green, Leaf Green, Antique White, Fawn, and Raw Umber
- Varnish; varnish brush

> **TIP**
> - Some of the solvents for cleaning brushes used for oil-based paints are expensive. It is economical to use a cheap brush and discard after use.

1 *Choose the areas where you want the paint to crackle and outline them with chalk. Apply crackle glaze to these areas. Leave to dry.*

2 *Apply the top, contrasting coat of cream-colored paint to the whole fountain. When going over the crackle-glazed areas, paint lightly and use only one or two strokes. If overworked, the crackle glaze will not craze correctly.*

3 *Leave the container to dry, preferably overnight. The crackle glaze will start to work immediately, cracking the paint.*

4 *Trace the trailing ivy design on to the tracing paper. At this point, transfer only the outline of the leaves—and not the veins—to the container.*

6 *Replace the traced designs and slide the transfer paper under the tracing paper. Transfer the veins on to the leaves, painting these in Leaf Green with the script brush.*

5 *Using the No. 4 brush, paint in the leaves using Hooker's Green, Ocean Green and Salem Green, with Leaf Green for the underleaf areas. Leave to dry.*

7 *To complete the design, paint the roots in Raw Umber, and the tendrils in Hooker's Green, once again using the script brush. When dry, apply a coat of varnish.*

GILDED TRAY

This project allows you to try your hand at using gold leaf. The black and gold combination gives a rich finish. Here, I have used a Russian technique with an early American pattern.

You will need

- Tray (primed and painted black)
- Transfer Dutch metal leaf
- Gold size
- Brush to apply size
- Cotton
- Shellac or sanding sealer
- Brush to apply shellac
- Tracing paper
- Transfer paper
- Stylus
- Masking tape
- Nos. 2 and 4 round artists' brushes
- No. 5/0 script artists' brush
- Palette or plate for paint
- Acrylic paints in Black, Turquoise, and Yellow Oxide
- White polish
- Brush to apply polish
- Soft cloth

TIP
- Unlike real gold leaf, Dutch metal leaf is less expensive, but it will tarnish and a coat of shellac will be required to prevent this.

1 *Apply a coat of gold size to the center of the tray where the gold leaf is to be laid. Follow the picture here as a guide.*

2 *Test for tack with your knuckle; it should have the same stickiness as adhesive tape.*

3 *Take a sheet of transfer Dutch metal leaf and, holding it by the backing paper, lay it carefully on to the tray.*

4 Before removing the backing paper, rub your fingers over the metal leaf to check it is stuck down. When applying the next piece, overlap the first piece by ½ cm (¼ in.).

5 Repeat steps 1 and 2 when going round the edges of the tray. Cut the metal leaf into strips, overlapping the pieces as you apply them. Leave overnight.

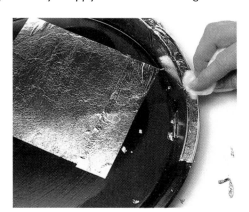

6 Use cotton to gently rub over the tray, removing any loose leaf. Apply a coat of shellac or sanding sealer.

7 Trace the design on to tracing paper and attach to the tray with masking tape. Slide the transfer paper underneath and trace down the design with the stylus.

8 Paint in the background of the design with black paint using the No. 4 brush.

9 Paint in any fine lines with the script brush.

10 *Using the No. 2 brush, paint in the detail on the large flowers. Now take the Script brush and paint the tendrils in Turquoise. Use the Turquoise also to edge the lower leaves on the border of the tray.*

11 *Using the No. 2 brush, finish with a little Yellow Oxide to the edges of the buds. Give the tray an application of white polish and buff with a soft cloth.*

Tin Trunk

Antiqued with crackle varnish, this quaint little storage trunk has been decorated with a Swedish-inspired cream and blue design. The colors work so well because the various shades of blue harmonize beautifully together.

You will need

- Trunk (primed)
- Base coats in cream and blue
- Brush to apply basecoats
- Old toothbrush
- Paper towel
- Tracing paper
- Transfer paper
- Masking tape
- Stylus
- No. 5/0 script artists' brush
- No. 4 round artists' brush
- Palette or plate for paint
- Acrylic paints in Adriatic Blue, Bonnie Blue, Blue Wisp, and Cape Cod Blue
- Two-part crackle varnish
- Brushes to apply crackle varnish
- Tube of raw umber oil paint
- White spirits
- Soft cloth
- Oil-based varnish
- Varnish brush

1 Measure about halfway up the sides of the trunk and mark with chalk or pencil. Paint in contrasting colors.

2 Using the darker color and a toothbrush, spatter the top, lighter half of the trunk. Spatter by dipping the toothbrush in some watered-down paint, dabbing off the excess on paper towel and running your finger along the brush. Practice before using on the piece.

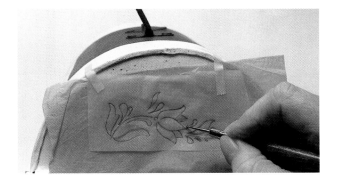

3 Trace off the design on to tracing paper and attach it to the trunk. Slide the transfer paper underneath and transfer the design on to the front and sides.

4 *Paint in the smallest leaves and the stalks in Adriatic Blue, using the No. 4 brush for the leaves and the script brush for the stalks.*

5 *Paint in the larger leaves in Bonnie Blue.*

6 *Paint the tulips with Blue Wisp.*

7 *Paint the commas on to the tulips using Cape Cod Blue.*

8 *Paint the trunk with the first coat of the crackle varnish and leave until the varnish is nearly dry.*

9 *Test to see if the varnish is ready for the second coat to go on: press it lightly with your fingers. It should feel almost dry, but with a slight stickiness. Apply the second coat and allow to dry, preferably overnight. Apply heat with a hairdryer; a web of cracks will appear but will be difficult to see until the Raw Umber is applied.*

10 *Mix some Raw Umber oil paint with a drop of white spirits and rub on to the trunk. Take a piece of paper towel and rub off the excess. Varnish with oil-based varnish.*

TIP
■ If the crackle varnish does not turn out as you hoped, remove the top, water-based coat by washing it off. You can then start again with the first coat of varnish without damaging the underlying painting.

Box of Fruits

A simple technique that makes use of bronze powders. The wonderful luster of these metallic powders lifts any design from the ordinary to the special. I have based the motif on an early New England pattern.

You will need

- Round tin (primed and then painted in black paint)
- Tracing paper
- Transfer paper
- Masking tape
- Stylus
- Gold size
- Small, old brush to apply the size
- White spirits
- Bronze powders in gold, bronze and antique bronze
- No. 4 round and No. 4 flat artists' brushes
- Any large, soft brush
- Cotton
- Palette or plate for paint
- Acrylic paints in Salem Green, English Yew Green, Adobe Red, Straw, Leaf Green, Plum, and Antique Rose
- Varnish
- Varnish brush

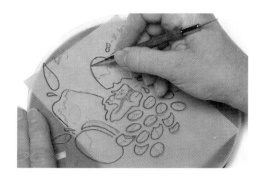

1 Trace the fruit on to tracing paper and attach this to the side and lid of the tin with masking tape. Slide transfer paper underneath and transfer the design on to the tin using the stylus.

2 Paint the gold size sparingly into the smaller areas of the fruit. Leave for 5 minutes to "set". While you are waiting, clean the brush in white spirits.

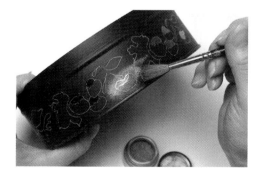

3 Take the large, soft brush and dust bronze powder across the sized areas of the cherries on the side of the tin. Leave for about an hour and then dampen some cotton and wipe off the excess powder.

4 Apply size on to the lid, as in Step 2. Using the large brush, dust the antique bronze on the leaves and stalks. Do the same with the gold powder on the fruit. Leave for an hour and wipe off excess powder with cotton.

6 Paint in the leaves and stalks on the border in normal, undiluted colors using Salem Green, English Yew Green and Leaf Green.

5 Using the No. 4 round brush, paint in the first washes of color (50 per cent water, 50 per cent paint) on the fruit; pat the color in roughly to make a textured finish. When dry, give a second coat.

7 Take the No. 4 flat brush and paint a border around the lid with the Adobe Red. Varnish the tin when it is completely dry.

UMBRELLA STAND

A florist's vase gave me the idea for an umbrella stand. An immensely practical yet decorative item for any lobby area. The decorative bands are adapted from a design used on an antique New England tray.

You will need

- Container (primed and painted with khaki green base coat)
- Tracing paper
- Transfer paper
- Masking tape
- Stylus
- Chalk and ruler
- Nos. 2 and 4 round artists' brushes
- No. 5/0 script artists' brush
- Palette or plate for paint
- Acrylic paints in Adobe Red, Straw, Leaf Green, Salem Green, Cayenne, Putty, Burnt Umber, and Antique Gold
- Varnish
- Varnish brush

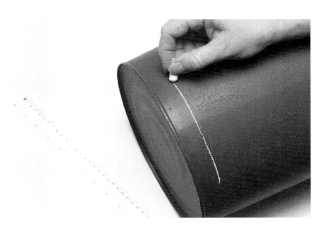

1 *To position the band and keep it level, first measure with a ruler along the container to the required place and chalk in a line.*

2 *Trace the design on to tracing paper and attach it to the container with masking tape, using the chalk line as a guide. Slide the transfer paper under the tracing paper and transfer the design with the stylus. At this point do not trace the details on the leaves or roses.*

3 *Using the No. 4 brush and the Putty acrylic, paint in the beige-color commas.*

4 Now take the script brush and the Cayenne paint to describe the border lines.

5 Paint in the leaves, using Leaf Green and a No. 4 brush.

6 Thoroughly rinse the No. 4 brush and, using the Adobe Red, paint in the daisies.

7 Complete the daisies by patting in the centers using the No. 2 brush and the Antique Gold.

8 The old yellow roses are base-coated in the Straw paint. Use a No. 4 brush.

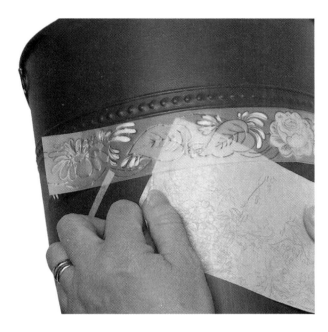

9 Take your traced design once more and reposition it over the painted areas. Slide the transfer paper underneath the design and transfer the details on to the leaves and the roses.

10 Finally, using the script brush, paint in the veins on the leaves with Salem Green and the details on the rose using Burnt Umber. When the container is completely dry, apply at least one coat of varnish.

LADLE

A nest of bluebirds in the bowl of the ladle, together with more birds and hearts decorating the handle, make this a simple but effective design for beginners to tackle. Finish the ladle with a flourish of colorful ribbons and hang it in the kitchen or family dining area.

You will need

- Ladle (primed and painted with cream-colored base coat)
- Tracing paper
- Transfer paper
- Masking tape
- Stylus
- Nos. 2 and 4 round artists' brushes
- Palette or plate for paint
- Acrylic paints in Antique White, Cerulean Blue, Bold Red, Yellow Oxide, and Black
- Varnish
- Varnish brush

TIP
- Some skill is required with the paintbrush. Practice the brushstrokes on a scrap of paper before you begin.

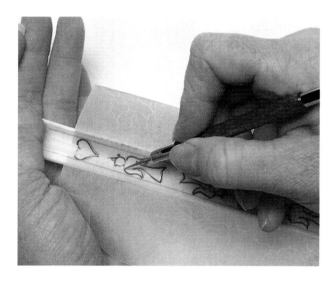

1 *Transfer the three parts of the design on to tracing paper. Place the first part of the tracing on to the handle of the ladle using masking tape to hold it in position. Insert the transfer paper under the tracing paper and, using the stylus, copy the design on to the handle.*

2 *Transfer the other two parts of the design to the inside and outside of the bowl of the ladle, again using masking tape to hold the tracing in place and carefully sliding the transfer paper underneath the tracing paper.*

3   Work on the handle using a No. 4 brush, and paint in the bluebirds in Cerulean Blue and the little hearts in Bold Red.

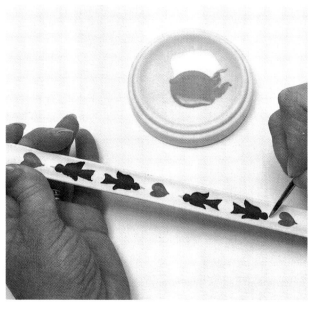

5   Acrylic paints dry very quickly, so you can now paint in the beaks of the bluebirds on both the handle and the bowl using a No. 2 brush and Yellow Oxide.

4   On the bowl, paint in the bluebirds in Cerulean Blue and the heart, nest and leaves in Bold Red.

6   Mix some Antique White with Cerulean Blue to make a pale blue. With the No. 2 brush, paint in the lines on the bluebirds' wings on the bowl's inside as well as outside.

7 Using the handle of the No. 2 brush, and the Bold Red paint, put in the dots on the heart and the nest.

8 Take the stylus and, using the pale blue, put in the dots on the bluebirds' wings. Clean the stylus, and with the black paint, dot in the eyes on the bluebirds. Make sure the design is completely dry before applying a coat of varnish. Red ribbons add an attractive flourish.

FLAT IRON

Rescued from an old junk shop, this rusting
flat iron was washed and scrubbed with a
wire brush before being painted with rust
inhibitor and then primed. The design is based
on old-English, traditional barge painting, a
naive style of strong brushstrokes that can
look most effective.

1 *Using Holly Green and the flat brush, paint the handle as indicated. Paint a green band on the base of the iron.*

You will need

- Flat iron (primed and painted with black basecoat)
- Tracing paper
- Transfer paper
- Masking tape
- Stylus
- Nos. 2 and 4 round artists' brushes
- No. 6 flat artists' brush
- Palette or plate for paint
- Acrylic paints in Bright Green, Holly Green, Bright Red, Crimson, Antique White, and Butter Yellow
- Varnish
- Varnish brush

2 *Trace the three parts of the design for the handle, base and foot on to tracing paper. Using masking tape, slide the transfer paper beneath the tracing paper. Trace the design on to the foot. Do not trace any dotted lines now.*

3 *Trace the leaves and daisies on to the handle, and the scalloped border on to the base, as in step 2.*

4 Work on the handle using a No. 4 brush, and paint in the bluebirds in Cerulean Blue and the little hearts in Bold Red.

6 Using Bright Red and a No. 4 brush, paint in the rose petals with comma strokes. This will form the petals of the flower.

5 Replace the tracing and transfer papers to the foot of the iron and trace in the dotted lines on to the roses.

7 Paint the lower scalloped border on the base of the iron in Bright Red and, using the stylus, finish with an edging of white dots.

8 Work on the handle and foot of the iron, painting in green leaves with a No. 4 brush and Bright Green. Use a No. 2 brush, Antique White and the comma stroke to paint in the daisies. Leave to dry.

9 For the decorative detail, take the Butter Yellow and apply with a No. 4 brush to add the comma strokes. Then use the No. 2 brush and the same yellow to put in the stamens on the roses. Use the stylus to add the centers of the daisies to the handle and the foot. Varnish when completely dry.

KITCHEN TIDY

This wall vase has been transformed into a
handy kitchen tidy. To give it a settled-in
homely look, I have antiqued it using a
rubbing-down technique. This removes one
layer of paint to reveal another beneath. The
pattern is taken from a late 17th century
biscuit box.

You will need

- Container (primed and then painted with
  contrasting base coats)
- Methylated spirit
- Paper towel
- Tracing paper
- Transfer paper
- Masking tape
- Stylus
- Nos. 2 and 4 round artists' brush
- No. 5/0 script artists' brush
- Palette or plate for paint
- Acrylic paints in Blue Wisp, Sandstone,
  Adriatic Blue, Yellow Oxide, Pigskin,
  Blue Haze, Butter Yellow, Burnt Umber,
  and Brown Velvet
- Varnish
- Varnish brush

1 *Make a piece of paper towel into a ball and dip it into
some methylated spirit. Then rub the container, using a
circular motion, in the areas that you wish to look
"faded". The longer you rub, the more paint will come
off, exposing the contrasting paint underneath.*

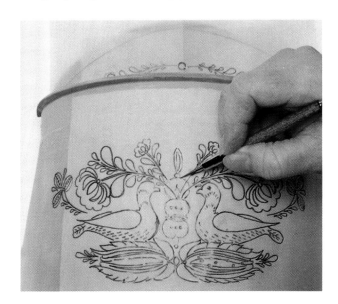

2 *With the tracing paper, trace off the designs and
attach to the container with masking tape. Slide the
transfer paper beneath and trace the design with the
stylus. Do not trace down the markings on the birds.*

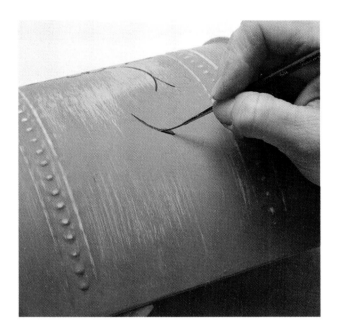

3 Paint in the stalks and central design with Brown Velvet, using the script brush.

5 Paint in the birds and the flowers on the back of the container. Use the No. 4 brush and Adriatic Blue and Blue Wisp.

4 Use the No. 4 brush and the Burnt Umber and paint in the leaves.

6 Paint in the flowers at the edge of the design, with a No. 2 brush using Butter Yellow and Yellow Oxide.

7 Using Sandstone, paint in the larger flowers.

9 Use the Blue Haze and script brush and paint in the details on the birds. Also, use the Blue Haze to dab in some dots on the flowers on the back of the container. Use the stylus for this.

8 Using the No. 2 brush, paint in the sepals of the larger flowers using Pigskin.

10 Rinse off the stylus and apply the Yellow Oxide to add some dots on the lower leaves. Varnish when completely dry.

BATIK

Batik is an ancient method of applying colored designs to fabric. It is called a "resist" method because traditionally hot wax is used to penetrate the cloth to prevent or "resist" the dye spreading to areas so protected. Rice paste or mud is sometimes used instead of wax. Designs may be of one color or of many colors, depending on the number of times the resists are applied and the fabric is dipped into baths of different dyes. Modern, simple-to-use dyes facilitate the technique of "pool" batik. Here, wax is applied to surround complete areas of fabric and to prevent the dye spreading from one area to another, which means that colors can be used next to each other.

The precise origins of batik are disputed. There is early evidence of batik in the form of garments depicted in Indian wall paintings; linen cloth dating to the 5th century has been excavated in Egypt; in Japan, batik was made into silk screens from the 8th century; and in Java, 13th-century temples show figures possibly wearing batik cloth. It is more certain that as early as AD 581 batik was being produced in China and probably being exported to Japan, Central Asia, the Middle East and India via the Silk Route.

The Javanese developed the canting (pronounced "chanting") to facilitate the application of wax. It is a metal bowl to hold the hot wax, with a spout through which the wax flows out, attached to a wooden handle.

The word "batik" derives from the Javanese *tik*, meaning "spots" or "dots". Early batiks were executed by means of tiny dots of wax. By the 13th century it was a highly developed art, a leisure pastime for women of noble birth.

The batik fabric was brought to Europe via Holland, after the colonization of Java by the Dutch in the early 17th century. By the 1830s, several factories had been established in Europe.

By the 1840s the Javanese were using caps (pronounced "chaps"), a form of block to print the wax on with. These were adapted from an Indian technique, and they made the process faster. In the 1920s modern dyestuffs started to replace traditional vegetable dyes, changing the appearance of batik fabric by bringing deeper, darker and more varied shades to the range of possible colors.

Batik is undergoing a revival in appreciation and interest in the West. In addition to the traditional uses of batik fabric for clothes and soft furnishings, the medium's potential is being explored and applied as a fine art, with artists seeking expression through dye instead of paint.

EQUIPMENT AND MATERIALS

In the projects described in this chapter you will gradually gain the requisite knowledge to accomplish a wide variety of batik pieces. All of the projects use a number of basic pieces of equipment and materials, and I have listed these below, together with the quantities you will need.

Chemicals, dyes and hot wax should all be treated with respect. Abide by the safety tips throughout the book.

Below *Traditional batiked material from Indonesia.*

You will need

- Plastic sheet to protect your work surface. Large bin liners, cut open, can be used.
- Cotton wool.
- Sponge, 1 in. (2.5 cm) thick by 12 in. (30 cm) square.
- Rubber gloves—the thin ones like hairdressers' gloves are best.
- Iron—preferably use an old one in case you get some wax on it.
- Newspaper.
- Measuring spoons.
- Dyes—1 oz (25 gm) pots of MX 4G (brilliant yellow), MX G (turquoise), MX G (peacock blue), MX 5B (cerise), and Kenactive Black 2647. Apart from the black, these are Procion fiber-reactive dyes; there is not a readymade Procion black.
- 2 pt (1 liter) measuring jug.
- 1 lb (500 gm) sodium carbonate (washing soda) or soda ash.
- 1 lb (500 gm) sodium bicarbonate (baking soda).
- 1 lb (500 gm) urea.
- 2 lb (1 kg) batik wax—this quantity should be sufficient for all of the projects.
- Wax pot—if you are going to do a lot of batik, you should buy a wax pot from a specialist shop. I have used a wax pot set on mark 5 for all the projects in this book.
- Natural bristle brushes, small and medium sizes and both flat and round.
- Cantings—small, medium and large spouts should be sufficient, with perhaps one novelty multi-spout.
- Soft, absorbent cloths (rags will do).
- Scouring kit—a large saucepan, detergent and wooden tongs.
- Fabric—6 yd (5.5 m) of 36 in. (90 cm) wide fine cotton should be ample for all the projects in the book. It must be 100 per cent cotton, not polycotton. You will also need 1 yd (1 m) silk, although 46 cm (18 in.) would be sufficient. All fabric has to be prepared—that is, scoured and ironed—before you start a piece of work. Do **not** boil silk.

BATIK

Left A wax pot, caps, cantings and wax brushes.

Below The five basic dye colors you will need.

Chemicals, dyes, hot wax should all be treated with respect. Follow the safety tips throughout the book and you will have fun and peace of mind.

TIP
■ Do not inhale the fine dye powder, and if it comes in contact with your eyes rinse them immediately in plenty of clean water.

GREETINGS CARDS

The simplest kind of batik you can do is on paper using ordinary white household candles to apply the wax resist. You can use almost any kind of paper as long as it is not coated with a shiny finish and it is not too flimsy—photocopying paper, which is usually about 80 gsm, is suitable. Making these greetings cards introduces you to working with the soda solutions, mixing and applying dyes, ironing out and the "halo" that results from wax seeping when you iron your work.

You will need

- Basic equipment, first 11 items
- Sheets of white paper, A4, 11½ x 8¼ in.(297 x 210 mm)
- Hair dryer (optional)
- Two or three white household candles
- Card to make a viewing window (use an empty cereal packet)
- Readymade, cutout window cards to mount your finished work
- Stick glue or spray adhesive for fixing

So that the dye penetrates the paper properly you should prepare it with a solution of 1 teaspoon baking soda and 1 teaspoon washing soda dissolved in 1½ pt (900 ml) warm water. You can use soda ash instead of washing soda, but it is twice as strong so you need add only ½ teaspoon to the water. If kept in an airtight container, this solution remains usable for 10-14 days.

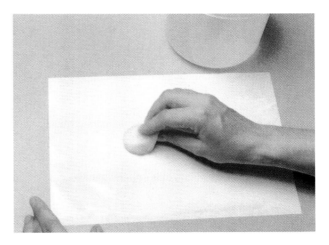

2 Lay a sheet of paper on a flat, non-absorbent surface, such as formica or glass. Use cotton wool to apply the soda solution evenly over the paper. Soak the paper thoroughly, but do not rub it very hard. Leave the paper to dry; wax will not penetrate where there is water. If you want to speed up the drying use a hair dryer, or iron the paper between sheets of newspaper with the iron set to low. Ironing may cause the paper to crinkle, but this often adds interesting effects.

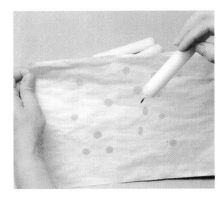

3 *Place your paper on the work surface. Light a candle and, as the wax melts, let it drip onto the paper. Experiment, holding it 3 in. (7.5 cm) above the paper, and then at 12 in. (30 cm). Tip the paper at an angle, and move the candle quickly across the sheet.*

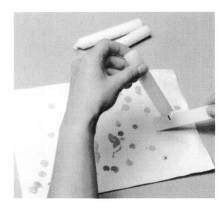

4 *Use a piece of cardboard to push the molten wax around the paper.*

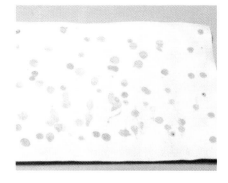

5 *Notice the changes in the tone and degree of transparency of the paper as the hot wax cools.*

6 *Cover your work surface with plastic sheeting to protect it from the dye. Mix ¼ teaspoon yellow dye powder to a paste with a few drops of the soda solution. Add 2 tablespoons (30 ml) soda solution to this paste. For a paler color dilute the powder further.*

7 *Use a large brush or a piece of cut sponge to color two stripes of yellow on your waxed paper. Wear rubber gloves when you do this or your fingers will go yellow, too.*

TIP
- Good ventilation is important at all times, but especially when you are ironing off wax. Work with your iron to one side so that your face is not directly above it. You may even wish to wear a mask as protection against the wax fumes released by the heat of the iron.

8 *Mix blue or turquoise dye powder in the same way and paint or sponge on two blue stripes. Leave to dry.*

11 *When the dye has dried completely, use a viewing window to select areas, and you will have three or four "alien landscape" cards to send to your friends.*

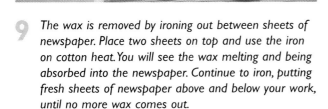

9 *The wax is removed by ironing out between sheets of newspaper. Place two sheets on top and use the iron on cotton heat. You will see the wax melting and being absorbed into the newspaper. Continue to iron, putting fresh sheets of newspaper above and below your work, until no more wax comes out.*

10 *When the wax is ironed out, it also spreads into the paper around the waxed areas, creating a "halo" effect. These "halo" areas resist the dye, leaving abstract shapes, which can be dyed a third color.*

Gift Wrapping

How about making some exclusive wrapping paper for a present or a waterproof jacket for a book? You can melt candles or use batik wax, which comes in the form of granules and is a mixture of paraffin (candle) wax and beeswax. Paraffin wax is brittle and cracks easily. Beeswax is soft and pliable when it is cool, and adheres well to fabrics. The combination of the two balances out their properties so that the wax will crack to give the traditional batik effect when it is folded. The ratio is about 70 per cent paraffin to 30 per cent beeswax. This project involves using a soft bed, mixing colors, and applying extra wax to remove "halos".

You will need

- Basic equipment
- Sheets of soda-treated paper, A3, 16½ in. x 11½ in. (420 x 297 mm)
- Small blanket or towel
  Cap-making kit
- Masking tape
- Scissors/craft knife
- Empty cereal packets
- Boxes
- Corrugated card
- Kitchen rolls
- Corks

TIP
- If you ever get hot wax on your skin, plunge it immediately into cold water. This will solidify and cool the wax, which is then easy to peel off.

I *Whichever kind of wax you decide to use, you will need a way of melting it and keeping it hot. The safest, most reliable equipment is one of the thermostatically controlled, electric wax pots that are available from specialist suppliers. Here, the batik wax granules are beginning to melt.*

2 *To apply the wax make some home-made versions of Indonesian caps, the copper printing blocks developed by the Javanese to print repeat patterns on lengths of fabric. Your caps can be made from cardboard rolls or from cut and folded card, held with masking tape if necessary. Cutting with pinking shears gives an interesting tool, and corrugated card is a good material to use because the loops serve as a reservoir for the wax.*

3 *To get the best print, place a soft surface under your paper. Lay a folded blanket or towel under the plastic sheeting on your work surface to give a soft bed.*

4 *Lay a sheet of paper on top of your printing bed. Heat the wax until it has melted, and put your cap into the wax. Cardboard sometimes fizzes the first time you put it in, so don't worry.*

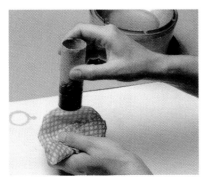

5 *As you lift it, gently shake off the excess wax. Hold a pad of material beneath to catch any further drips.*

6 *Print the wax onto the paper by pressing the cap down firmly. If the wax stays white and opaque, it is not hot enough. The paper should go darker and become more translucent when it comes into contact with the wax.*

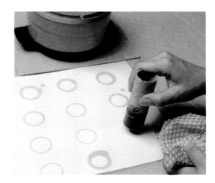

7 *You can do more than one print before going back to the wax pot, but each successive print will leave a finer deposit as the wax is used up and cools. Three or four impressions are usually the maximum.*

TIP

WAX POTS

Cheaper alternatives to a purpose-made wax pot:

- A double-boiler saucepan (bain-marie) in which boiling water in the bottom container melts the wax above. The water must be constantly checked to avoid boiling dry.
- An old saucepan on a thermostatically controlled hot plate. You must clean spilt wax on the hot plate regularly.
- A second-hand electric frying-pan with a temperature control.

8 *Combine different cap prints to build up a pattern.*

9 *Mix the dye using $1/4$ teaspoon of dye powder and 2 tablespoons (30 ml) soda solution for each color (see page 173). Red, yellow and blue have been used here. You can apply the dye in stripes or paint different colors inside the various wax-surrounded shapes.*

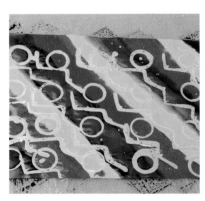

10 *When the dye is dry, iron out the wax. If you do not want the "halo" shapes, cover the unwaxed areas with wax while they are still warm from ironing, and then iron out again. All the "halos" will disappear.*

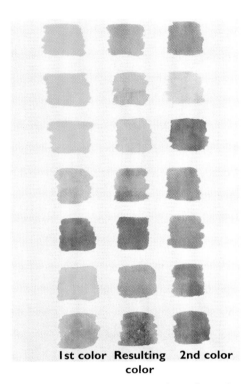

**1st color Resulting 2nd color
color**

11 *Try mixing your dyes to see what other colors you can get.*

The colors and patterns you achieve will be as varied as your imagination.

TIP

- Whichever way you use to melt the wax, do not allow it to smoke—the fumes are unpleasant, and unhealthy to breathe in for long periods and unnecessary. A temperature of 270° F (132° C) is an ideal constant temperature, and you can test this with a wax thermometer.
- If the wax becomes overheated and ignites, smother the container with a fireproof lid. Never introduce water, which will spit and spread.
- Always work in a well-ventilated area.

SUN CALENDAR

Working on fabric is slightly more complicated than producing batik paper. The fabric must be 100 percent natural fiber—cotton, linen, silk, for example—or viscose rayon. Any manmade fibers in the fabric, as in cotton polyester, may appear to take up the dye only for it to wash out at a later rinse stage. When the dyes are mixed with an alkali (the solution of sodas), a chemical reaction takes place allowing a permanent bonding of dye and fiber—hence the name, fiber-reactive dyes. Once the chemical reaction between dye and alkali has begun it lasts for 2-4 hours, after which the dyestuff is no longer fiber-reactive.

You will need
- Basic equipment, plus
- 2 squares in prepared fabric, 8 x 8 in. (20 x 20 cm) and 3 x 3 in. (7.5 x 7.5 cm)
- Small blanket or towel

Cap-making kit
- Masking tape
- Scissors/craft knife
- Empty cereal packets
- Boxes
- Corrugated card
- Kitchen roll

1 *Burning a fabric sample is a good way to test the fiber content, and the kitchen sink is a safe place to do this. Hold a lighted match to a piece of the fabric. Synthetic threads will burn quickly and leave a hard plastic residue; natural fibers burn slowly, leaving a soft ash.*

2 *You will need a piece of prepared cotton about 8 in. (20 cm) square. Any oils or dressings in the fabric may prevent the dye from penetrating, and they must be removed by scouring. Boil the fabric for 5 minutes in a solution made to the proportions of 2 teaspoons detergent to 2 pt (1 liter) water. Rinse the fabric in clear water, allow it to dry and iron to a smooth finish. The fabric is now prepared and is also pre-shrunk.*

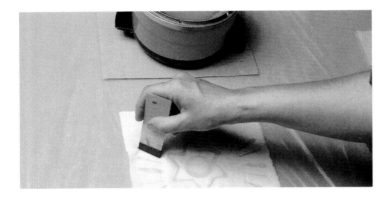

TIP

BRUSHES

- Hot wax takes a heavy toll on brushes, and natural bristle are longest lasting. Never leave them sitting in hot wax for a long time or let them become set in the cooled wax, or they will lose their shape.
- Dipping your brushes in boiling water when you have finished waxing helps to lengthen their lives. Make sure they are thoroughly dry before you put them into wax again, otherwise you will get lots of spitting.
- Place a brush in melted wax for a few seconds, press out the excess against the side of the wax pot, and carry over to the fabric with a pad of cloth underneath to catch any unwanted drips.

3 Lay the prepared fabric on a soft bed and heat the wax to approximately 270° F (132° C). Have your home-made caps ready, and wax the areas you wish to remain white. If the wax is at the right temperature, you will see the change in the tone of the fabric just as you did with the paper.

4 Mix ¹/₄ teaspoon yellow dye with 2 tablespoons (30 ml) soda solution (see page 173).

6 Dye the test piece for experimenting with overdyeing later. Leave it to dry naturally; this will depend on the temperature of your room. You can speed up the drying time with some warm air, placing the fabric in an airing cupboard, for example, or hair dryer—taking care not to melt the wax. Apply wax to the dried fabric in the areas you want to keep yellow. The facial detail can be added with a small brush.

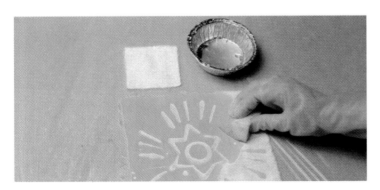

5 Apply the dye with a piece of cut sponge. Remember to wear rubber gloves.

7 *Mix red dye as the yellow above. Try it out on your test piece of fabric. Add more dye powder if the color is too weak, or more soda solution if the color is too strong. Apply to your square and allow to dry.*

9 *Mix blue dye and test it on your sample piece before applying it. When the dye has dried completely, remove the fabric from the plastic sheeting and iron out the wax between sheets of newspaper.*

8 *Use a brush and cap to wax the areas you want to stay orange.*

You can mount your finished piece and perhaps attach a calendar below it. You can buy readymade window mounts, or you could get the piece mounted at your local art shop.

CALENDAR

DOLLY BAGS

Painting on the dye in "pools" of fabric surrounded by wax, gives tremendous possibilities for color combinations. Using the dye in this way requires the addition of urea, which is a by-product of natural gas. In this process, small amounts of dye are painted onto the fabric, rather than the fabric being immersed completely in a dye bath, and urea is used to delay the drying process. Fibers and dye react while the fabric is wet, and the longer this process takes the better the fixation of the dye will be. Urea also helps to dissolve the dye more thoroughly, maximizing the color intensity.

1 To make up a urea solution, dissolve 1 teaspoon of urea with 1 pt (600 ml) warm water. If you mean to use it straightaway, do not use water warmer than 122° F (50° C) since fiber-reactives are cold dyes. The solution is usable for 10-14 days if kept in an airtight container.

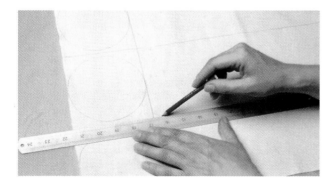

2 Using the selective dyeing method, you can make three bags with different color schemes. The bases are 5 in. (12 cm) in diameter and the sides are 5 x 15³/4 in. (12 x 38 cm). Mark the strips and bases on the prepared cotton with a soft pencil and lay it on a soft bed.

You will need

- Basic equipment, plus
- Prepared cotton, 21³/4 x 16¹/2 in. (52 x 39 cm)
- Lining material, 21³/4 x 16¹/2 in. (52 x 39 cm)
- Blanket or towel
- 2 wooden sticks, 6 in. (15 cm) long
- Small paint brush (optional)
- Soft pencil, 4B
- Ruler

Cap-making kit
- Masking tape; cardboard tubes
- Corrugated paper/cereal box card
- Scissors/craft knife

Making up the bags
- Scissors
- Pins
- Sewing machine or needles; thread
- 1 yd (1 m) lacing for the drawstring handles

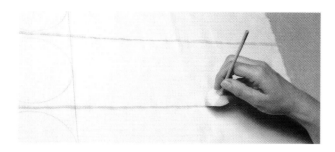

3   *Push one of the wooden sticks into a piece of sponge and strap it with masking tape. Trim it to a point. The sponge will hold more wax than a normal brush. This home-made tool is also excellent for applying dye. Heat the wax and use your sponge "brush" to apply it, following your pencil lines, to separate the three strips.*

4   *Make your cap prints in each section, making sure that each shape has a continuous wax boundary. If the wax sticks to the plastic beneath the fabric you know it has penetrated! It will also keep your work in place while you are dyeing.*

5   *Color fastness is obtained by combining the urea solution with the soda solution in the ratio of 1 part urea to 2 parts soda. For this project add a few drops of urea solution to 1/4 teaspoon of dye powder, then add 2 teaspoons urea solution and 4 teaspoons soda solution. For paler colors reduce the dye powder.*

6   *When all waxing and dyeing is completed and dried, remove the fabric from the plastic sheet and iron out the wax. You will notice that the fabric becomes soft while it is warm from ironing, but stiffens again as the residue of wax in the fibers cools. If you want the fabric less stiff, more wax can be removed by boiling the fabric in water in an old saucepan for 5 minutes, and then plunging it into cold water, using wooden tongs to transfer it from saucepan to bowl. The wax solidifies on the surface of the cloth and can be rubbed or scraped off. This process can be repeated to remove more wax. Finally, boil in soapy water to remove all surplus dye. Allow the dye to set in the fabric for 24 hours before using this method. Leave the saucepan of water to cool, and the wax will form a skin on the surface, which can be removed, dried and used again. You must dry wax thoroughly before reusing it, otherwise it will spit in the wax pot.*

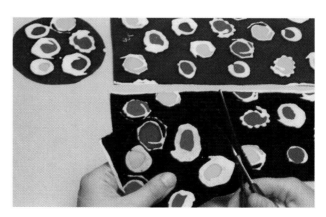

7   *Once the wax has been removed, cut out the fabric ready to make up your bags. Allowing 1/4 in. (5 mm) seams, sew the sides together. On each side, make a buttonhole 1/2 in. (1 cm) long and running from 3/4 in. (2 cm) to 1 1/4 in. (3 cm) from the top edge.*

8 *With right sides together, sew the base to the bottom edge. Turn right-side out. Cut and sew the lining material in the same way, but omit the buttonholes. Leave unturned.*

9 *Put the lining inside the bag, turn in ¹/4 in. (5 mm) seams on both and sew together. Sew two lines of stitching around the top of the bag, one at the top edge of the buttonholes and the other at the bottom edge, to provide a channel for the drawstring. Thread through the drawstrings, one entering and one exiting from each buttonhole. If you want to make a larger bag, multiply the radius of the base by 6.284 (approx. 6¹/4) to give you the appropriate length side.*

DYEING TIP

- If you want to mix all your colors before you start to dye, mix them just with 2 teaspoons urea solution. They will remain usable for 24 hours, and you can add the soda solution to each color just before use to give fresh, potent dyes.
- Do not saturate the fabric until puddles of dye form underneath, because these may run over the surface of your wax boundaries to the neighboring areas. Water has only so much surface tension before it breaks down and spreads.
- If you paint on the lightest colors first, you can cover any mistakes by a darker color afterwards.
- If your wax boundaries allow dye to seep, let the dye dry, wax the color you want to keep, and then overdye with a darker color.

TIP
REMOVING DYE

- An easier and more effective way of removing wax is to put your work through a dry-cleaning machine. The chemicals dissolve all the wax but the brightness of the color is not lost.

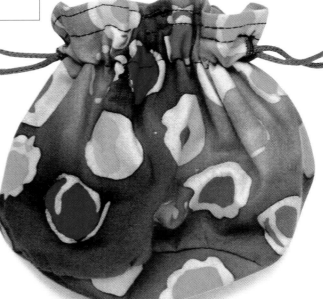

Garment Fabric

Large pieces of fabric can be quite easily batiked. The waxing is done in stages on a soft bed, and the fabric is then immersed in dye to ensure full penetration and evenness of color.

You will need

- Basic equipment, plus
- Blanket
- Plastic bucket, minimum capacity 1 gallon (4.5 liters)
- Bowl, minimum capacity 1 gallon (4.5 liters)
- Paper and fabric for experimenting with caps and dyes
- 2 yd (2 m) prepared fine cotton

Cap-making kit
- Masking tape
- Scissors/craft knife
- Empty cereal packets
- Corrugated card
- Kitchen roll
- Empty card from wide roll of adhesive tape

TIP
FIXING COLORS
- Fixing is improved in a humid atmosphere. Short bursts of steam from an electric kettle, introduced intermittently over the 2-3 hour drying period, can provide the necessary humidity.
- The evenness of color can be enhanced by adding the salt in three stages in the first 15 minutes of the dyeing process. However, the fabric must be removed each time more salt is added.

1 *Make some cardboard caps and experiment on paper with them until you have a design you are happy with.*

2 *Try the caps on fabric to see how many prints you can get from each dip in the wax and how they change as the wax cools and runs out.*

3 *Make as large a soft bed as your blanket and work surface will allow. Lay down the first section of your fabric, and arrange a chair at either side to hold it off the floor while you are waxing. Lift the fabric at intervals to prevent it from being stuck to the plastic.*

CALCULATING THE DYE BATH INGREDIENTS

Multiply the dry weight of fabric before waxing by 20—e.g., 6 oz (150 gm) x 20 = 120 fl oz (6 pt)/3,000 ml (3 liters). For each 2 pt (1 liter) of dye bath you need:

- ½-2 teaspoons dye powder
- 2 tablespoons (50 gm) salt
- 2 teaspoons (5 gm) soda ash or 4 teaspoons (10 gm) soda crystals

4 When the first waxing is complete prepare the dye bath. These ingredients are enough for about 6 oz (150 gm) dry weight of fabric, which is about what 2 m (2 yd) cotton should weigh. Dissolve 6 tablespoons (150 gm) salt in 3 fl oz (100 ml) warm water and set aside. Dissolve 6 teaspoons (15 gm) soda ash (or 12 teaspoons/30 gm soda crystals) in 3 fl oz (100 ml) warm water and set aside.

5 Make a paste of 1½-6 teaspoons yellow dye powder in water not warmer than 122° F (50° C). Add some more water so that it will pour easily.

6 Add 6 pt (3 liters) water to the dye and stir. Add the dissolved salt and stir. Salt is added to facilitate penetration, to promote an even quality of dyeing, and to get the best color.

7 Immerse the waxed fabric and test piece in clean, cold water and shake off the excess.

8 Transfer the fabric to the dye bath. Immerse it, agitating it to ensure good penetration of the dye.

9 Remove it after 15 minutes and put it in a bowl.

10 Add the dissolved soda to the dye bath, then immerse the fabric for a further 45 minutes, stirring occasionally. Remove the fabric, rinse in cold water until the water runs clear, then hang to drip dry.

11 When the fabric is dry, return it to the soft bed and do the second waxing. Wax everything you want to stay yellow.

12 Follow the same recipe and procedure as before, but using blue dye powder instead of yellow. Test the color on your sample piece first.

13 As the fabric moves around in the dye bath, some of the wax will be bent and crack, and dye will be able to penetrate. This gives batik its crackle effect. Wax cracks more readily and cleanly when it is cold, and this is why the fabric is soaked in cold water before it is immersed in the dye. The cracking is further controlled by crushing the fabric before and while it is being dyed.

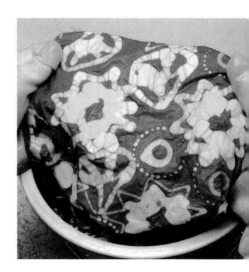

CUSHION COVER

As we have seen, it was the Javanese who invented the canting. Although it is not easy to use, once you have mastered the techniques you will find that the canting will provide a continuous flow of hot wax that will enable you to fine-line or dot work that would not otherwise be possible. There are many different shapes of these metal wax reservoirs available, but they all have one or more spouts through which the wax flows. The diameter of the spouts is one of the factors dictating the width of a line or the size of a dot of the wax applied to the fabric; speed, heat and angle of use are others.

Wax can be most easily applied to fine cottons and silks because it can penetrate more quickly than on thicker or more coarsely woven fabrics like linen. You will draw a more confident, freer and finer line if the tool can move smoothly across the surface. If you go more slowly to allow wax to penetrate a thicker fabric, you will be more likely to produce wobbly, uneven and thicker lines. The heat of the wax also affects the speed with which it flows through the spout and how much it spreads in the fabric—this is more evident when working on fine fabrics, such as silk.

An abstract design, which will give you maximum freedom to experiment with the cantings, is suggested for a cushion cover. Lay the prepared piece of cotton on your work surface and use a soft pencil to mark the diagonal and horizontal crosses lightly as a guide to keep the design symmetrical.

You will need

- Basic equipment, plus
- Soft pencil, 4B
- Wooden frame
- Drawing pins
- Prepared cotton, 17 x 17 in. (43 x 43 cm)

TIP
USING A CANTING
- If you get some unwanted drips, do some on purpose to match on the other side so that the "mistakes" are incorporated into your design or used to accentuate a motif.
- Do not travel so fast that the wax does not have time to soak in at all. Experiment with the lines and marks that the different cantings can make.

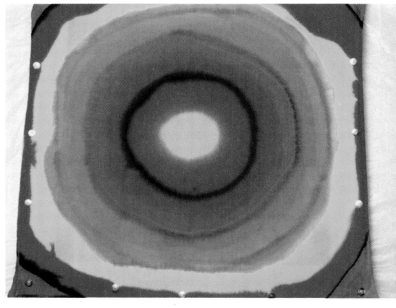

4 Keep the colors light and bright. Allow the fabric to dry completely.

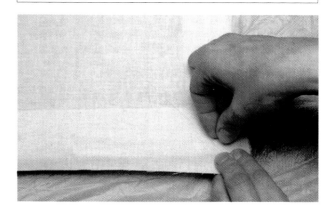

2 At first you will find that canting work is easiest on stretched fabric. You can use an old picture frame, if it is firmly jointed and not warped. Pin the center of each side and then the corners. The fabric needs to be taut, but take care that you do not pull the weave out of alignment, or the image will be distorted when you take the fabric from the frame.

3 Before you begin waxing, mix the dyes—6 tablespoons (90 ml) of each should be plenty. I have used red, yellow and turquoise. Apply the dyes to the fabric, allowing them to mingle with each other at the edges to create a colorful, softly diffused effect.

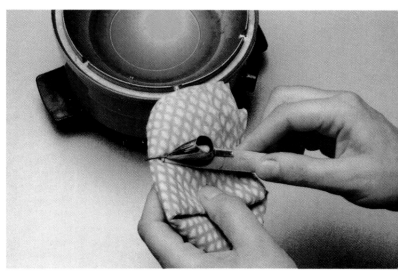

5 Heat the wax and put the canting in it for at least 30 seconds so that the metal bowl can warm up and help to keep the wax hot. Fill the reservoir about half full so that wax does not flow over the top while you are working. Use a piece of soft, absorbent cloth to remove excess wax and to catch any drips as you carry the canting from the wax pot to the fabric.

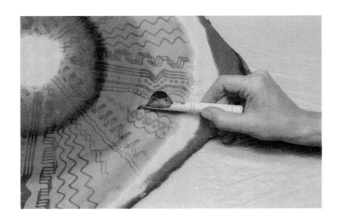

6 Rest your frame at an angle and also hold the canting at an angle as you work. The angle affects the flow of wax from the spout, and you will have to experiment to get the flow you want, but do not hold it at such a sharp angle that wax flows out of the back onto your fingers!

7 When waxing is complete, mix up 3fl oz (90 ml) of black dyestuff using $^1\!/_2$ teaspoon dye powder. Apply it over the fabric with a sponge. Place a sheet of plastic beneath to catch any drips, and remember to wear rubber gloves. Fiber-reactive dyes gain in intensity when they are overdyed, and this is especially true with black, which looks richer when applied twice, as was done here to cover the bright dyes. When the fabric is dry, iron out and dry-clean before making up into a cushion cover.

WINDOW BLIND

When cotton batik is held against the light, the effect is similar to that of stained-glass windows. A window blind is, thus, a good way of displaying your batik expertise.

This project covers an area 26 in. (66 cm) wide and 44 in. (112 cm) long. The materials allow ½ in. (12 mm) at the side edges for turning and 4 in. (10 cm) at the top and bottom for fixing to the blind kit. The fabric may shrink when boiled, so cut about 1 in. (2.5 cm) more all round than the measurements given.

You will need

- Basic equipment, plus
- Prepared fabric, 27 x 52 in. (69 x 132 cm)
- Wooden frame, 27 x 27 in. (69 x 69 cm)
- Drawing pins
- Tape measure
- Long ruler or straight edge
- Mashing tape
- Soft pencil, 4B

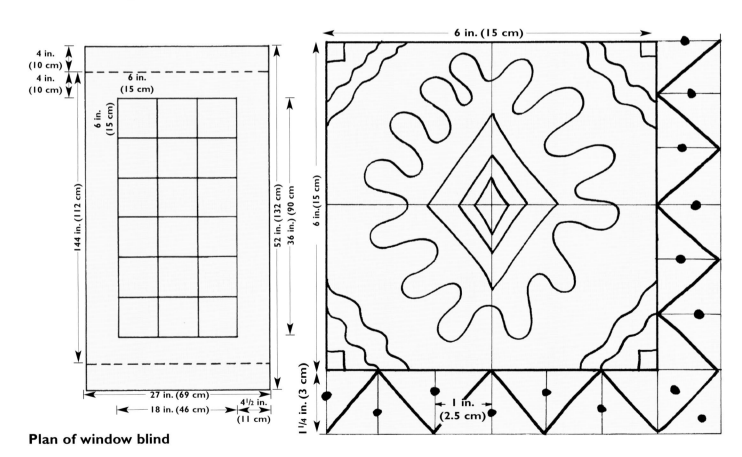

Plan of window blind

1 Lay the fabric on a firm surface and use a soft pencil to mark off 4 in. (10 cm) at top and bottom. Draw a margin inside these lines of a further 4 in. (10 cm) and on each side a margin of 4½ in. (11 cm). The inside area is 18 in. (46 cm) by 36 in. (90 cm), so the repeat motif has been made 6 in. (15 cm) square to fit three times across and six times down. Mark these squares. The border pattern needs only a ruler's width line marked in to keep the width of the snake line constant, with the points 1 in. (2.5 cm) along the edges.

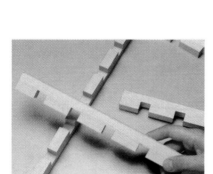

2 A frame about 27 in. (68 cm) square would be ideal for stretching your fabric, so that it can be worked in two manageable sections. These adjustable frames, which slot together, are available from most craft shops in a range of sizes; however, you could use an old picture frame.

3 Wax in the border pattern. When the first section is complete, move the fabric up the frame and position the second half. Move it carefully so that you do not crack the wax lines; otherwise, the colors will seep where you do not intend them to. The only extra guides you might need are the vertical and horizontal crosses—so that you can place the points of the diamond shapes in each square. Let your canting run freely. They will all look sufficiently similar to work well visually, but different enough to add interest.

4 It is easier to apply dye if the fabric is in a complete length. If it is laid on a plastic sheet, the dye may collect and cross over the wax lines. Laying it on an absorbent surface, such as newspaper, can make this less likely, but this tends to suck the dye away from the fabric. If you can suspend the material in some way there will be fewer color accidents, and the finished design will look more the way you intended. You can suspend the fabric from a shelf or door lintel, which is how I applied the smaller areas of color here. Remember to work from light to dark with your dyes, and wax them as they dry to prevent any accidents with darker colors later.

5 The final background was applied with a sponge while the fabric was suspended between two lengths of 2 in. (5 cm) square wood resting on the work surface.

7 *When the dye is dried, wax all over to avoid "halos", lifting the fabric between applications. Iron out and leave the fabric stiff and waterproof—or get it dry-cleaned after ironing and spray it with fabric protector and water repellant, so that the blind can be wiped down. Your batik fabric is ready to turn into a roller blind.*

6 *It is better to work horizontally when larger areas are being dyed because the fabric will hold the dye, which will not drain away to the base—and also not lead to any color loss at the top.*

PORTRAITS

The techniques used to make the Sun Calendar can be used to reproduce photographs. This time, instead of using caps on cotton, you will wax with a canting onto silk. Silk is used because it allows you to see the image easily through the fabric. Choose an image with a lot of contrast. It doesn't matter if it is in black-and-white or color.

You will need

- Basic equipment, plus
- Image
- Enlarged photostat of the chosen image
- Acetate
- Prepared silk, 1 in. (2.5 cm) wider all around than projected finished image
- Cardboard frame with inside dimensions of projected finished image
- Unprinted newsprint

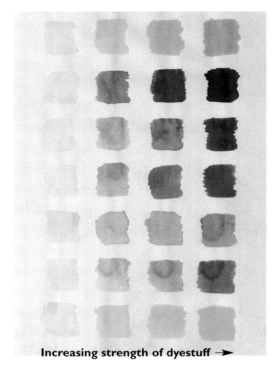

Increasing strength of dyestuff →

2 *Plan for three tones besides white. You might prefer tones of one color by mixing different strengths of dyestuff.*

1 *Enlarge the image on a photostat machine. As a guide, increase the face to measure at least 6 in. (15 cm) from crown to chin. Cover the image with acetate.*

3 *Prepare and attach your silk to the cardboard frame. Tape the image in position behind the stretched silk and draw the line of wax around the image area. Wax in the areas to be kept white using a brush or sponge. Soften the edges by applying the wax as dots with the canting.*

4 Remove the silk from the image ready to dye the first tone. Mix the lightest dye (tone 1) and apply it with a piece of sponge. Do not overload the sponge with liquid or the wax outline to your image will be unable to contain the dye. Remember to wear rubber gloves.

6 Mix the next dye, tone 2 and test on the reverse side of the picture.

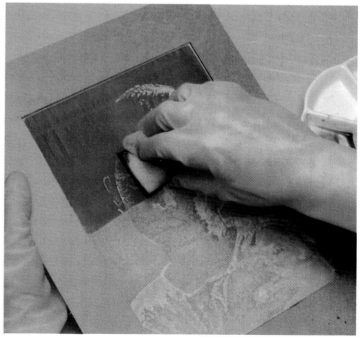

5 Use the dotting technique to wax the areas to be saved as tone 1.

7 Apply the tone with a soft sponge.

8 *Apply wax to save the areas of tone 2.*

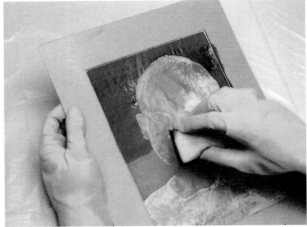

9 *Mix the darkest dye, tone 3, and apply. When it is dry, wax the remaining areas to avoid "halos" forming.*

Iron out the wax, leaving the silk to lie flat until it is cool. Mount for display.

WALL HANGING

Bleach can be used to increase the possible range of colors when you are working on images you do not want to be outlined by a white wax line.

When you do successive immersions in dye, some colors are lost—for example, if the first color is yellow, subsequent dyeing with blue will create green. In this project, which uses red and blue dye, the discharge process is used to regain the blue.

You will need

- Basic equipment, plus
- Prepared cotton, 24 x 36 in. (60 x 90 cm)
- Soft pencil, 4B
- Blanket
- Plastic bucket and bowl, each with minimum capacity of 1 gallon (4.5 liters)
- Cork
- Kitchen roll (cardboard)
- Plastic tray
- Bleach
- Sodium metabisulphite
- 2 pieces of $1/2$ in. (14 mm) dowel, each 2 ft (60 cm) long

To make up
- Scissors
- Pins
- Sewing machine or needles; thread

1 *On the prepared fabric use a soft pencil to mark margins of 2 $1/2$ in. (6.5 cm) at the top and bottom to form the channels for the rods to fit in, and a 1 in. (2.5 cm) margin on either side for a hem. These lines will act as guidelines for waxing. Lay the fabric on a soft bed and wax the white border pattern with cork and kitchen roll caps.*

2 *Draw an oval in the center. Position the eyes about halfway up the "face". Support this area over a frame so that you can hold the fabric at an angle to wax in the white part of the eyes.*

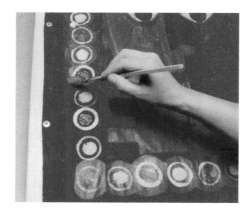

3   *Prepare a red dye bath. Test to try out overdyeing colors and discharge strengths. For the border, use a brush to wax areas to stay red. Use a sponge "brush" to wax the side of the mask face that is to stay red.*

4   *Prepare a blue dye bath. Test it on your sample.*

5   *To avoid too much crackle on the face, use a tray to hold the dye. It will be easier to keep the fabric flat.*

6   *When the fabric is rinsed and completely dry, return it to the work top and wax the areas that are going to stay purple. To avoid wax sticking to the plastic sheeting, lift the material as you wax. You may find it easier to mount the fabric on a frame.*

7   *Mix a medium strength solution of bleach, preparing enough to cover the unwaxed areas and using proportions of 1 tablespoon bleach to 6 tablespoons water. Test on your sample piece to check the timing. You will find that the red dye discharges completely before the blue, so as soon as all the red is gone you can rinse out the bleach solution. Neutralize and rinse.*

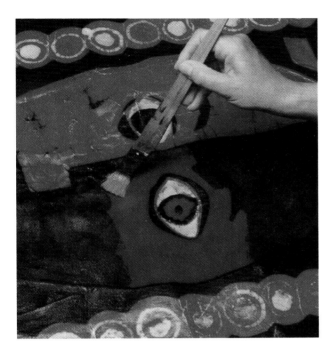

8 *If you want to intensify the blue dye, apply it as in pool batik. When it is completely dry, wax over to avoid "halos" forming after ironing out.*

9 *If you want to iron out so that the fabric retains a residue of wax for waterproofing, do so on a surface that is large enough to accommodate the whole piece so that it will cool flat. Otherwise, such a large piece may distort like silk.*

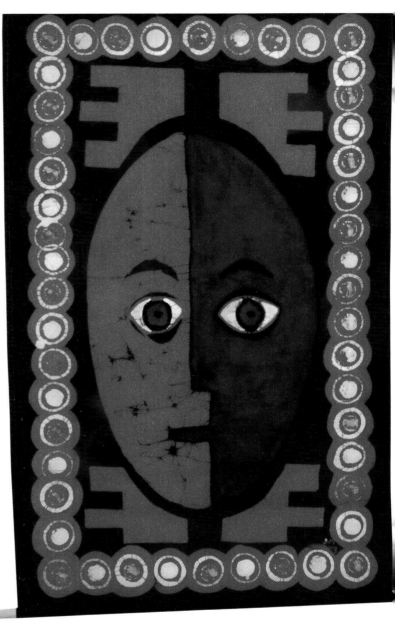

Turn in and sew the sides. Turn over wide hems at the top and bottom to take the wooden dowel by which the finished piece will hang. The bottom rod will weight the work, making it hang better. If you prefer a softer finish have the work dry-cleaned, then spray it with a fabric protector.

FABRIC PAINTING

Painting on fabric offers you the opportunity to create sensational effects on ordinary household items. Liven up a dull T-shirt or an old pair of jeans; and design table linen to match your china, or cushions to match your wallpaper. Many simple and effective designs can be done freehand. As your skills develop you can attempt more ambitious designs that require a steady hand, such as copying a motif from a magazine, or even making up your own design.

There are numerous ways of applying the paint to the fabric. Stenciling is an excellent way of covering a large area or creating a repeat pattern. Printing with sliced vegetables, fruits and flowers is a novel way of creating abstract patterns— simply apply paint to the surface or edge of the object with which you are painting and print it directly onto the fabric. Throughout this chapter there are projects that incorporate masking, sponging, printing and painting on dark fabric so you become familiar with a whole range of fabric painting techniques.

PAINTED ESPADRILLES

Plain espadrilles come in a variety of bright colors, and they are inexpensive to buy. Decorating lighter colors—pale blue, green, pink and white—tends to be more successful than applying paint to darker shades. I have suggested using masking tape as a guide, but you may feel confident enough to apply the paint freehand.

You will need

- A pair of plain espadrilles
- Newspaper
- Masking tape
- Scissors
- Fabric paints (I used red, yellow, and blue)
- Mixing palette
- Brushes (small and medium sizes)
- Tailor's chalk or colored pencil)
- Iron
- Cloth

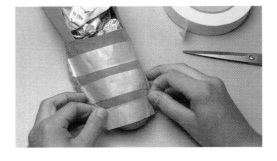

2 *Place three strips of masking tape across the front of the shoe, varying the distance between the pieces or using narrower tape if you want narrower or wider lines.*

3 *Begin with the blue paint and use short strokes to paint the first stripe. Do not water down the paint or it will bleed.*

Put some scrunched-up newspaper into each espadrille so that the surface is smooth and taut.

4 *When you have painted the red and yellow stripes, leave them to dry before removing the masking tape.*

5 *Add the details to the stripes.*

7 *Use tailor's chalk or a colored pencil to draw a pattern of random circles on the sides of each espadrille.*

6 *I added bumps to give a wavy effect; this can be done freehand.*

8 *Paint in the circles using a small brush to give a neat outline.*

9 *Place a piece of cloth over the espadrille and iron to seal the paint.*

CUSTOMIZED JEANS

This project is an ideal way of experimenting with some of the more specialized fabric paints that are available these days—puff, glitter and fluorescent paints, for example. It is also a great way to liven up an old pair of jeans, and there are endless possibilities to try.

You will need

- Pair of jeans
- Newspaper
- Fabric paints (including puff, glitter, and fluorescent)
- Mixing palette
- Paint brushes (various sizes)
- Hair-drier

2 Use puff paint to draw zigzag lines around the pockets.

3 Add green dots to the inside of the zigzags.

1 Place a few sheets of newspaper inside the jeans to protect them from paint seeping through.

4 Paint on a patch using a mixture of yellow and white. Draw on some crosshatched squares using a mixture of blue and purple paint.

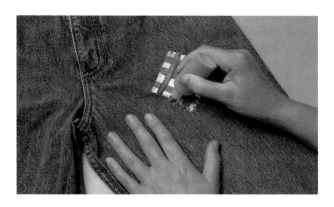

5 *Paint on "stitches" around the patch using pink puff paint.*

7 *Add green puff paint crosses inside the heart and white dots around the edge. Add more patches down the legs of the jeans if you wish. When the paint is completely dry, puff up the paint using a hair-drier.*

6 *Draw another motif on the other leg of the jeans—a pink heart, for example. Use green puff paint to draw a border around the heart.*

ABSTRACT PATTERNS

This is an ideal way of decorating lengths of plain fabric to make them up into curtains, table linen, cushion covers, or even clothes. Look around your home and you are sure to find countless bits and pieces—sponges, combs, jar lids, pegs—that can be used to make interesting patterns. You could also experiment with food—pasta, for example—to create unusual designs.

You will need

- Items for printing—combs, cotton reels, pen tops, etc.
- Newspaper
- Fabric
- Masking tape
- Fabric paint
- Mixing palette
- Paintbrush (medium size)
- Iron
- Cloth

Assemble the items you think would make interesting shapes. You might find it helpful to make a rough sketch of your overall design before you begin.

2 *Cover your work surface with newspaper and lay out the fabric. You may use masking tape to keep it in position.*

3 *Mix the colors you want to use in a palette.*

4 *Apply paint to the object—I used a comb. Avoid too much paint, or the outline will not look crisp and neat.*

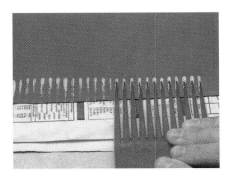

5   *Use the comb to transfer the paint to the fabric. Continue all around the edge of the fabric, then leave to dry for about 20 minutes.*

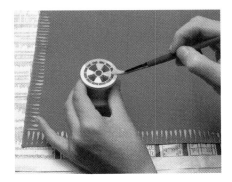

6   *Take your next object—I used a wooden cotton reel—and paint the surface with a different color.*

7   *Incorporate the shape into your design. Leave to dry.*

8   *Use a different color with your next object. I used a small piece of sponge, which gives an interesting and uneven texture.*

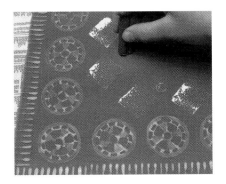

9   *Leave the third color to dry before you apply the next series of colored shapes. When you are satisfied with the pattern, iron under a cloth to fix the paints.*

VEGETABLE-PRINTED APRON

Vegetables with distinctive shapes, such as cabbage, mushrooms, chilies and broccoli, are ideal for fabric printing. Cut them in half and use them to decorate a plain calico apron of the kind you find in do-it-yourself or catering shops. Experiment with halved fruit too.

You will need

- A selection of vegetables
- Kitchen knife
- Pencil
- Plain paper
- Plain calico apron
- Newspaper
- Fabric paints
- Mixing palette
- Paintbrush (medium size)
- Fabric paint pens
- Iron
- Cloth

2 Draw a rough sketch on plain paper of how you want the apron to look.

3 Lay the apron on sheets of newspaper and prepare the paints. Use a paintbrush to paint the surface of, say, the cabbage.

1 Cut the vegetables in half with a sharp knife. Include the stalks and cut more than one of each so that you can use several colors.

4 Test the cabbage on rough paper to check that the surface is smooth. You will need to press firmly to get a good print. Do not put too much paint on the vegetable, or the pattern will smudge.

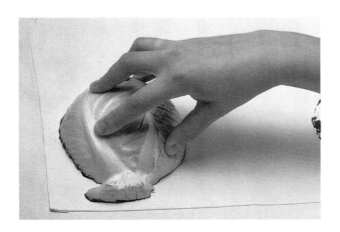

5 *Print the cabbage on the apron.*

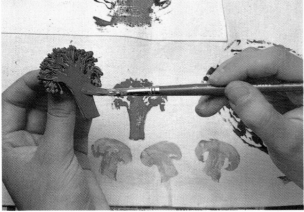

6 *Add more vegetable prints to build up your design, taking care not to move the vegetable as you apply pressure. Add fresh paint for every print.*

7 *Use a fabric marker pen to draw a line around the edge of the apron and to highlight the pocket edge. Iron under a cloth to fix the paints.*

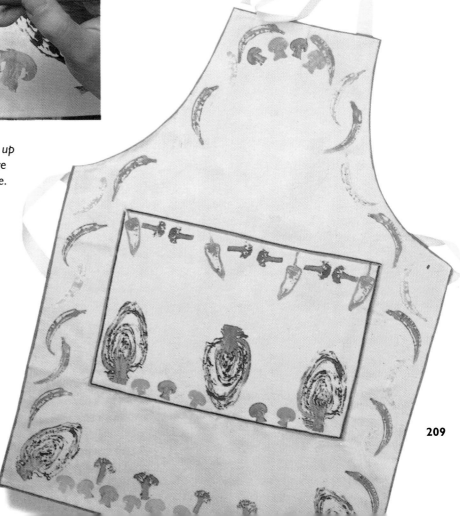

PRINTING WITH FLOWERS

This project uses flowers and leaves to decorate fabric, which can be used for cushion covers, table linen, and even curtains. Some plant materials work better—flowers and leaves with sturdy outlines give more successful prints than more delicate shapes. Try buddleia, ivy and conifer leaves, and flowers such as daisies. The backs of leaves with prominent veins work especially well.

You will need

- Rough paper
- Colored pencils
- Newspaper
- Fabric of your choice
- Masking tape
- A selection of flowers and leaves
- Fabric paints
- Mixing palette
- Paintbrush (medium size)
- Iron
- Cloth

Position the flowers and leaves in a design. Make a rough sketch of the design and color in the shapes so that you have a reference when you start to print.

2 Cover your work surface with newspaper and spread out your fabric, taping it in position if necessary. Mix your paints and paint some of the leaves.

3 Using your sketch as reference, place a leaf on the fabric, pressing it firmly but gently. After 10 seconds, raise an edge to see if the impression has printed. If successful, carefully lift the leaf to avoid smudging the paint. Build up the design with other leaves.

4 Paint a flower, placing it as indicated on your rough sketch. Fill in any gaps in the design and don't worry if some of the flowers look rather abstract. Leave to dry, then iron under a cloth to fix the paints.

FOLK ART PICTURE

This charming image is achieved by applying a series of stencils, one after the other, and painting each in a different color. You could frame the completed image, as I have done, or you could paint two and make up a pair of cushion covers.

You will need

- Tracing paper
- Pencil
- Stencil card
- Masking tape
- Craft knife or scalpel
- Piece of canvas or calico, approximately 13 x 11 in. (33 x 28 cm)
- Scissors
- Newspaper
- Stencil brush ¼ in. (5 mm) or ½ in. (12 mm)
- Fabric paint
- Mixing palette
- Iron
- Cloth
- 4 buttons

1 Trace the stencil designs, drawing each of the outlines onto equal sized sheets of paper so that they will all fit together accurately.

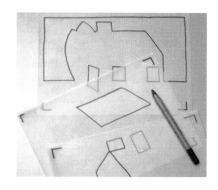

2 Tape each traced stencil onto a separate piece of stencil card, taking care to position each outline in the same position on each piece of card. Cut out the holes in each stencil.

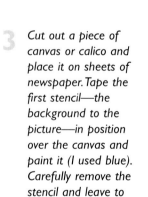

3 Cut out a piece of canvas or calico and place it on sheets of newspaper. Tape the first stencil—the background to the picture—in position over the canvas and paint it (I used blue). Carefully remove the stencil and leave to dry for a few minutes.

4 Tape the second stencil—the house front and chimney piece—accurately in position and apply dark-blue paint. Use a paintbrush to paint around the window areas.

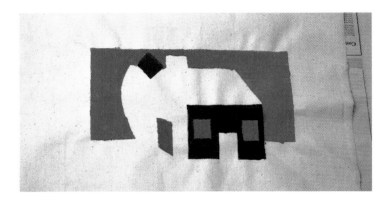

5   *Leave the paint to dry before you use the next stencil.*

7   *Tape the next stencil in place and paint the side of the house in purple. Leave to dry before using the last stencil, the foreground and trees, painting in green.*

6   *Tape the next stencil—the front door and roof—in place. This time use brown paint. Again, leave to dry.*

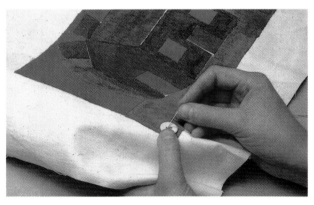

8   *Iron under a cloth to fix the paint and sew a button in each corner.*

CHILD'S WALL-HANGING

This charming parade of stenciled animals would look great on a child's bedroom wall. The project uses simple hand-stitching and stenciling, to give an old-fashioned, slightly folksy effect. You could also use numbers or letters instead of animals.

You will need

- Tracing paper
- Pencils
- Stencil card
- Masking tape
- Craft knife or scalpel
- 8 pieces of cream-colored fabric, each measuring about 5 x 5 in. (12.5 x 12.5 cm)
- Fabric paints
- Mixing palette
- Stencil brushes ¼ in. (5 mm) and ½ in. (12 mm)
- Sponge (natural sponge is best)
- Iron
- Cloth
- 2 pieces of colored fabric, each measuring about 50 x 8 in. (128 x 20 cm) [I used blue]
- Pins
- Scissors
- Needle
- Colored embroidery silks
- 2 buttons
- Bias binding, tape or ribbon, approximately 4 in. (10 cm)

1 Trace eight animal shapes. Place each animal tracing on a piece of stencil card and hold it in place with masking tape.

2 Use a craft knife or scalpel to cut out each shape. Discard the tracing paper.

3 Cut out eight squares of cream-colored fabric.

4 Use masking tape to hold each cutout animal in position on a square of fabric.

5   *Prepare your paints, then color the pig's body using a stencil brush.*

8   *Add some yellow and orange to the feathers in the cockerel's tail.*

6   *Color the pig's feet brown and add a band of brown across its body.*

9   *Color the cow's body black and its hooves and udder pink. Make some spots by sponging on some white paint.*

7   *The cockerel has a blue-green body and a bright-red comb.*

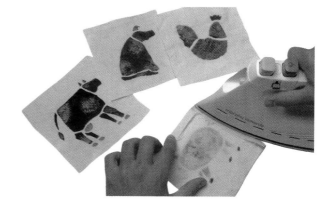

10   *Paint the rest of the animals, using the photograph of the finished wall hanging as a guide. Turn under the edges of each square and iron under a cloth to fix the colors and press down the turned-back edges.*

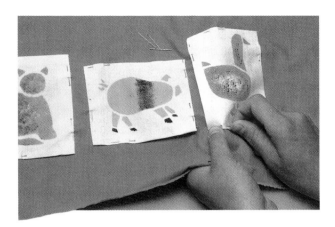

11 Place the two rectangles of fabric together and pin. Space the eight animal pictures evenly along one of the long rectangles of fabric, pinning them in position.

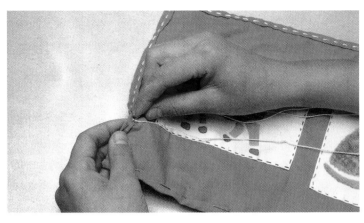

13 Turn the edge of the large rectangle into a neat hem on the front and hand-sew with yellow embroidery silk.

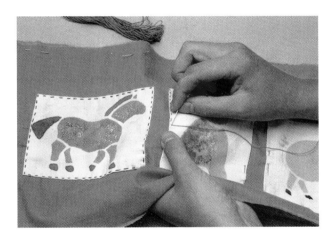

12 Use colored embroidery silk and straight-stitch to sew each square in place.

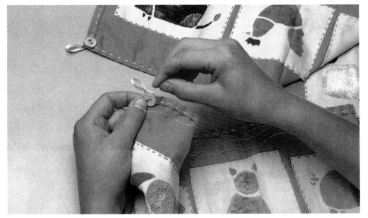

14 Sew a button in each of the top corners and add loops of tape, bias binding, or ribbon from which to hang it.

ANIMAL CUSHIONS

Scatter these lively animal cushions on a child's bed or arrange them in a group on a chair. Watered-down fabric paints have been used to achieve the background colors, while thicker paints are used for the detailed markings. Simple embroidery stitches in brightly colored threads have been added to enhance the details of feathers, whiskers, and so on.

You will need

- Tracing paper
- Pencil
- Scissors
- Pins
- White cotton fabric, approximately 20 x 10 in. (51 x 25 cm) for each cushion
- Newspaper
- Fabric paints
- Mixing palette
- Paintbrushes (small and medium)
- Colored embroidery silks
- Needle
- Sewing thread
- Sewing machine
- Kapok or other toy stuffing
- Buttons for eyes
- String for pig's tail

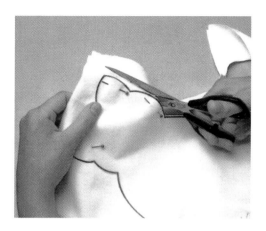

1 Trace the animal shapes and cut out. Pin each template to a double layer of fabric and cut around it.

2 Place each animal shape on some newspaper and prepare your paints.

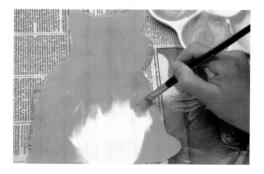

3 Water down the paints that you are going to use for the background—for example, use orange for the cat—but do not make the color flat; it will look more natural if it is quite streaky.

4 Add spots on the back and head and a nose and tail.

7 The cockerel is more difficult. The background is a combination of green, purple, pink and yellow. Apply each color separately, but try to achieve a soft, feathery effect with no harsh edges.

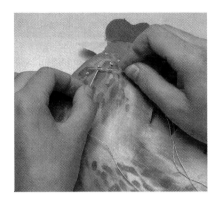

10 Use embroidery silks to stitch details on the cockerel's neck feathers.

5 Make the pig in the same manner and remember to include two ears.

8 Add a yellow beak and bright-red comb.

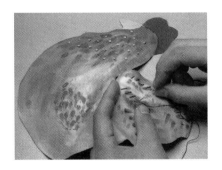

11 Stitch some additional feather detailing to the cockerel's back.

6 Use brown paint for the pig's feet and the spots on its flanks.

9 Iron both sides of each of the animals under a cloth when you have finished them to seal the paints.

12 Stitch around the spots on the cat and embroider the whiskers. Remember to stitch the cat's paws.

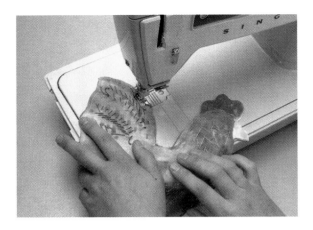

13 Pin the two pieces of the cushion together and use a sewing machine to stitch around the edge, leaving about 5 cm/2 in. open along the bottom edge.

15 Turn the cushion to the right side, using the wrong end of a paintbrush to push out the seams, especially around the cockerel's beak and comb. Fill the cushion with soft toy stuffing material, pushing it into the head and tail with a piece of wooden dowel.

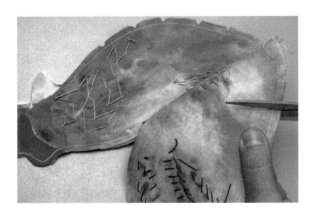

14 Carefully snip the curved edges up the stitching line so that the seams lie flat.

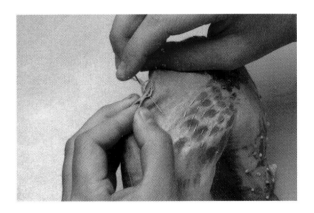

16 Sew up the open seam. Repeat steps 13-16 for the pig and cat.

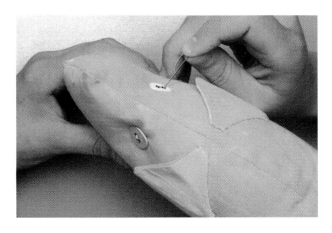

17 *Stitch on buttons for eyes and remember to add the pig's ears.*

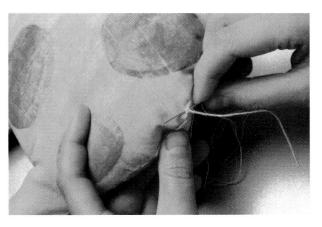

18 *Make a tail for the pig by painting some string pink and sewing it onto the pig's back.*

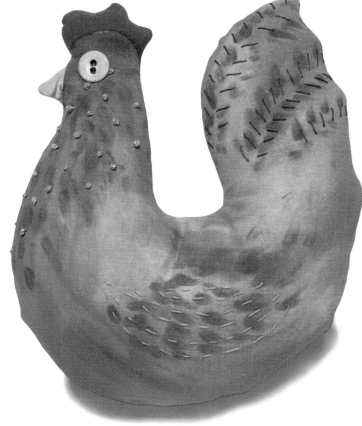

DOLL

This simple doll makes a delightful gift for a child older than five or six years of age. You could design a different outfit if you preferred, or you could base the doll's appearance on someone you know. If you wish, you could add extra details such as a hair ribbon, a hat, or a piece of jewellery.

You will need

- Sewing machine
- Sketch pad
- Sewing thread
- Colored pencils
- Fabric paints
- Tracing paper
- Mixing palette
- Pencil
- Paintbrushes (various sizes)
- Piece of white fabric, 13 x 10 in. (33 x 25 cm)
- Iron
- Pins
- Cloth
- Scissors
- Needle
- Newspapers
- Buttons
- Kapok or other toy stuffing

1 Sketch a design for your doll's clothes, keeping to the shape of the doll.

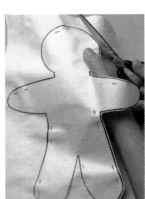

2 Trace the doll's template and cut out. Fold the white fabric in half (so it measures 13 x 5 in./33 x 12.5 cm) and pin the template to it, with the pins going through both layers. Cut out the outline, adding a seam allowance of ⅛ in. (3 mm) all round.

3 Using your sketch as a reference, pencil guidelines on the cutout doll—hairline, top, trousers, shoes, and so on. Add the details to the front and the back.

4 Cover your work surface with newspaper and paint the front of the doll. Begin with the background color of the blouse (I used blue).

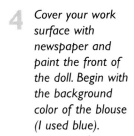

5 Next, paint in the shoes and trousers, and then the mouth, cheeks and hair.

6   *Allow the paint to dry, then add details such as the flower pattern to the top and the frills around the neck and trousers.*

7   *Paint the face pale-pink and leave to dry. Paint the back of the doll to match. Iron.*

8   *Place the two pieces, right sides together, and machine-stitch all the way around the doll, leaving a gap of about 2 in. (5 cm) under one arm. Carefully snip into the curves, up to the sewing line, at the neck, between the legs, and at the ends of the arms and legs, so that the seams lie smoothly.*

9   *Turn the doll the right way out. Fill it with soft toy stuffing, using a piece of wooden dowel to push down into the arms and legs. Stitch up the underarm seam opening.*

10   *Sew on buttons for the eyes.*

11   *Paint on the eyebrows.*

TIE-DYEING

Tie-dyeing is seen as a "resist" method of dyeing, similar to batik. An array of patterns can be achieved by binding or folding the fabric, then immersing it in a dye bath. Multicolored patterns can be made by refolding and rebinding the fabric when a new color is added. As with other surface patterning forms, the best results are obtained when the fabric is decorated before it is made up into the garment.

Early evidence in the *sima* charters from Indonesia mention tie-dyers as one of the five different groups of textile workers producing fabric in the early 10th century. One of the earliest techniques of tie-dyeing to be used was *ikat*—a method of tying resist material around yarn and dyeing before weaving—which added subtle variations of color to simple geometric designs.

Pelangi, the technique most often associated with tie-dyeing, produces the familiar circular and striped patterns. One of the more complicated methods is *teritik*, which involves stitching areas of the fabric to resist the dye. The use of stitching means that a more controlled, sometimes even pictorial, pattern can be achieved. More recently, western designers have been adapting the traditional methods to produce elaborate and subtly colored patterns.

EQUIPMENT AND MATERIALS

The projects in this chapter have been designed to demonstrate a variety of tie-dyeing techniques. You will find most of the required equipment in your home. Several different kinds of fabric dye are available, although those most suitable for tie-dyeing are the cold-water dyes. In general, it is easier to dye 100 per cent natural fibers—silk, cotton, wool and linen, for example, or a combination of these. Synthetic fabrics or mixes of natural and synthetic fibers do not dye evenly, and you will have to use special dyes for these fabrics.

You will need

- Old newspaper or a plastic sheet to protect your work surface
- Scissors and a craft knife
- As wide a variety of winding materials as possible—string, thread, wool, twine, strips of fabric (from old sheets, etc.), and elastic bands
- 30 wooden or plastic clothes pegs (those with metal springs are best)
- 50 paper clips in various sizes
- Glass marbles or balls or stones (about 30 small, 10 medium-sized and 4 large)
- 5 corks in various sizes
- Old buttons in various sizes
- Rubber gloves (the thin, surgical ones are best)
- Plastic bucket or large plastic bowl
- Electric kettle or saucepan and hot plate
- 1 teaspoon (5 ml measure) and a 1 tablespoon (15 ml measure)
- Large, heat-proof measuring jug that holds 2 pints (1 liter)
- 1 lb (500 g) table salt
- 1 pint (0.5 liter) vinegar

When you select your dyes, weigh the fabric and check the quantity of dye you need for each item or items. Each manufacturer gives specific recipes and instructions for its own products. The quantities given in these mixing instructions will dye approximately 64 x 64 in. (270 x 270 cm) of fabric.

MIXING DYES FOR COTTON

1   *Mix each dye, checking the manufacturer's instructions for the dye that you are using. Approximately you will need to add 1 tsp (5 g) of dye to each 1 pint (0.5 liter) of boiling water in a heat-proof jug.*

2   *Add 2 tbsp (30 g) of salt and mix thoroughly.*

3   *Add the solution to a bowl containing 4 pints (2 liters) of hot water and stir. Check the strength of the dye by placing a strip of the fabric you are using in the dye bath for 10-15 minutes. If the color is too strong, add more boiling water; if it is too weak, add more dye.*

MIXING DYES FOR SILK AND WOOL

1   *Add 1 tsp (5 g) of dye to each 1 pint (0.5 liter) of boiling water in a heat-proof jug.*

2   *Add 2 tbsp (30 ml) vinegar and mix thoroughly. Add this to a further 2 pints (1 liter) of hot water and stir.*

TIP
Tie-dyeing is a safe craft. However, never forget that all powder dyes, hot liquids, small objects and sharp tools should be handled with care, and young children should always be supervised. Remember:
- do not inhale the fine powder dye
- do not inhale the vapor given off when the dye is dissolved
- always wear gloves when handling dyed fabric

If the dye comes into contact with your eyes, rinse thoroughly in clean water and seek medical advice.

TYING METHODS

There are numerous ways of tying fabric to achieve patterns, and each one will produce a different end result. Even if you tie several pieces of material in the same way, you will not be able to produce exactly the same pattern each time, and this is one of the exciting things about tie-dyeing—you never know exactly how a piece will turn out, and every one is individual and personal.

CHECK PATTERN

Evenly pleat the fabric and iron it, then secure the pleats with clothes pegs.

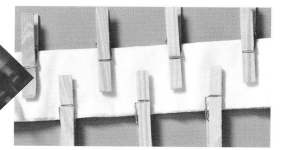

STRIPES

Fold the fabric in half, pleat it and bind it in the center with string.

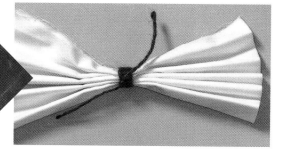

SMALL CIRCLES

Tie small round objects—marbles or stones—into the fabric.

MARBLED PATTERN

Crumple the fabric into a hard ball and bind it with twine or string. For each different color, re-crumple the fabric in a different way. When you are dyeing larger pieces of material, bunch the fabric along its length and bind it into a sausage-like shape. You can add greater definition to the pattern by brushing fabric paint onto the fabric after it is dry—but before untying it.

VIGNETTE EFFECTS

Roll the fabric tightly around a cord, then ruche it. Repeat the process by wrapping the fabric in opposite directions and re-dyeing it with a different color.

FRAGMENTED PATTERN

Pinch the center of the fabric and allow it to fall into drapes like a closed umbrella. Cross-bind it with thread or twine.

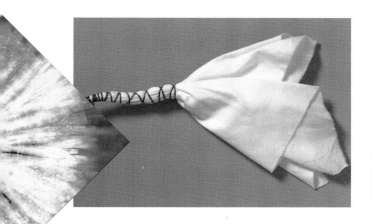

RIBS

Make neat folds and secure the pleats at regular intervals with paper clips.

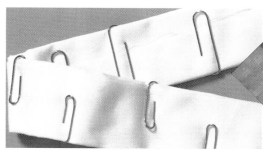

VARIABLE STRIPES

Fold the fabric in half, pleat it and bind it at intervals with twine or thread.

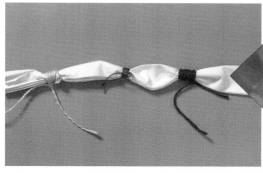

ELABORATE CIRCLES

Wrap a champagne cork into the fabric and tie it with thin twine or thread.

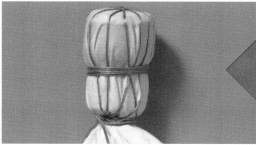

CONCENTRIC PATTERN

Pinch the center of the fabric and have it fall into drapes like a closed umbrella. Bind it at intervals lengthways.

ASYMMETRIC PATTERN

Knot each corner with a piece of fabric from the center of a square of material. This technique is best done with lightweight fabrics.

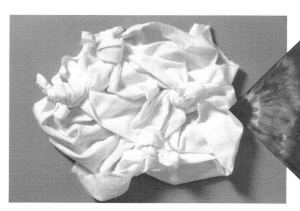

SQUARES

Take a square of fabric and fold it diagonally twice so that it makes a triangle. Pleat the fabric lengthways and bind it with thread.

FRACTURED GLASS PATTERN

Fold the fabric once or twice, then twist and allow it to twist back on itself before binding it with twine.

BOLD STRIPES

Simply knot the fabric at intervals.

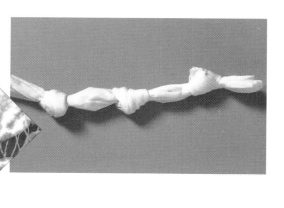

CARDS AND JEWELRY

You can combine several techniques, including over-dyeing, to produce intricate, multicolored patterns. Mastering the basic binding and dyeing techniques will make it easier for you to visualize the end results, and make personalized gift tags, greetings cards, and jewelry.

You will need

- 2 pieces of habutai silk, finely woven, each 12 x 12 in. (30 x 30 cm)
- 15 ft (5 m) heavy thread or embroidery thread
- ½ tsp (2.5 g) each of red, yellow, and blue dye
- 3 tbsp (45 ml) vinegar (but check manufacturer's instructions)
- 6 ft (2 m) twine
- 5 small marbles or glass balls
- 2-3 bowls, each large enough to hold 1 pint (0.5 liter)
- Electric iron
- A sheet of A1 (33⅛ x 23⅓ in.) card or readymade greetings card and gift card blanks
- A pair of earring findings or blanks
- 2 brooch findings
- 4 blank button covers, ¾ in. (22 mm) across
- Scissors and a craft knife
- Clear, all-purpose adhesive

1 Scrunch a piece of silk into a tight ball and bind it with embroidery thread. Tie marbles into the second piece with embroidery thread. Mix the blue dye in 1 pint (0.5 liter) of boiling water in a heat-proof jug, and add 1 tbsp (15 ml) vinegar. Since silk does not react well to boiling water, let it cool to about 120° F (50° C) before pouring the dye into the bowl. Place the silk bundle in the blue dye.

2 Mix the yellow dye in the same way and place it in the fabric with the marbles tied into it. Leave both pieces for about 20 minutes. Remove each bundle and rinse thoroughly under the cold tap until the water runs clear. Untie each bundle and allow the silk to dry flat, you can iron damp silk with a medium-hot iron.

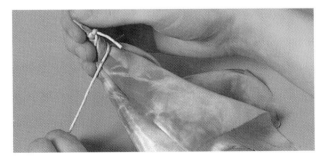

3 When the blue square is dry, find the center and pinch it so that the fabric falls into folds like a closed umbrella. Cross-bind it down three-quarters of its length, starting at the pinched center.

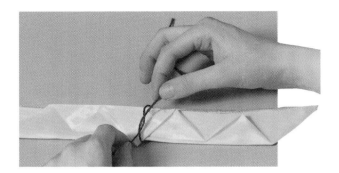
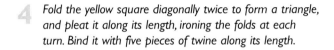

4 Fold the yellow square diagonally twice to form a triangle, and pleat it along its length, ironing the folds at each turn. Bind it with five pieces of twine along its length.

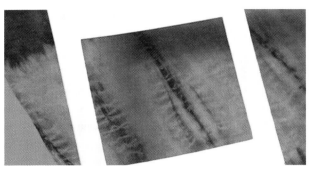

6 Use a viewing window or two L-shaped pieces of card to select areas to cut and mount for your cards and gift tags.

5 Mix the red dye, allow it to cool, and place the blue square in the red dye. Place the yellow square in the blue dye. Leave both pieces for at least 20 minutes. Rinse each piece thoroughly in cold running water. Untie, allow to dry completely and iron.

7 We used a round wooden brooch blank and a semicircular metal blank and oval earring drops. If you use adhesive to hold the fabric in place, take care not to get it on the front of the silk, which will be spoiled.

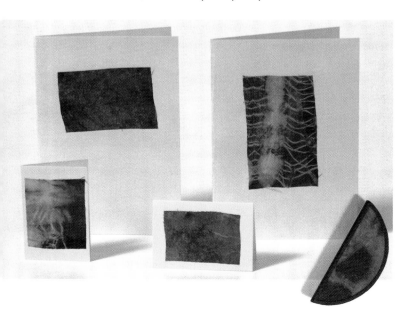

8 Button blanks usually have removable backs. Make sure that you keep the fabric taut and even over the front while you clip in the back sections.

Socks and Hair Scrunchies

The basic principles of tie-dyeing apply no matter what object you choose to decorate. When selecting a method, consider the construction of the piece you are planning to make, because some patterns are more effective on a larger scale. In addition, some fabrics, such as cotton jersey and non-woven materials, stretch when they are wet.

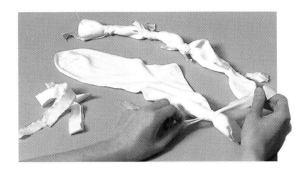

Cut one of the strips of fabric into eight pieces and tie four pieces at intervals around each sock.

You will need

- 1 pair of white, plain flat-weave, cotton socks
- 3 pieces of fabric, each 39 x 1 in. (1 m x 2.5 cm)
- 2 hair scrunchies
- 39 in. (1 m) string
- ¼ tsp (1.25 g) each of orange, light-green, and violet dye
- 1 tsp (5 g) salt
- 2 tsp (10 ml) vinegar

Use the remaining two strips to cross-bind each sock tightly along its length.

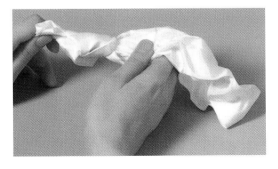

Tie three knots along the length of the first hair scrunchy. Cross-bind the second scrunchy with string along its length.

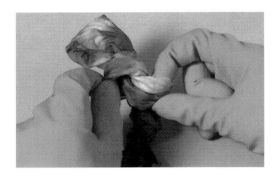

4 *Cross-bind the second scrunchy with string along its length.*

5 *Remove the items from the dyes, rinse thoroughly and allow to dry. If the socks have stretched slightly, try drying them in a tumble dryer to shrink them back into shape.*

TIP

- When you buy articles like socks, avoid those made of ribbed cotton jersey, which may stretch out of shape when immersed in water. A small amount of nylon—about 10 percent—will help to prevent the socks from twisting and bagging.

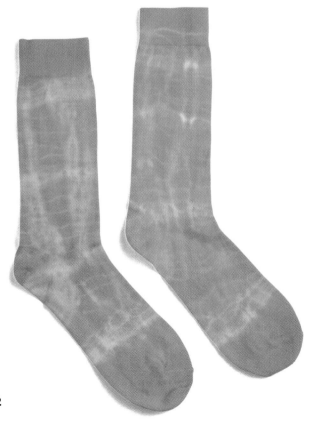

MAKING 2 HAIR SCRUNCHIES
You will need

- 2 pieces medium-weight habutai silk, each 28 x 4 in. (70 x 10 cm)
- Needle and sewing cotton
- 4 in. (10 cm) fine string
- 14 in. (35 cm) fine elastic
- Bodkin or safety pin

- With right sides together, stitch the two short ends of one piece of silk together to form a circle, then fold the fabric in half lengthways.
- Still with right sides together, stitch along the long edge to form a tube, leaving a small opening. Turn the silk back to the right side and repeat the process with the second piece of silk. Dye the scrunchies as described above.

- When dry, tie a piece of fine string to the elastic and use a bodkin or safety pin to thread it through the opening in the tube.
- Untie the string, pull up the elastic and tie the ends together, over-sewing them for extra security. Neatly oversew the opening.

SILK SCARF

There are many different kinds of silk available. You may also prefer to personalize a scarf that you already own. We have used three colors and two tying methods to produce a subtle, delicately shaded pattern.

> **TIP**
> - If you are using dye colors that are either very strong or very dilute, you may wish to alter the dye to water ratios. In general, the final color is determined both by the concentration of the dye and by the length of time that the object is immersed in the dye.

You will need

- 36 x 36 in. (90 x 90 cm) undyed, lightweight habutai silk
- Electric iron
- 13 ft (4 m) twine
- 6 ft 6 in. (2 m) heavy thread or 2-ply wool
- 1 tsp (5 g) each of deep rose, golden yellow, and marine-blue dye
- 6 tbsp (90 ml) vinegar
- 1 bowl, large enough to hold at least 2 pints (1 liter)

Before binding your scarf, iron it to remove any creases. Fold the silk square diagonally to form a triangle, then fold it in half again to make a smaller triangle.

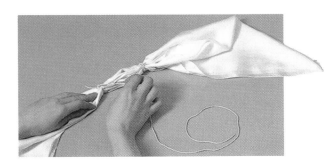

Pleat the silk lengthways and bind the folded strip with pieces of twine, placed at intervals of about 2½ in. (6 cm), and fasten securely. Midway between each piece of twine, tie lengths of heavy thread tightly around the silk.

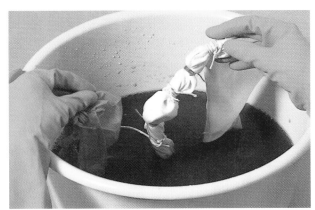

Mix 1 tsp (5 g) deep rose dye in 2 pints (1 liter) of hot water and allow it to cool to about 120° F (50° C). If the dye you are using requires the addition of vinegar when silk is dyed, add 2 tbsp (30 ml). Place the pleated and bound silk scarf into the dye bath, making sure that the bowl is large enough to allow the material to move freely and that the dye solution is sufficiently deep to cover the material completely.

> **TIP**
> - If you choose to dye a scarf that is already colored, remember that the original color of the fabric will affect the result. A blue scarf dyed with yellow will, for example, become green.

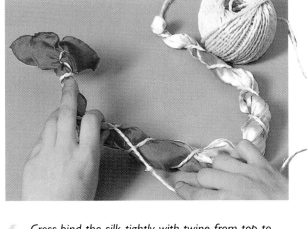

6 Cross-bind the silk tightly with twine from top to bottom, mix the yellow dye, and proceed as before.

4 Leave the scarf in the bowl for at least 15 minutes, stirring it occasionally. When you have achieved the shade you want, remove the dye from the bowl and rinse the scarf under cold running water until the water runs clear. Then untie the twine and thread.

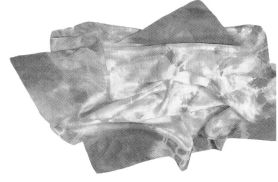

7 Rinse thoroughly, untie and dry before ironing to remove the creases.

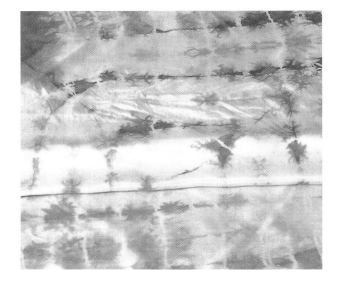

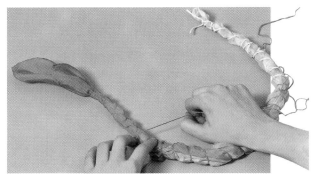

5 Allow the silk to dry flat. You may iron it when it is still slightly damp to remove all creases. Find the center of the square, pinch it and allow the silk to fall into drapes as if it were a closed umbrella.

8 Pinch and fold the silk as in step 5 and use twine to bind the top half. Bind the bottom half more tightly with heavy thread so that more blue dye reaches the center. Mix the blue dye and place the scarf in the bowl. You may dilute the blue dye since marine blue can be rather strong.

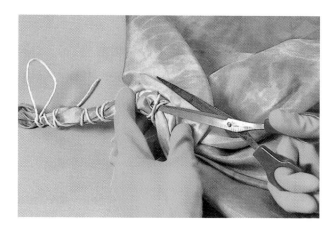

9 *Rinse the silk thoroughly before untying the scarf and allow it to dry.*

COLOR WHEEL

■ Dyes behave differently from pigment-based colors—paints and inks, for example—because they rely on some form of chemical agent such as salt or vinegar to make them permanent. This attribute makes it difficult to judge accurately what the end result will be, and tie-dyeing colored fabric or an already dyed item of clothing can add to this unpredictability. In general, however, you should be able to anticipate more or less what the end result will be, and you can use this wheel as a guide.

CUSHION COVERS

Different materials accept dyes differently. When they are bound and dyed, cotton and thicker fabrics take on a softer, almost dusty pattern, which tends to be stronger on one side. This quality makes them acceptable for use in soft furnishings, where only one side of the fabric is visible.

You will need

- 4 pieces of fabric, each 26 x 26 in. (65 x 65 cm)
- Electric iron
- 13 ft (4 m) twine
- A packet of dye in each of golden yellow, marine blue, and copper (or colors to suit your furnishing scheme)
- A bowl, large enough to hold 3 pints (1.5 liters)
- 2 cushion pads, each 18 x 18 in. (45 x 45 cm)

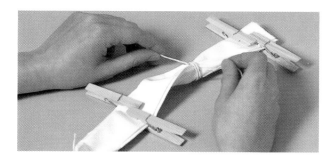

1 *Iron the squares of material to remove any creases, and for the first cover, fold the material in half and pleat it lengthways, making the pleats about 1¼ in. (3 cm) wide. Iron again. Secure the pleats with clothes pegs, spacing the pegs at intervals of about 2½ in (6 cm). Bind the fabric with twine between each peg.*

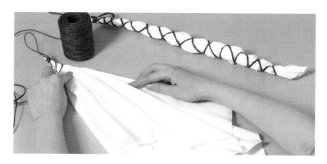

2 *For the second cover, pinch the material in the center and allow it to fall into drapes. Twist the fabric slightly, then tightly cross-bind it along its entire length with twine to limit the amount of dye that comes into contact with the material. This technique is especially useful for adding small splashes of color.*

TIP

- Some colored twines—those that are sold for garden use, for example—may stain fabrics when they are dampened by the dye solution. Wooden clothes pegs may also retain traces of dye, and if you re-use them you may find that minute quantities of the original color are transferred to your new pattern. These colors may enhance your design or they may ruin it—so take care.

MAKING A CUSHION

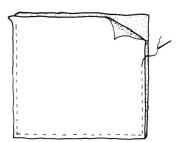

- Place two matching squares together, right sides facing, and stitch around three sides, leaving a seam allowance of about 1¼ in. (3 cm), although the seam may vary if your material has shrunk slightly during the dyeing process.

- Fold down and iron a 1 in. (2.5 cm) hem along both edges.

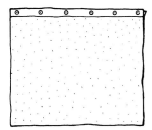

- Add a zip fastener, Velcro or press-studs to close the opening before turning to the right side and inserting the cushion pad.

TIP

- If you are making larger cushion covers, remember to increase the amounts of water and dye you mix, and to use a large bowl so that the pieces of material can be completely submerged.

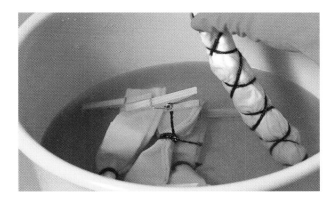

3   *Mix the yellow dye, using a bowl large enough to accommodate all the pieces of fabric. Add the salt to the dye bath, if recommended. Place both covers in the dye and leave for 15-20 minutes, stirring occasionally. Remove the covers, rinse thoroughly and untie.*

4   *Dry the fabric and iron it. If the fabric is very creased, you may use the steam setting on your iron or dampen the material slightly to make ironing easier.*

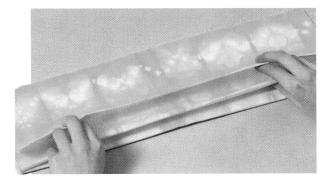

5   *Take the first square and fold it in half across the dyed lines, and then pleat it.*

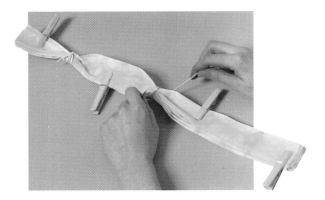

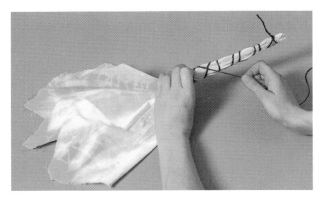

6 Iron and pleat the square, securing it with pegs and twine as before. Mix the blue dye and place the folded and tied material in it. Leave for 15-20 minutes, rinse thoroughly, untie and dry.

7 Take the second, ironed cover and pinch it in the center to drape it in an umbrella shape. Cross-bind it halfway down its length with twine. Mix the copper dye and place the tied material in it. Leave for 15-20 minutes, rinse thoroughly, untie and dry.

TIP

■ If you make cushions that are backed with plain fabric, make sure that the material you choose for the backs shrinks at the same rate as the patterned square. Otherwise, the cover will twist when it is laundered.

ALL-IN-ONE COTTON BODY

Combining several techniques in one item of clothing can produce fairly spectacular results. Although the final pattern can look complicated, the tie-dying process means that decorating in this way is relatively straightforward. Here, we have dyed a white all-in-one cotton body by using two colors and two different techniques to produce a three-color pattern. This project also demonstrates how easy it is to isolate a pattern and color on the same article.

You will need

- A white all-in-one cotton body
- A large marble or glass ball
- 24 in. (60 cm) string
- 4 strips of fabric, each 5 ft x 1 in. (1.5 m x 2.5 cm)
- 1½ tsp (7.5 g) each of bright pink and violet dye
- A bowl large enough to hold 6 pints (3 liters)
- 2 tbsp (30 g) salt

TIP
- Remember that the poorer the quality of the article you are dyeing, the cooler the dye solution should be before you place the item in it.

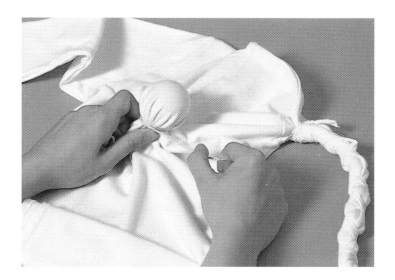

1 Bind the large marble into the chest of the cotton body, making sure that you bind the string from the front of the garment, which will give slightly different circular patterns on the back and the front. Take each arm, twist it slightly, and then tightly cross-bind each one with strips of fabric. You will need two strips for each arm. Twisting the fabric before binding stops the dye from saturating the whole of the sleeve.

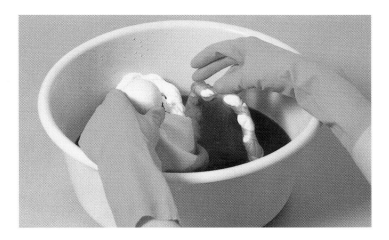

2 Mix the pink dye in 1 pint (0.5 liter) of boiling water. Add the solution to a bowl containing 5 pints (2.5 liters) of warm water. Add the salt and allow to cool. Dye the whole garment, stirring it to help prevent patchy coloring and leaving it for a further 20-30 minutes. The longer you leave it, the brighter the color will be. Rinse thoroughly in cold running water.

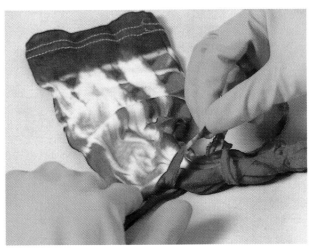

3   *Wring the excess water from the garment and mix the violet dye. Place the gusset end of the body, up to the waist, and the bottom half of the sleeves into the dye. Leave for a further 20-30 minutes.*

4   *Remove from the dye, rinse thoroughly and untie. Tumble dry and iron to remove creases and any stretching that may have occurred.*

ECRU COTTON TOP

Mixing and matching different kinds of fabric within one project is an effective way of adding spots of color and texture to a design or item of clothing. We have chosen to pattern a long-sleeved ecru cotton top in a single color and then appliqué a piece of multicolored silk to the chest. Back the silk with medium-weight cotton to stop it from twisting.

You will need

- A long-sleeved cotton top
- 10 ft (3 m) string
- 2 tsp (10 g) black dye
- 2 tbsp salt
- A bowl large enough to hold at least 6 pints (3 liters)
- A piece of medium-weight habutai silk, 12 x 12 in. (30 x 30 cm)
- Electric iron
- 10 elastic bands
- ½ tsp (2.5 g) each of navy-blue and orange dye
- 4 tbsp (60 ml) vinegar (but check manufacturer's instructions)
- A bowl large enough to hold at least 2 pints (1 liter)
- 24 in. (60 cm) heavy thread
- A piece of fine ecru cotton lawn, 5 x 5 in. (13 x 13 cm)

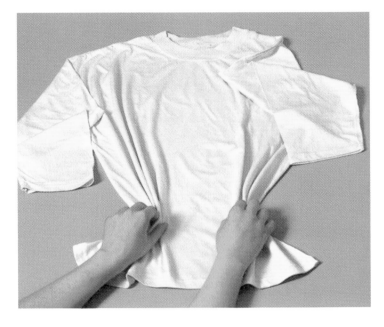

Lay the top on your work surface, with the neck furthest away from you. Take a side of the body in each hand and pleat the sides towards the center.

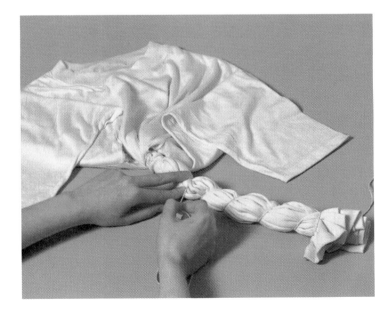

Use 5 ft (1.5 m) of string to cross-bind the body from 10 in. (25 cm) down from the neck to the bottom hem.

3 *Take each arm and cross-bind them separately, pleating them as you did the body and binding from 1 in. (2.5 cm) up from the wrist to the shoulder seam.*

4 *Mix the black dye and salt in 2 pints (1 liter) of boiling water and add it to a bowl containing 4 pints (2 liters) of hot water. Test the strength of the dye by dipping a strip of cotton into the bowl for about 10 minutes. To obtain a dense black you may add more dye.*

6 *When the top is as dark as possible, which may take 45 minutes, remove it from the dye, rinse thoroughly and untie. You may want to put it through the tumble dryer if it has stretched slightly.*

5 *Allow the solution to cool so that the fabric does not stretch, and add the top, stirring occasionally to encourage the dye to spread evenly. The longer you leave the garment in the dye, the darker the shade of black that will be produced.*

TIP
- When you are appliquéing fabric that is different from the garment or base material, remember that they may shrink at different rates. If you are unsure, wash, dry and iron both pieces separately before you begin.

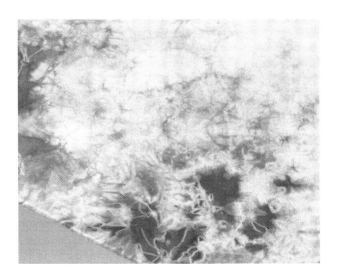

9 Cross-bind it tightly with heavy thread. Mix the orange dye as in step 8 and add the silk. Leave the silk for 15-20 minutes before rinsing thoroughly, untying and ironing. Take the piece of cotton lawn and turn under and iron a hem of about ½ in. (12 mm) all round.

7 While the shirt is drying, dye the silk. Scrunch it into a tight ball and bind it with embroidery thread. Mix the blue dye in boiling water and add 1 tbsp (15 ml) vinegar. Allow the dye to cool to about 120° F (50° C) before adding the silk, which should be left for 15-20 minutes. Remove the silk from the blue dye, rinse thoroughly and untie.

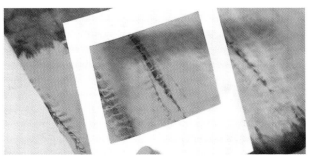

10 Use a viewing window to cut out a 4 x 4 in. (10 x 10 cm) section of the patterned silk.

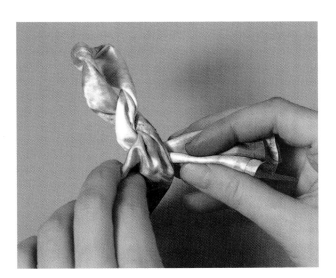

MAKING THE PATCH

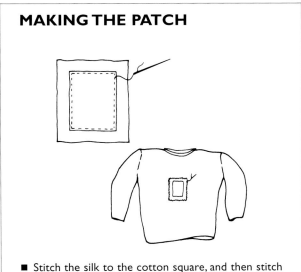

■ Stitch the silk to the cotton square, and then stitch the mounted silk onto the front.

8 Dry the silk, ironing it with a medium-hot iron to speed the process. Fold it in half, twist it, and allow it to fold back on itself.

SHORT-SLEEVED SILK TOP

Silk is a versatile fabric, and there are dozens of ways in which it can be woven to produce different types of material, each with its own properties. This project involves dyeing a silk crêpe de chine top. The material is slightly stretchy, but it takes dye well and gives a lustrous finish. To build up texture, we initially bind and dye the silk with a light color, and although this shade will not be obvious when the other color is added, it provides subtle variations of tone that become visible in certain lights.

You will need

- 1 *crêpe de chine* short-sleeved top
- 5 corks
- 6 ft 6 in. (2 m) heavy thread
- 2 tsp (10 g) each of citrus yellow and bright-red dye
- 8 tbsp (120 ml) vinegar (but check manufacturer's instructions)
- A bowl large enough to hold at least 6 pints (3 liters)
- 36 in. (90 cm) thick cord (nylon washing line is best)

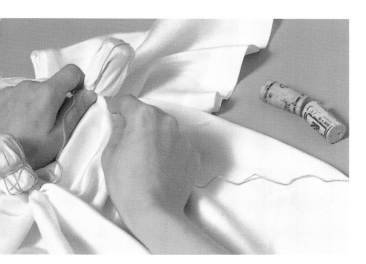

1 Randomly bind all the corks into the top. If you prefer, use other objects such as egg cups or buttons.

2 Mix the citrus yellow dye in 2 pints (1 liter) of boiling water and add 4 tbsp (60 ml) of vinegar. Add this to a basin containing a further 4 pints (2 liters) of hot water. Allow the dye to cool to about 120° F (50° C) before adding the silk. Leave in the dye for 30 minutes, stirring occasionally.

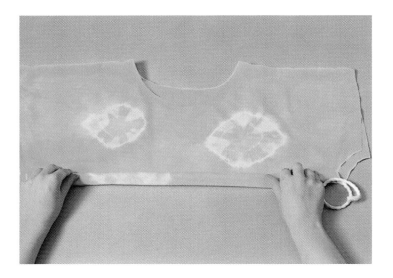

3 Once the silk has dyed, remove it, rinse it thoroughly and untie it. Dry the silk, ironing it to remove creases. Place the top on your work surface with the neck away from you, and roll the garment around the thick cord, leaving about 10 in. (25 cm) at the top unrolled.

4 Hold one end of the rolled material and ruche the top along the cord as far as you can. Tie the two ends of the cord together firmly in a double knot.

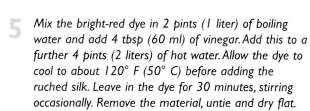

5 Mix the bright-red dye in 2 pints (1 liter) of boiling water and add 4 tbsp (60 ml) of vinegar. Add this to a further 4 pints (2 liters) of hot water. Allow the dye to cool to about 120° F (50° C) before adding the ruched silk. Leave in the dye for 30 minutes, stirring occasionally. Remove the material, untie and dry flat.

SILK GEORGETTE SHIRT

Different weights of fabric accept dyes in different ways. When they are tie-dyed, lighter weight materials and loosely woven fabrics tend to yield softer patterns, and it is worth considering the weight and density of the weave before you decide on your tying methods. For example, sharp, pleated designs are most effective on tightly woven, flat fabrics. Silk georgette, on the other hand, is a soft, open-weave silk, rather similar to chiffon or silk muslin, and you could use either of these materials or cotton cheesecloth or cotton muslin instead.

You will need

- A silk georgette shirt, either readymade or one you have made yourself
- 10 ft (3 m) string
- 1 tsp (5 g) each of dusky rose and dark-gray dye
- 4 tbsp (60 ml) vinegar (check manufacturer's instructions and if you are using cotton, remember to use salt instead)
- A bowl large enough to hold at least 3 pints (1.5 liters)

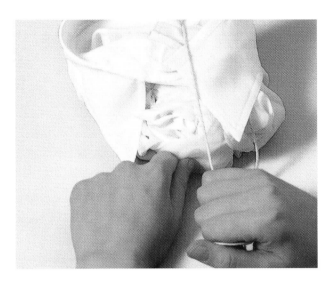

1 *Bunch the shirt into a ball—secure it by wrapping string tightly. Do not roll it, because this will limit the area exposed to the dye. Mix the dusky-rose dye in 1 liter (2 pints) of boiling water. Add 2 tbsp (30 ml) of vinegar (salt if you are dyeing cotton) and add the mixture to a further 1 pint (0.5 liter) of hot water. Allow the solution to cool to about 120° F (50° C) before adding the shirt. Leave in the dye for 20-30 minutes.*

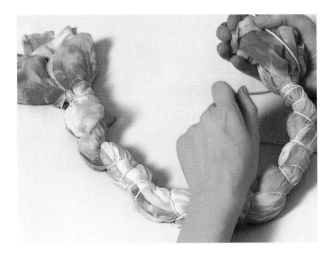

2 *Remove the bundle from the dye, rinse thoroughly and untie. Dry the shirt flat to help avoid creasing and shrinking. When the shirt is dry, bunch the collar and neck into a ball and bind it with string. Loosely twist the body and sleeves together, and cross-bind the entire length of the garment with string.*

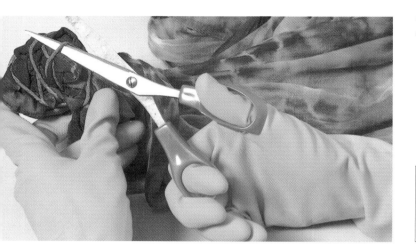

3 Mix the dark-gray dye as in step 1 and, when the dye has cooled, add the shirt to the bowl and leave it for a further 20-30 minutes. Remove the shirt from the bowl, rinse thoroughly, untie the string, and leave the shirt to dry flat.

TIP
- Many open-weave silk and cotton garments contain a dressing or stiffener, and you will get better results if you wash the article before you attempt to dye it.

DUVET COVER AND PILLOWCASES

This duvet cover is built up in patterned panels separated by plain panels of cotton lawn. Constructing large pieces in this way overcomes the problems of color matching or under-dyeing that can occur with large quantities of fabric.

TIP

- Working with large amounts of fabric poses certain problems, especially when it comes to binding the material effectively and achieving an even color. When a project requires a large amount of cloth, you may find it easier to dye the fabric in panels and make the pieces into the item afterwards. Trying to color-match panels that have been dyed in separate dye baths is, unfortunately, one of the drawbacks of attempting to apply a pattern to a large item in this way. However, even if you were able to fit the whole piece of fabric in one dye bath, you would probably find that the color was unable to penetrate through to all areas of the fabric simply because of the mass of material.

You will need

- 4 pieces white cotton, each 6 ft 6 in. x 30 in. (2 m x 75 cm)
- 2 pieces white cotton, each 26 x 20 in. (65 x 50 cm)
- Electric iron
- 52 clothes pegs
- 13 ft (4 m) string
- 3 tsp (15 gm) dusky-rose dye
- 1 tsp (5 gm) cornflower-blue dye
- 4 tbsp (60 g) salt
- A bowl large enough to hold at least 4 pints (7 liters)
- 2 pieces lightweight ecru cotton lawn, each 6 ft 6 in. x 30 in. (2 m x 75 cm)
- 2 pieces lightweight ecru cotton lawn, each 26 x 20 in. (65 x 50 cm)

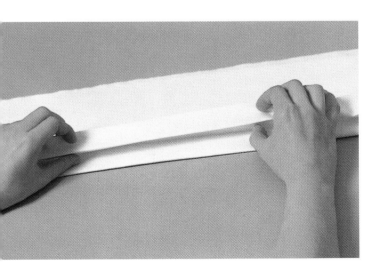

1 Iron the pieces of white cotton to remove any creases, then fold them, separately, in half lengthways and pleat them. Each pleat should be about 1¼ in. (3 cm) wide.

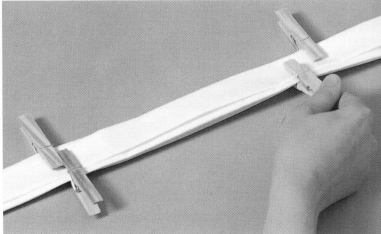

2 Iron the pleats and secure them with clothes pegs on both sides of the pleat, spacing the pegs at intervals of about 12 in. (30 cm).

ASSEMBLING THE DUVET

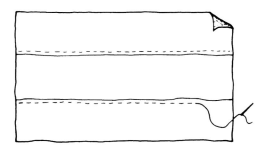

- When the pieces are dry, iron them flat. Assemble the duvet cover by stitching one piece of ecru cotton between two patterned panels for the front.

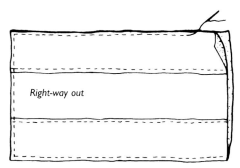

Right-way out

- Repeat this for the back, then lay the two squares, wrong sides together, one on top of the other, and stitch three sides.

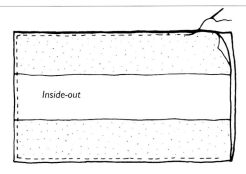

Inside-out

- We have allowed fairly generous seams in case the fabric shrinks during the dyeing process, but you have ample material to stitch French seams—that is, once you have stitched the three sides, turn the duvet cover so that the right sides are together and stitch around the same three sides to trap the raw edges in the hem.

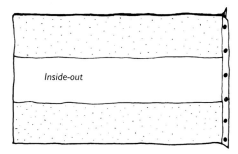

Inside-out

- Turn in and hem the open edge and add fasteners.
- Make the pillowcases in the same way, stitching a patterned piece to a plain ecru piece and hemming the open seams.

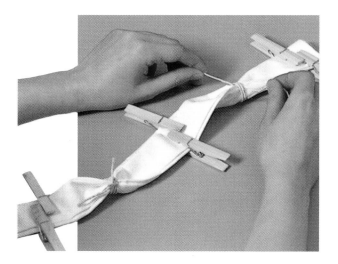

3 *Halfway between each peg, bind the fabric with pieces of string about 9 in. (23 cm) long.*

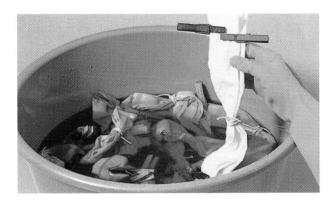

4 *Mix the dusky-rose dye in 2 pints (1 liter) of boiling water and add 2 tbsp (30 g) of salt. Add this solution to a further 12 pints (6 liters) of hot water. You must use a bowl large enough to hold the fabric and the dye comfortably. Place all the bound white fabric in the bowl while the dye is still hot, if you want a particularly vibrant color. Leave it for 30-45 minutes. When the fabric is dyed, remove the bundles from the dye and rinse thoroughly—but do not untie the bundles.*

5 *Mix the cornflower-blue dye in 2 pints (1 liter) of boiling water and add the salt. Add this to a further 6 pints (3 liters) of hot water. Drape the pleated fabric over the bowl so that only the ends are in the dye— about 18 in. (45 cm) each end for the duvet cover and 8 in. (20 cm) each end for the pillowcases. Leave for a further 30 minutes. Remove the fabric from the dye, rinse thoroughly and untie.*

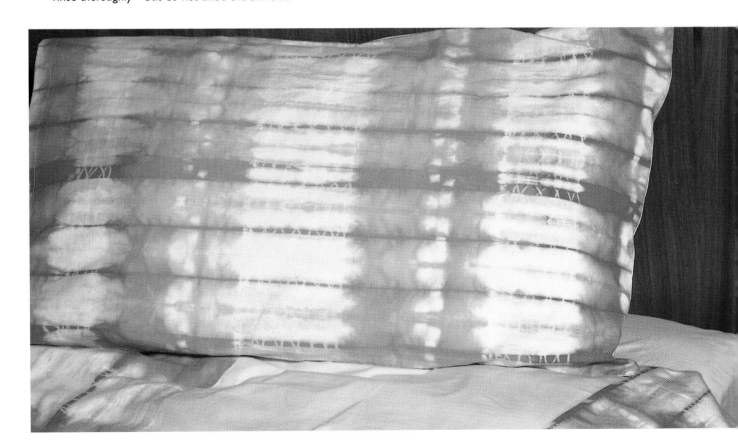

PICTURE FRAMING

One of the great appeals of framing is that it takes so little time to learn. With only a couple of pieces of wood and some glass you can make a present for a friend, or a frame for a favorite photograph.

The frame is important because any picture needs to be confined within a clearly defined area. When there is no frame, the eye tends to wander and it is difficult to focus on the image and to appreciate it properly. The finishing edge—that is, the mount and the frame—should complement the picture, but they must not be so intrusive that they are the first thing you look at.

You may find it helpful to visit art galleries, museums and shops to look at the ways different frames and moldings can be used to create different effects. If you look at Victorian watercolors, for example, you will see how the overall balance is maintained by the use of light-ivory or cream-colored mounts, often decorated with wash lines, together with a fairly dark wooden or deep-gold frame. Traditional framing has a long and rich history, but new products, which make techniques such as gilding and distressing so much easier, have changed people's attitudes to the craft and encouraged new fashions.

Equipment and Materials

If you are lucky, you will find that you already have most of the tools and equipment you will need in your household tool cupboard. There are, however, two items that you will probably have to buy—a miter box or clamp and a mount cutter—but in general, you should think about buying new tools only as you need them.

MOLDINGS

There is a wide range of moldings available to the amateur framer these days. When you are choosing a molding, consider the size of the picture and such aspects as whether it is boldly colored or finely drawn.

You will need

To make the frames described in this book, you will need the following:

- Pin hammer
- Tenon saw
- Screwdriver
- Pincers/pliers
- Nail punch
- Set square
- Hand drill and bits
- Panel pins
- Miter box or clamp
- Metal ruler
- Plastic ruler and pencil
- Craft knife
- Wood glue

Since hard wood has become much scarcer in recent times, plastic moldings have been introduced. These have the great advantages that they do not warp or suffer from woodworm. They also take gilding and colored finishes well, though they do not, of course, have the wonderful smell and feel of real wood.

MOLDING FORMULA

- This simple formula can be used to work out fairly accurately how much molding you will need. Add together:

  The height of the picture x 2
  The width of the picture x 2
  The width across the top of the frame (i.e., of the molding) x 8

  You need the additional width of the molding for the miter cuts that are made at the ends of each of the four pieces.

  For example, say that you are framing a picture measuring 12 x 10 in. (31 x 25 cm) and that the depth of the molding is ½ in. (1 cm):

  12 in. (31 cm) x 2 = 24 in. (62 cm)
  10 in. (25 cm) x 2 = 20 in. (50 cm)
  ½ in. (1 cm) x 8 = 3½ in. (8 cm)
  = 48 in. (120 cm)

  Add an extra 2 in. (5 cm) to be on the safe side, which means you will need 50 in. (125 cm) in total.

USING THE CLAMP AND SAW

When your saw is new you may find that a little oil will make it run smoothly when you are cutting molding. Try not to put a lot of pressure on the saw when you are cutting. Aim to use short, light, even strokes and to let the saw do the work. When it is not being used, always keep the saw in its cover to protect the teeth.

1 Fix the clamp to a wooden base. You will need a piece of $\frac{1}{2}$ in. (1 cm) plywood measuring about 8 x 7 in. (20 x 18 cm). Cut a length of 1½ x 1 in. (3.5 x 2.5 cm) timber to 8 in. (20 cm), and screw it along the longer side of the piece of plywood to form a lip that will butt up against the edge of your working surface.

USING A MITER CLAMP

- Make sure that the molding is sitting flat on the base before you tighten up the screws.
- Use small pieces of card or off-cuts of wood at the end of the clamp screws to protect the molding from any damage.
- If the base moves around too much when you are sawing pieces of wood, use a clamp to hold the base firmly to your working surface.
- When you have cut a corner and you need to smooth the edges, gently rub the cut edge on the rough side of some hardboard instead of using sandpaper, which may be too severe.

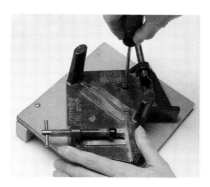

2 Screw the metal miter clamp on to the plywood base so that the lip is on the other side.

3 Before you use a clamp for the first time, you may find it helpful to draw a line on the rubber insert of the base of the clamp to indicate the central cutting line.

USING CORNER CLAMPS

Frame corner clamps held with a cord can be rather awkward to work with. They can be useful, however, especially if you are making small or very narrow frames that are difficult to pin.

Take the four cut pieces of the frame and glue the ends of the long sides. Lay the frame on the surface and put the four corner clamps in place. Pull up the string until it is very tight, clean off any glue that has seeped out, and put to one side until the glue is dry.

MOUNTING

Your choice of mount can affect the final appearance of the painting even more than the frame itself. If the mount is too small, it can appear to squeeze and confine the picture, so, at least at first, you should make the mount slightly larger than you had planned.

You will need

- Cutting mat
- Mount cutter with ruler
- Compasses
- Pencil
- Adhesive tape
- Plastic ruler and pencil
- Scissors
- Craft knife
- Mapping pen and paint brush

You must make sure that the blade of your mount cutter is sharp. Keep a supply of spare blades and replace the worn one as often as necessary, but certainly every 5 or 6 mounts.

Remember that the bottom edge of the mount is usually deeper than the top and sides, which should be the same depth. Thus, if the top and sides were 3½ in. (8 cm) deep, the bottom should be 4 in. (10 cm) deep. The difference helps to lead the eye into the picture.

There is a huge range of mounting boards and cards available.

Being sepia, this photograph has been treated like a drawing, and so has a large mount. However, they generally look best in small, dark mounts.

In general you should pick a light color, especially if you are framing a watercolor painting. Pick a color from the painting itself and match the tone of the color with a light green, soft brown, ivory, and so on. If the

color seems too bland, wash or crayon lines can be added. A brightly colored painting may look best with a pale mount, but with a more vividly colored frame.

Prints require special treatment. If they are original, they will have a plate mark impressed on the paper, all around the

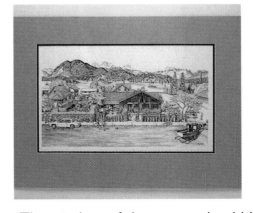

image. The window of the mount should be large enough for the mark to be visible, which usually means leaving a margin of white about ½ in. (1 cm) wide around the actual printed image.

Choosing your mount thoughtfully and cutting it precisely, will make all the difference to the final look of the picture. The different types are:

- A normal window mount
- A double mount, in which about ½ in. (1 cm) of the color of the underlying mount can be seen around the edge of the top mount
- A float, in which the picture lies on a colored mount with about 1 in. (2-3 cm) of the mount showing all round the edge of the picture
- A float and mount combined, in which the picture lies on the lower mount while the window in the top mount is cut to reveal about ½ in. (1-2 cm) of the bottom mount around the picture
- Fabric-covered mounts, when silk or hessian is used over the mount
- Paper-covered mounts
- Wash mounts

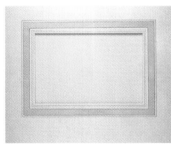

TIP
- Your choice of mounting technique can radically alter the final appearance of the picture or photograph, as can be seen from this picture, which has been mounted in three different ways.

  A normal window mount
  A float
  A double mount

CUTTING A MOUNT

We are mounting a brightly colored painting, which needs a quieter colored mount so that the painting stands out. We later added a colored frame, which tied the scheme together.

You will need

- Cutting board
- Scraps of card
- Sharp pencil and ruler
- Set square
- Mount cutter
- Craft knife or razor blade
- Backing board
- Masking tape
- Acid-free tape (optional)

Measure the picture and fix the area you want to show in the window of the mount. Here the window is 13 x 9½ in. (33 x 23.5 cm). The width of the mount at the top and both sides is 3 in. (7.5 cm), and the width at the bottom is 3½ in. (9 cm). To calculate the total area of mount, add the width of the window to twice the width of the side and add the depth of the window to the top and the bottom widths of the mount. Here, that is 13 + 6 in. (33 + 15 cm), which gives an overall width of 19 in. (48 cm), and 9½ + 3 + 3½ in. (23.5 + 7.5 + 9 cm), which gives an overall depth of 16 in. (40 cm).

Lay the cutting board on a flat surface and place some scrap card on it. On the reverse side of the mounting card, draw a rectangle to the outside dimensions of the mount—in our example this is 19 x 16 in. (48 x 40 cm). Use a set square to make sure that the corners are exactly 90 degrees. Cut out the mount area. On the reverse side, draw the window opening. Measure in from the outside edge, in this case, 3 in. (7.5 cm) from the top and sides, and 3½ in. (9 cm) from the bottom. Cut the window. If the window does not fall out easily, use a sharp craft knife or razor blade to finish the corners.

Cut a piece of backing board the same size as the outside dimensions of the mount, and lay the mount face down beside the backing board, with the long edges abutting. Use small pieces of masking tape to hold the top edges together. Open out the mount and backing board and lay the picture on the backing board. Bring the mount over the picture and adjust the position of the picture. If your picture is a usual one, hold it in position under the edge of the mount with masking tape; a more valuable picture should be held with acid-free tape. Cut two pieces of tape and secure the picture at the top with these. Cut two more pieces of tape and cover the top ends of the tape.

USING THE MOUNT CUTTER

You should follow the instructions that come with your mount cutter, but the following guidelines apply to all makes.

- Make sure that the blade is sharp and that it is set so that it just cuts through the mounting card and into the scrap card beneath.

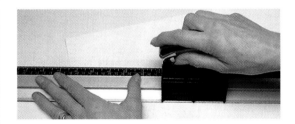

- Lay the ruler so that the blade follows the pencil line. Insert the blade just beyond the corner and pull it towards you, finishing just beyond the corner nearest to you.

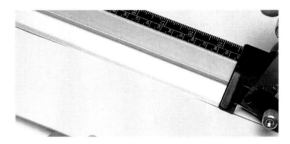

- Test to see if the cut is clean. Keeping the ruler in position, lift the edge of the card to check that the cut has gone right through. If it has not, slide the cutter down the line again.

Remember, when you have completed each cut, you should move the scrap card so that the blade does not get stuck in the groove made by the first cut.

HANGING MATERIALS

You will need a range of rings and eyes to provide secure hangers for your finished frames.

You will need

- D-rings
- Screw eyes
- Wire or cord
- Metal glass clips
- Plastic mirror clips
- Brown adhesive paper or masking tape

MAKING A CUTTING SURFACE

- Although you can buy special cutting mats, they are not cheap and are available in only a limited range of sizes. You can easily make your own, which will provide a suitable surface for cutting both the mounts and the glass.

- To make a cutting surface measuring about 30 x 36 in. (75 x 93 cm), which is large enough for most frames, cut a piece of hardboard and a piece of mounting card to the same size. Use an ordinary rubber-based adhesive to stick the mount to the shiny side of the hardboard, or, if you have one, use a staple gun to fix the two pieces together.

- Always place a piece of scrap card between the mount you are cutting and the surface of your cutting board.

CUTTING GLASS

Glass cutting is much easier than you may think, and unless your frame is very large you should be able to cut glass to fit all your frames.

You will need

- Glass cutter
- Wooden T-square or squaring ruler
- Pincers
- Felt-tipped pens

Buy a good glass cutter. The best kind have a little built-in reservoir to hold white spirit or glass-cutting oil, which keeps the cutting head clean and running smoothly. If your cutter does not have this feature, you will need to dip the head into white spirit before each cut.

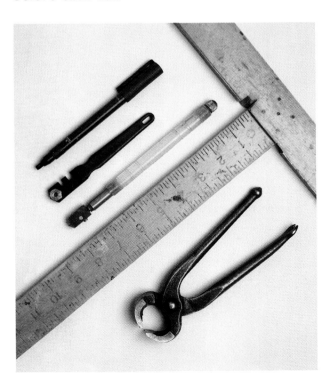

Picture frames take $\frac{1}{16}$ in. (2 mm) glass, which you can buy in small quantities from your glass merchant and which is much thinner and lighter than the glass used for windows. Buy a few off-cuts initially so that you can practice your cutting technique.

CUTTING GLASS TO SIZE

1 *Lay a small piece of glass on the flat surface and hold your cutter between your first and second fingers, supporting it with your thumb so that it is almost upright. If you find this uncomfortable, you can hold the cutter between your thumb and first finger.*

2 *Practice scoring the glass. Do this a few times on different parts of some spare glass until you feel comfortable with the cutter and you can hear the satisfying sound that indicates you have cleanly scored the glass every time. Throw away this piece of glass.*

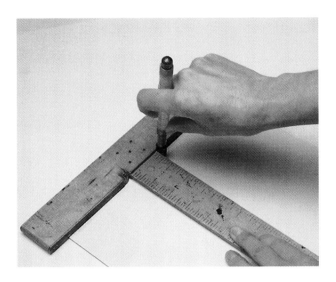

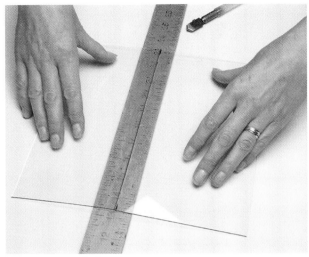

3 Put another piece of glass on your working surface. Lay the cross end of your T-square against the top of the glass so that the long piece is flat on the surface of the glass, with the top edge butted up against the edge of the glass. Take your glass cutter and, pressing down firmly, pull it down one side of the T-square. Do not go over the scored line a second time, or you will damage the cutter.

5 Place the fingertips of each hand on either side of the ruler and press down sharply. If your cut was good, the glass will break easily.

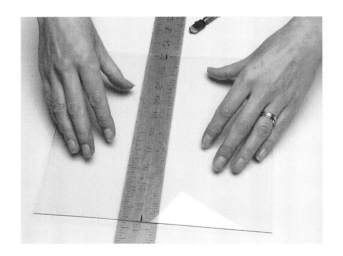

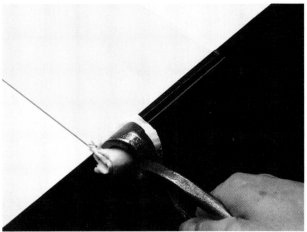

4 Carefully raise the glass at one side and slide the ruler under the cut, so that the edge of the ruler is exactly under the scored line.

6 If the glass does not break smoothly or if you need to cut a small sliver from the edge, place the glass so that the edge of your work surface aligns with the scored line (which you may, for once, need to go over with your cutter for a second time). Put a piece of cloth in the jaws of your pliers or pincers, grip the edge of the glass and snap it off.

BASIC FRAME

This first frame is for a print of a colorful Mediterranean scene, which looks good with white space around it. It will be framed to the edge of the paper without a mount. The molding is fairly wide wood, which is easier to work with than narrow, flexible molding—it is also easier to correct mistakes on wood.

You will need

- Molding (see page 254 for estimates quantity)
- Miter cutter and clamp
- Saw
- Plastic ruler and pencil
- Wood glue
- Drill and fine bit
- Panel pins
- Small hammer
- Nail punch
- $\frac{1}{16}$ in. (2 mm) glass
- T-square
- Felt-tipped pen
- Glass cutter
- $\frac{1}{16}$ in. (2 mm) hardboard
- Metal ruler
- Craft knife
- D-rings or screw eyes
- Masking tape
- Brown adhesive paper
- Wire or cord

1 Make the first miter cut by sliding the molding into the left side of the miter cutter, so that the screw clamp butts against the back of the frame. Protect the molding with card or off-cuts of wood and screw the clamp firmly.

2 Gently push the nose of the saw into the slit that is nearest to you and slide it into the further slit. Without putting a lot of pressure on the wood, slide the saw backwards and forwards, using small, even strokes.

3 Unclamp the molding and lay it on your working surface with the rebate side towards you. Working on the longest dimension first, use your ruler to measure from the inside of the corner you have just cut and mark the required length.

4 Slide the molding into the right side of the miter corner—that is, the opposite side from your first cut—and push the molding along until your pencil mark is on the center line of the miter cutter.

6 You now have to make a new 45-degree angle on the remaining piece of molding by cutting off the waste. Slide the molding into the left side of the clamp, screw it tightly in place and cut the new angle.

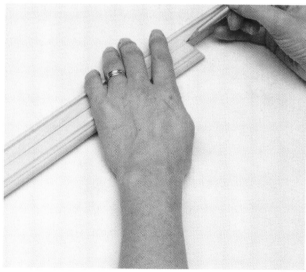

5 Clamp and cut it as the other side. Put the finished piece to one side.

7 Measure the second long side. Place the first piece you cut so that it is back to back with the second. Line up the corners and mark the length of the first piece on the back of the second. Slide the molding into the right side of the clamp, line up your mark with the center line of the clamp, tighten and cut.

8 Repeat steps 3-7 to make the two short sides. Then take a long piece and a short piece, and put some wood glue on the corner angle of the long piece.

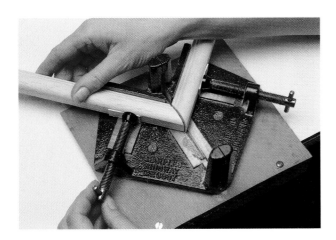

9 Place the two pieces, corner to corner, in the clamp, adjust and re-adjust until they fit neatly and tightly together and are firmly held.

TIP
- If the corners you have cut do not fit well together, hold them tightly in the clamp, with the corners as close together as possible. Insert your saw and re-cut the corner. The two pieces should now fit neatly together. You might have to carry out the same procedure on the other corners because you will have altered the size very slightly.

10 Use a drill with a fine bit to make small holes for the panel pins. When you lay a panel pin across the corner, it should be long enough to penetrate well into the other piece. A 1 in. (2.5 cm) pin is usually long enough, but if you are using wide molding you may need 2 in. (5 cm) pins.

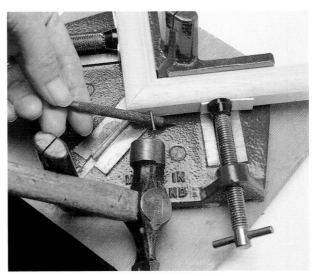

11 Using a punch, hammer the pins in gently. Repeat the steps for the opposite corner, making sure that the second long piece goes into the clamp on the same side as the first. You can now glue and pin the final corners to complete the frame.

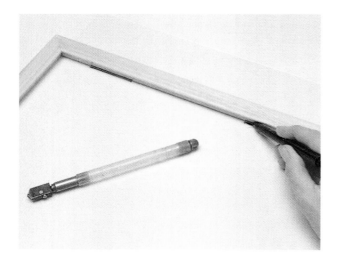

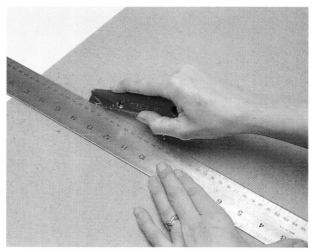

12 Cut the glass by transferring the dimensions of the picture to the glass with a felt-tipped pen, and lining your T-square against the marks before cutting on the inside of the marks by about ⅛ in. (3 mm) to allow for the width of the head of your glass cutter. Alternatively, simply lay the frame on the glass at a corner so that the frame butts up to the edges of the glass. Use a felt-tipped pen to mark the edges that are sitting on the glass and cut as before.

14 Lay a heavy metal ruler along the line and draw the blade of your craft knife down the line several times. Do not press too hard—you are not cutting right through the hardboard but scoring it. With the ruler held in the same position, sharply pull up one side of the hardboard. It should snap cleanly. If it does not, align the scored line with the edge of your working surface and snap it downwards.

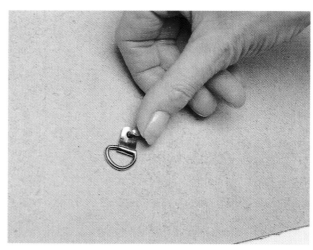

13 Lay the piece of glass on the hardboard. Draw around it so that it is exactly the same size as the cut glass.

15 Mark positions for two D-rings on the hardboard—these should be about one-third of the way down and 2-2½ in. (5-6 cm) in from the sides—and use a nail punch and hammer to make the holes.

16 Place the D-rings in place and push through the rivets. Turn over the hardboard and, resting it on a flat surface, split open the rivets with a screwdriver and hammer them flat. Cover the rivets with small pieces of masking tape. Sandwich the hardboard and glass together with the picture between them. Lay the components on your working surface and place the frame around them. Pick the whole piece up and turn it over. Hold the back in the frame by driving in a few small panel pins. Lay the pins on the hardboard and tap them into the frame.

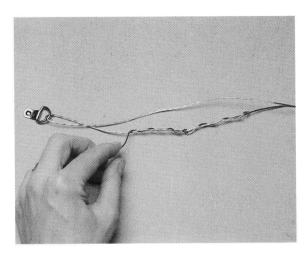

18 If you are using screw eyes rather than D-rings, insert them now, before attaching the wire or cord.

17 Use masking tape or brown gummed paper to cover the joins around the back, to help keep out insects and protect the picture from damp. A stamp roller is useful for moistening the gummed paper. Use a craft knife to trim off the ends of the tape or gummed paper.

TIP

■ When the four corners have been glued and pinned together, you can—if the frame is a wooden one—tidy them up by filling any gaps in the corners. Run a tiny amount of wood glue into the space and sand the area gently, pushing the sanding dust into the gap. You can finish off the frame with a coat of polyurethane varnish or polish it with wax.

19 *When it comes to painting the frame (see step 11), you can achieve great effects by matching one of the colors in the picture itself.*

GLASS AND CLIP FRAME

This is a simple way to display small posters and children's drawings. It is best used with items not larger than 24 x 24 in. (60 x 60 cm), because the clips exert pressure on the glass—if the glass area is too large, it may crack. This project uses plastic glass clips and a wooden frame. The picture has been floated on black, to give it a definite edge.

Measure your print—ours was 14 x 11 in. (35.5 x 28 cm) – and add ¾ in. (20 mm) all round. Cut a piece of mounting card to this larger size.

You will need

- Plastic ruler and pencil
- Mounting card
- Craft knife; saw
- Adhesive tape or double-sided tape
- 1 x 1 in. (2.5 x 2.5 cm) long wood molding
- Miter cutter and clamp
- Wood glue
- Drill and small bit
- Small hammer and nail punch
- ¾ in. (20 mm) panel pins
- Wood filler
- Sandpaper and wet and dry papers
- Paint
- Glass; glass cutter; glass clips
- T-square
- Felt-tipped pen
- Hangers

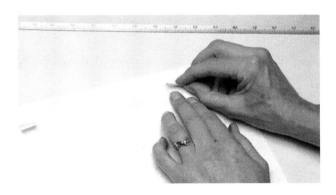

Use double-sided adhesive tape or make a hinge from ordinary adhesive tape to hold the picture in position on the mounting card. If it is held by a simple hinge rather than double-sided tape, it is easier to move the picture should you make a mistake.

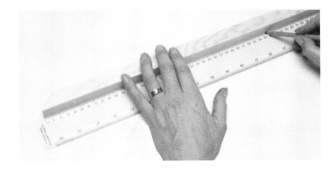

TIP
- For a larger frame, use a piece of hardboard as a backing for the mounting card for extra strength.

Cut the first angle on the frame, then measure along from the outside corner, using the long dimension first, and mark.

4 Slide the timber into the clamp, align the mark with the central cutting line, screw the arms tight, and saw. Because the timber has no rebate, you do not need to cut another angle—simply turning over the timber will give you the correct angle.

6 Apply some wood glue to one cut angle of a long side and place it in the clamp with a short side. Adjust and tighten when the angles sit neatly together.

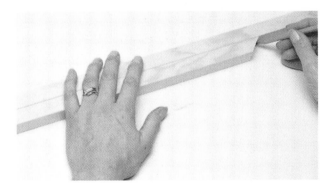

5 Use the first cut piece to measure the second long side, placing them back to back and marking the outside corners. Cut the two shorter sides in the same way.

7 Use a drill to make two small holes for the pins and drive them in, using a nail punch to drive them just below the level of the wood.

TIP

■ This frame uses the same method as the main project, but the picture fits into the other side of the frame instead of being clipped onto the front of it.

8   *Fill the holes with wood filler, leave to dry and smooth with sandpaper.*

9   *Paint the frame to suit your picture. We used black to match the mounting card, but you could use a color that harmonizes with the picture you are framing, or one that will complement your furnishings. Leave to dry.*

10   *Use the finished frame as a guide to cut the glass. Lay the frame against a corner of the glass and mark the other two sides on the outside of the frame with a felt-tipped pen.*

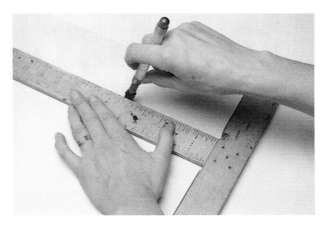

11   *Use a wooden straight-edged ruler to cut the glass to size, then smooth the edges with wet and dry sandpaper, taking especial care at the corners. Clean the glass and sandwich the glass, the picture and the card. Lay them on the frame.*

12   *Use two glass clips on each side, making sure they are placed opposite each other. Mark the position of the holes in the clips all the way round and use the drill to make the holes. Screw the clips into position. The clips must be screwed sufficiently tightly to hold the glass securely, but not so tightly that the glass cracks. Screw hangers in place on the back of the frame.*

from larger projects. To make a frame with glass and metal clips, cut the hardboard to size, then cut the glass to exactly the same size. Smooth the edges of the glass. Fit D-rings to the hardboard, position the picture and slide on the metal clips, digging the metal less into the back of the hardboard.

TIP

■ The shops are full of frames made with metal clips and hardboard, and they are so reasonably priced that you may not think it worthwhile to make your own, but they are a good way of using up the small pieces of glass and hardboard that are left over

FABRIC AND PAPER FRAMES

Frames made in this way are ideal birthday and Christmas presents, and they are the perfect way of displaying all those school photographs that seem to accumulate. You can use almost any paper you like—wrapping paper, handmade paper or lightweight cotton. You might want to practice on some less expensive material before using handmade paper, as we have done to make this double frame.

You will need

- Mounting card or equivalent
- Plastic ruler and pencil
- Mount cutter
- Polyester wadding
- Clear, all-purpose adhesive
- Sharp-pointed scissors
- Handmade paper or fabric to cover frames
- Double-sided adhesive tape

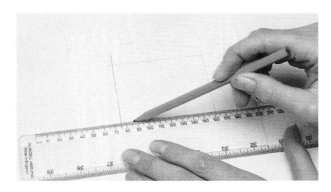

1 *Cut four pieces of card. In our example the outside measurements of each are 6½ x 5½ in. (16 x 14 cm). You will also need to cut a piece of card 6½ in. (16 cm) long by about ½ in. (1 cm) wide, which will form the spine of the frame.*

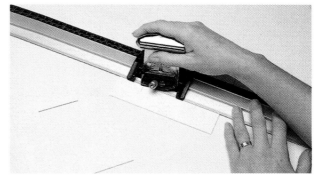

2 *In two of the larger rectangles of card, cut a window; ours measured 3¼ x 2½ in. (8 x 6 cm). (See page 260 for using a mount cutter.)*

3 *Cut two pieces of wadding to the same size as the window mounts, and use a small amount of adhesive to glue them to the fronts of the mounts.*

4 Snip a hole in the center of the wadding, then trim away the excess to the window edge.

7 Cut a strip of covering paper to cover the spine and glue it into position. Leave the adhesive to dry.

5 Cut a piece of handmade paper for the back—ours was 13½ x 7½ in. (34 x 19 cm) – and two pieces for the front—ours measured 7½ x 6¾ in. (19 x 17 cm).

8 Take the two smaller paper pieces and place them, wrong sides up, on the working surface. Lay the window mounts on this so that an even amount of paper shows all round. Glue down the paper all the way round, making sure that it is taut and the corners are neat.

6 Put the larger piece of paper on your working surface with the wrong side up. Lay the two backing cards on it with ¾ in. (20 mm) between them. Glue the thin strip of card into this space. Apply adhesive around the paper edges and neatly stick it over the card. Work on the top and bottom edges before turning in the sides. Pull the paper tightly over the edges. Trim the corners so that the paper lies neatly and flat.

9 With the back of the mount towards you, use sharp scissors to make a hole in the center of the mount. Make four cuts, just up to—but not right into—the corners.

10 *Trim off the excess triangles of paper and glue and fold the inside edges, making sure that the front edges are neat and that there are no creases, especially in the corners. Trim off any excess paper or, if you have used fabric, any loose threads and frayed edges.*

11 *Use double-sided adhesive tape to stick the two front sections carefully to the back, leaving the top open so that you can slide in the photograph.*

Box Frame

This kind of frame is useful for holding three-dimensional objects such as a piece of embroidery or collectable items such as badges or medals. There are several ways of making box frames, but this is a simple and effective method. The size of the frame is determined by the backing board, which can be covered with colored card or with polyester wadding and fabric. We have made the frame to display an arrangement of dried flowers mounted on card.

You will need

- Hardboard; card
- Plastic ruler and pencil
- Craft knife; scissors
- Polyester wadding
- Fabric
- Clear, all-purpose adhesive
- 1 in. (2.5 cm) hockey wood molding
- Miter cutter and clamp
- Saw
- Wood glue
- Drill and fine bit
- Panel pins; small hammer
- 1/16 in. (2 mm) glass
- Glass cutter
- T-square
- Masking tape or brown gummed paper
- Screw eyes
- Wire or cord

1 Cut a piece of hardboard to size—we used a piece that is 12½ x 8½ in. (32.5 x 21.5 cm). Cover the hardboard with polyester wadding and cut a piece of fabric that is about ½ in. (10 mm) larger all round than the hardboard.

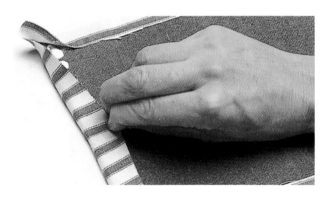

2 Stretch the fabric over the wadding and glue it firmly to the back, making sure that the corners are neatly mitered.

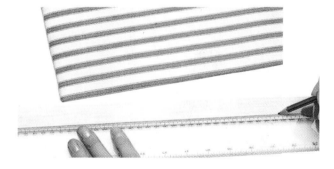

3 Cut the first miter in the molding and, working on a long side first, measure the covered hardboard. Transfer this measurement to the outside edge of the molding, measuring from one corner to the other.

4 *Slide the molding into the miter clamp and align the mark with the center line of the vice. Cut the other three sides and assemble the frame as described in page 263. Cut a piece of glass to fit inside the frame. Lay the frame face down, clean the glass and fit into the frame.*

7 *Place the frame over the backing board and carefully over the box.*

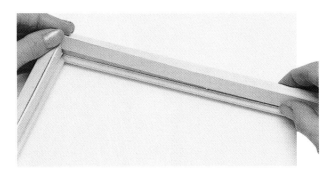

5 *Measure the depth of the side from the glass to the back of the frame—in our frame this was about ¾ in. (20 mm) – and cut four strips of thick card to this width and long enough to fit along the inside of the frame. Glue them in place, sticking the long pieces down first. The strips will hold the glass at the front of the box.*

8 *Use small panel pins, tapped through the backing board into the frame, to hold the back in place. Cover the join with strips of masking tape or brown gummed paper.*

6 *Attach the object or objects to the covered backing board. We used all-purpose adhesive to hold the card in place.*

9 *With your hand drill, make holes, about one-third of the way down, on each side of the frame and insert the screw eyes. Attach wire or cord for hanging.*

SHELL FRAME

You can revitalize an old wooden frame by covering it with shells, feathers, or even small bits of seaweed. Alternatively, you can make your own frame, although you will need to use a fairly flat molding or one that has only a gentle curve.

You will need

- Wooden frame
- White emulsion paint
- Acrylic paint
- Wire wool or a rag
- White candle (optional)
- Screw eyes
- Mirror
- Panel pins and hammer
- Masking tape or gummed brown paper
- Strong adhesive
- Interior wall filler (optional)
- Gold paint

2 *Mix the acrylic paint, diluting it with a little emulsion to give a smooth, runny consistency. Experiment until you have a shade you like. Paint the frame and before the paint is completely dry, use wire wool or a rag to drag some of the paint off.*

3 *An alternative method is to use the end of a candle to draw patterns on the dried base coat.*

1 *If the frame is going to be painted, apply a coat of white emulsion and leave to dry.*

4 *When you apply the acrylic paint, the wax will resist the paint and leave the white base coat showing through.*

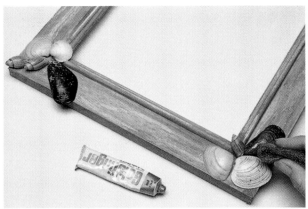

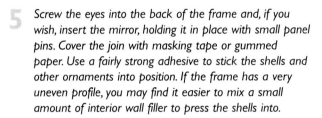

5 Screw the eyes into the back of the frame and, if you wish, insert the mirror, holding it in place with small panel pins. Cover the join with masking tape or gummed paper. Use a fairly strong adhesive to stick the shells and other ornaments into position. If the frame has a very uneven profile, you may find it easier to mix a small amount of interior wall filler to press the shells into.

6 When you are happy with the final arrangement of the shells, add a touch of gold tube paint to create highlights on the shells, wiping off any excess before it dries.

REVIVING AN OLD FRAME

You might see an attractive old frame in a junk shop, but when you get it home you realize that not only is it in a worse state than you had thought, but it also will not fit the picture you had in mind. Fortunately, you can use your newly acquired skills to take the frame apart and re-make it with new glass.

You will need

- Pliers
- Hammer; screwdriver
- Plastic ruler and pencil
- Miter cutter and clamp
- Saw; craft knife
- Wood glue
- Drill and fine bit
- Panel pins
- Fine wire wool
- Emulsion paint
- Gold paint (in liquid, powder, or tube form)
- 1/16 in. (2 mm) glass
- Glass cutter
- T-square
- Masking tape or brown gummed paper
- Screw eyes
- Wire or cord

TIP
- If the frame is an old wooden one, always sand and stain it before applying a wax finish.
- Make a plain frame by applying two coats of a solid, dark paint.

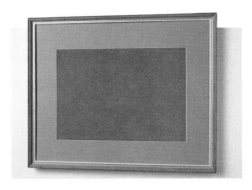

1 First remove the backing and the glass from the old frame. Take care because the glass may be old and fragile. Stand the frame on a corner, hold the opposite corner and gently push down until the corners crack.

2 If pins have been used, push the sides apart and wiggle them apart. If the frame has been underpinned, use a screwdriver and hammer to drive the pins out.

3 Once the frame is in pieces, use your pliers to remove any remaining pins. Working on one of the long sides, cut a new mitered corner.

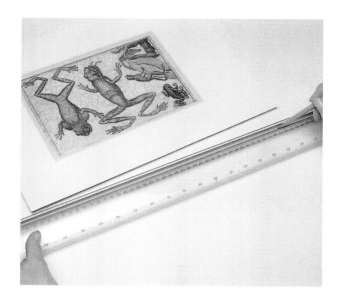

4 Measure the long side of the picture you want to frame and transfer the measurement to the inside of the newly cut side.

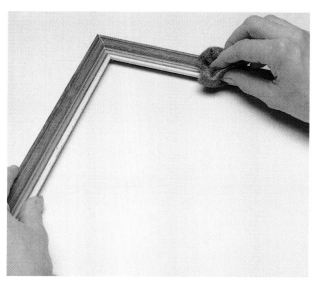

6 You can now decorate the frame, choosing a style that is in keeping with the picture. We have used an old print of some frogs and want the frame to look suitably distressed and aged. To achieve this, rub the frame all over with fine wire wool.

5 Slide the molding into the miter clamp and align the mark with the center cutting line. Cut all the sides as for the Basic Frame (see page 263) and re-assemble the pieces.

7 Apply a coat of dark brick-red emulsion all over the frame. Leave to dry. You may need to apply a second coat if the first did not cover the frame completely.

8   *When the paint is dry, smooth it carefully with fine wire wool, then apply a coat of liquid gold leaf or another proprietary gold paint. Some gold powders need to be mixed with shellac or button polish, so always check the manufacturer's instructions.*

9   *When the gold paint is dry, rub it gently with fine wire wool to give a distressed look, with the red paint showing through in places. Insert the glass and finish off the frame as described in the instructions for the Basic Frame (see page 267).*

PAPIER-MÂCHÉ FRAME

Making this frame for a mirror will allow you to combine your framing skills with the satisfying craft of papier-mâché. We have created a simple design, with fish swimming around the glass, although this is a technique that allows you to give your creative talents full rein.

You will need

- ½ x ½ in. (1 x 1 cm) plain wooden molding
- Plastic ruler and pencil
- Miter cutter and clamp
- Saw
- Craft knife
- Wood glue
- Drill and fine bit
- Panel pins
- Small hammer
- Tracing paper
- Mounting card or thick card
- Scraps of newspaper, torn into small pieces
- Masking tape
- Flour-and-water paste or wallpaper paste
- Masking tape or brown gummed paper
- Acrylic glue (optional)
- Clear, all-purpose adhesive
- White tissue paper
- Acrylic paint
- Polyurethane
- Screw eyes
- Wire or cord

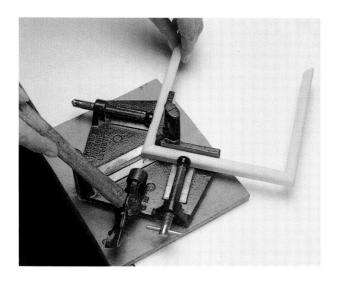

1 Use the wooden molding to make a three-sided frame, following the instructions for the Basic Frame (see page 263). We have made a square frame, measuring 6½ x 6½ in. (16.5 x 16.5 cm). Leave the opening at the top so that you can slip in the mirror.

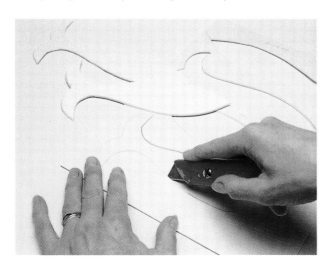

2 Trace a fish design (or any motif of your choice) onto a spare piece of card. Use a craft knife to cut out four fish shapes.

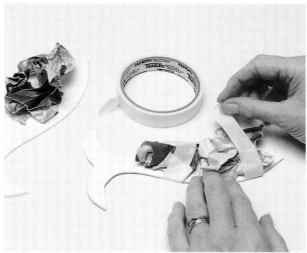

3 Tear up some pieces of newspaper and scrunch them up loosely. Use tape to hold them onto the parts of the fish bodies that you want to be fuller and more rounded.

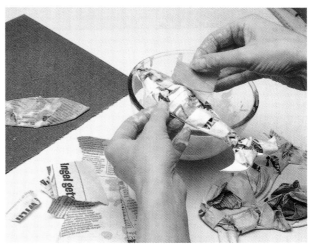

4 Mix the paste. If you use flour-and-water paste, you can add a small amount of acrylic glue to make it stronger. Dip pieces of paper into the paste and begin to cover the fish bodies. Do not let the paper become saturated with paste, and if you find that the paper is too wet, lay some dry pieces over the shapes. When you are satisfied with the overall shapes, smooth the surface of each fish and leave them somewhere warm until they are absolutely dry.

5   *Take the frame and arrange the fish on it. When you are satisfied with the positions they are in, use a lot of adhesive to stick them, nose to tail, around the frame.*

8   *When the fish are dry, paint them in colors of your choice. Leave the paint to dry, then apply a coat of clear polyurethane.*

6   *The fish at the top should be attached by its nose and tail. Place under a weight and leave until the adhesive is dry. Check that the mirror will slide into the frame, but do not leave it there yet. Add more layers of pâpiér mâché to the fish, using strips of paper across the back of the top fish to make sure it is firmly attached to its neighbors. Put back in a warm place to dry.*

9   *Insert the mirror and apply screw eyes on the sides to hang up the frame.*

7   *To finish the fish, cover them completely with two layers of white tissue paper. The paint colors will be much brighter and clearer if applied over a white base.*

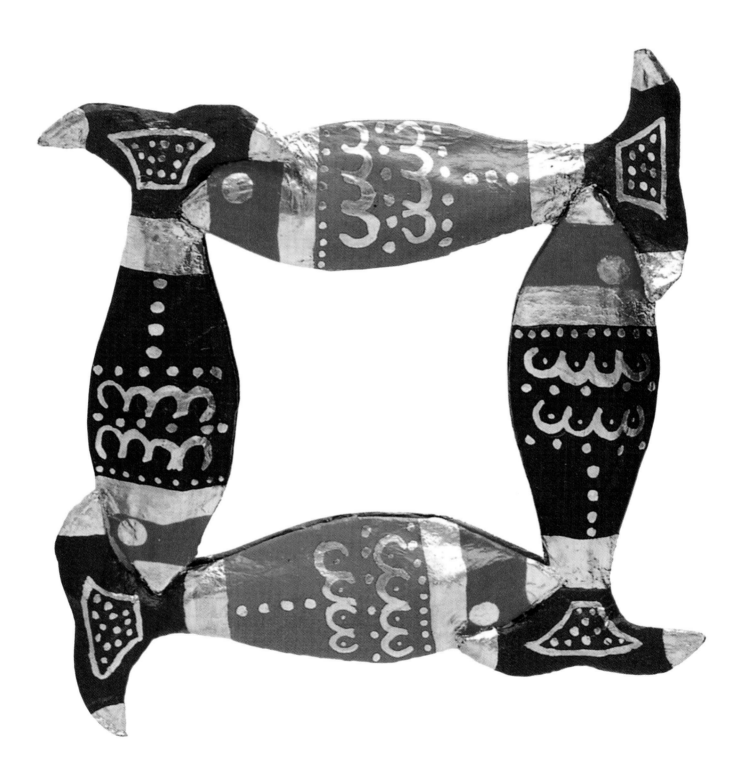

Gilded and Painted Frame

Naive paintings and prints usually have a strong image, often in good, clear colors, and they do not usually need a mount if they are in a wide frame. We chose to frame a print of a sheep, which measures 16 x 12 in. (40 x 30.5 cm). The frame can either be simply painted, or it can be finished with gold to give it extra sparkle.

You will need

- Molding
- Miter cutter and clamp
- Saw
- Plastic ruler and pencil
- Wood glue
- Drill and fine bit
- Panel pins
- Small hammer; nail punch
- Shellac and paintbrush (optional)
- Red emulsion paint
- Fine wire wool
- Masking tape
- Emulsion and acrylic paints
- Gold paint (in liquid, powder, or tube form)
- Shoe polish and soft cloth (optional)
- Metal gold leaf and size
- Soft, long-handled brush

TIP
- If you need to tone a color down, add a little black acrylic paint rather than more of the base color.

1 Make the frame in the molding following the Basic Frame instructions (see page 263). You may seal the wood by applying a coat of shellac. Apply two or three coats of red paint, leaving each coat to dry completely before you paint on the next. Gently rub the surface with fine wire wool.

2 If you are going to have a gilded edge, apply strips of masking tape around the center of the frame.

3 Mix the emulsion and acrylic paints. We used dark green, made by mixing green acrylic with a little white emulsion paint to give it body. Apply the paint to the outer edge of the frame, taking care that it does not seep under the masking tape.

4 When the paint is completely dry, rub it gently with wire wool to distress it. If you wish, you can leave the frame as it is.

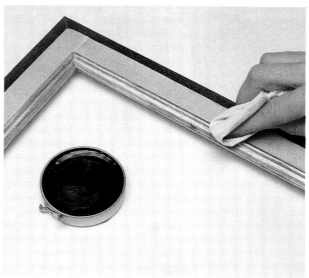

6 If you want the gold to look "aged", apply a tiny amount of dark shoe polish and rub it carefully with a soft cloth. If you prefer, use wire wool to remove part of the gold to give an even more distressed appearance.

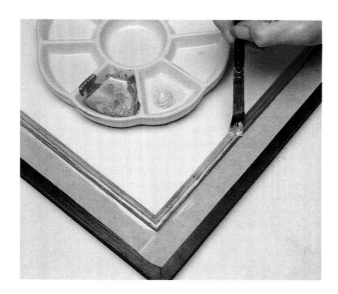

5 If you want to add a gold edge, remove the masking tape and put new strips of tape over the area you have just painted. Following the manufacturer's instructions for the gold paint you are using, paint the edge of the frame and leave this to dry.

7 If you prefer, you can apply quick gilding with metal gold leaf, which is quick and easy to use. Apply fresh strips of masking tape as in step 5. Working on small sections of the frame, apply some gilding size and wait until it becomes tacky.

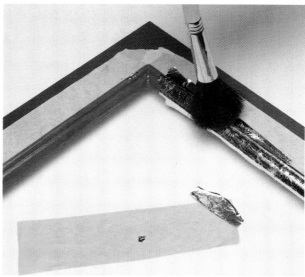

8   *Cut a piece of gold leaf large enough to cover the edge and leave the paper backing on it. Use your fingertips to carefully position the gold leaf and to press it down gently.*

10   *Continue to work around the frame, overlapping the gold leaf by about ⅛ in. (3 mm) each time. If you find you have missed any, use small scraps of gold leaf to cover the gaps or, when the size has dried completely, use gold paint to fill in the gaps. Use a soft, long-handled brush to remove any loose particles.*

9   *You may find it helpful to use a soft brush to make sure you have pressed it down completely. Carefully remove the backing paper.*

11   *Leave to dry for a few hours or, ideally, overnight—until the size is quite dry. Use a ball of cotton wool to buff the gold leaf until it gleams.*

TIP

■ When it comes to the corners, take care not to overlap the gold leaf too much, otherwise they will be very bulky. Again, use a soft brush to remove loose particles.

FRAMING AN OIL PAINTING

Oil paintings need to be treated rather differently from watercolors, but it is still important to have a space between the image and the frame. A simple way of doing this is to float the painting on a board covered in a material such as hessian or coarse linen. The fabric is stretched taut over hardboard and the painting is fixed to the covered board. An alternative, which we are using, is to make an inner slip and an outside frame. The slip can be wood, gold or silver, or, as we used, linen, and it serves the additional purpose of holding the glass slightly away from the painting surface if you choose to glaze it, although traditionally oil paintings are not glazed.

You will need

- Ruler and pencil
- Linen slip molding
- Masking tape
- Miter cutter and clamp
- Saw
- Wood glue
- Drill and fine bit
- Panel pins
- Small hammer; nail punch
- Outer molding
- D-rings or screw eyes
- Wire or cord

1 *Measure the painting. Ours was 23 x 17 in. (58.5 x 43 cm). Working on the long measurement, add about 1/8 in. (3 mm) and cut a piece of linen slip molding to this length. Cover the cutting area with masking tape before cutting.*

2 *Follow the instructions for making the Basic Frame (see page 263), but before you drill the holes for the panel pins lay the pieces around the painting, holding them in position to check that the frame will fit. Oil paintings are not always perfectly square and you may need to make some fine adjustments.*

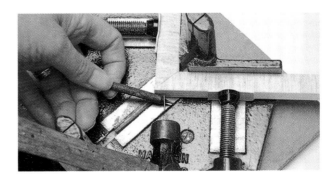

3 *Finish off the frame (see page 267). Use a nail punch to drive the panel pins securely into the corners.*

4 *Make the outer frame, using the inner frame as a guide to mark the measurements. Do not allow any extra because the frames should fit tightly together. Make the outer frame as the inner frame.*

5 *Fit the oil painting into the slip frame and carefully insert panel pins to hold it in place. Place the outer frame over the slip frame. Pin the back by driving panel pins in upright, then tapping them until they bend over. You will need about two pins along each side.*

6 *Make holes for the screw eyes or D-rings on each side of the outer frame.*

WOODCARVING

Carving wood, a natural and most attractive resource, has held a fascination for mankind since the beginning of time. We often see wonderful examples of this craft, which might lead us to assume that it is not for us. However, reality is quite the reverse—a sharp knife, a piece of wood, some varnish or paints, a desire to learn, and a little imagination are all that are required to embark upon a craft that will give you countless hours of pleasure and amaze your friends. All the projects in this chapter have been designed so that they can be achieved with no previous experience. The plans are drawn to scale so they can be copied or traced to use as simple templates. The finished carving can be either varnished or painted, and clear illustration and instruction is given on both of these techniques. The projects have been designed to quickly increase your skill and confidence as you work your way through the chapter. All you need to bring is enthusiasm and a desire to learn—so let's go!

EQUIPMENT AND MATERIALS

TOOLS

Would-be carvers are often put off by the thought of having to purchase and maintain a large variety of woodcarvers' chisels and accessories. However, the projects in this book have been designed to enable you to complete them by simply using a knife.

STAINLESS STEEL CRAFT KNIFE SET

This is the simplest to use and probably the least expensive to buy. The blades are interchangeable and should be replaced when they become blunt.

STEEL CRAFT KNIFE SET

This is similar to the set just described, but the blades can be sharpened. The basic techniques of sharpening are described later.

FOLDING OR FIXED BLADE KNIVES

These knives can be either purpose-made fixed blade knives or the simple folding penknife. Both these types can be sharpened.

CHISELS

While the carvings in this book can be completed simply with a set of knives, they can of course be produced by using carving chisels. A basic set would comprise of $3/4$ in. (18 mm) shallow gouge, a $3/8$ in. (9 mm) shallow gouge and a 6 mm ($1/4$ in.) "V" tool.

Carving knives

Craft saw

Pencil

Fixed blade craft knife and blades

Fixed blade stainless steel craft knife and blades

Larger gouge carving chisel

Smaller gouge carving chisel

"V" tool

WOOD

There is a bewildering number of timbers in the world, all having their unique properties of texture and color. In practice some will be more suitable for carving than others. An ideal wood for our projects would be straight-grained, not too dense and light in color. Examples include English Lime, American Basswood, Canadian Yellow Pine and Malaysian Jelutong—all of which I have used to good effect. Good craft outlets should be able to assist you in obtaining the right wood and there are many published magazines on woodwork generally to point you in the right direction.

However, since the projects are quite small and do not require enormous amounts of wood to be removed, you may find that experimenting with that bit of scrap wood you were about to throw away also works quite well.

PAINTS AND BRUSHES

Acrylic paint works very well on light wood and a small basic set of colors, and two or three brushes is all you need.

VARNISHES

Many wood varnishes are sold and I would recommend acrylic, water-based varnish. It can be used on the bare wood directly or as a finishing coat to a painted carving. Acrylic varnish is easy to apply with a brush and I suggest a satin finish rather than a high gloss.

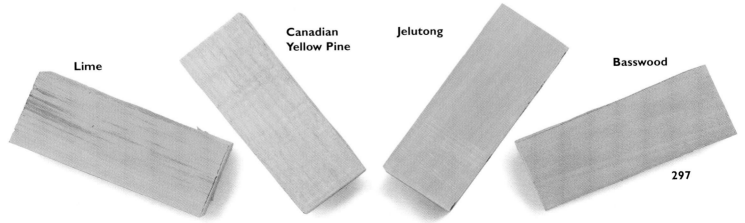

Lime

Canadian Yellow Pine

Jelutong

Basswood

TECHNIQUE AND SAFETY

Since knife carving involves holding both the knife (which must always be sharp) and the wood in your hands, it is essential that due regard is given to safe and effective cutting techniques.

It is important to ensure that wherever possible you keep your hands away from the line of the blade, whether you are cutting away from or towards yourself.

Your thumbs play a very important part in knife carving, as they provide both power and control at the same time. When using a chisel it is important to have both hands on the chisel at all times.

Another point to note is to try to understand how the grain runs. Wood grain can be likened to thousands of tiny straws compacted together. You can safely cut with them and even across them, but you cannot cut directly into them without splitting.

Cutting away from yourself with the grain.

Cutting towards yourself with the grain.

Using the chisel for heavy work.

Using the chisel for light work.

Cutting across the grain.

Cutting into the grain will split the wood.

MAINTENANCE

Whatever craft you embark upon, looking after your equipment is essential—be it keeping your pencils sharp or your brushes clean and dry. Keeping your cutting edges sharp is an essential part of woodcarving.

If you are using pre-sharpened stainless steel craft knives, do not continue using the blades when they are blunt. Throw them away and insert new ones.

If your knife is not the pre-sharpened type, you will need to obtain a good edge on it and keep it that way.

Sharpening a knife is fairly simple. You require an oilstone to get the blade to the right shape and a leather strop for a smooth razor-edge finish. The strop can be made from a piece of leather or old belt and an oilstone can be had from hardware stores.

The oilstone needs to be held firmly in place, a smearing of lubricating oil applied, and the blade drawn across the stone several times on each side. The blade should be held almost flat and the process repeated until the metal becomes rather ragged along its full length. This burr (or rough edge) can be felt carefully with the finger.

The next step is to repeat the process on the leather strop after it has been smeared with any metal-polishing agent. Tubes of polishing paste can be found in most hardware or car accessory stores and work very well. Stropping the blade from side to side is continued until the burr is smooth and the blade is sharp. Clean it with a cloth or paper towel if necessary.

Using the oilstone to sharpen a blade.

Using the leather strop to get a razor edge. Sharpening chisels follows the same basic principles, but due to the variety of shapes the process is more involved. I would recommend reference to more specialized books for information.

MINIATURE BOTTLES

This is an ideal project for a beginner. If you keep the lines fairly straight, it is quite an effective subject and provides you with a good introduction to some simple techniques.

You will need

- Block of wood 1 1/2 x 1 1/2 x 3 1/2 in. (3.8 x 3.8 x 8.9 cm)
- Knife
- Varnish or paint to finish

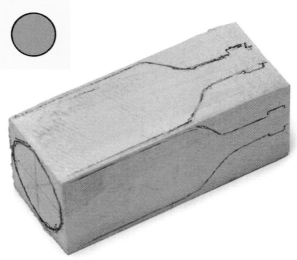

TIP
- To help draw the circles at either end, mark lines diagonally from corner to corner, then mark lines horizontally and perpendicularly.

1. Trace around one of the plans to create a template, then transfer the outline to a block of wood. Draw the bottle's end shapes on the top and bottom of the block.

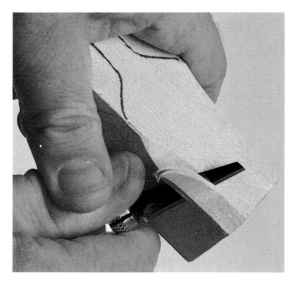

2. Start shaping around the base. You can carve away from or towards yourself, whichever feels more comfortable.

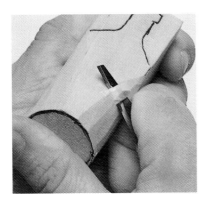

3 *Complete the bottom of the bottle.*

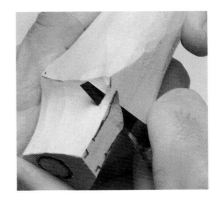

6 *Continue to carve the neck to completion.*

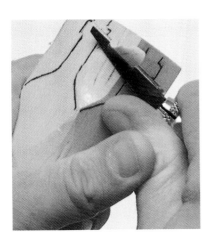

4 *Start shaping the neck and shoulders.*

7 *Compare your progress with the template.*

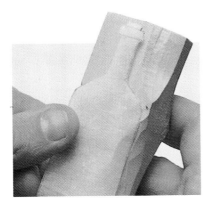

5 *Use your template to re-mark the neck and shoulders where the original marks have been carved away.*

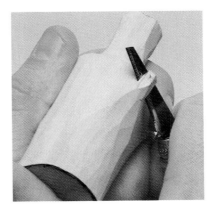

8 *Complete the shaping of the shoulders.*

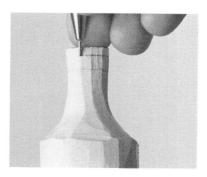

9   *Refer to your plan and mark in the lip around the top of the neck.*

10   *Score in the bottom part of the lip, holding your knife firm and rolling the bottle around the blade.*

11   *Carefully remove the wood from below the scored line.*

TIP
- Find the depth you require and use your second finger as a depth gauge—carpenter style!

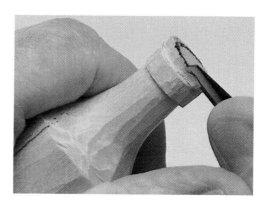

12   *Do the same on the top line of the lip.*

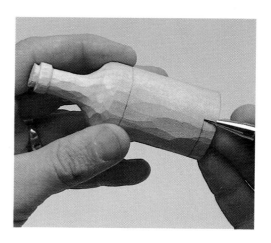

13   *Add a little more interest by carving in a label—mark with your pencil.*

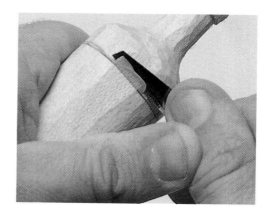

14   *Score in the drawn line.*

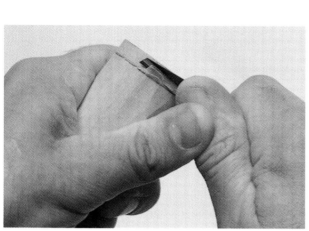

15 *Carve wood away from around the label.*

16 *Varnish or paint to finish.*

FRUIT

Carving fruit, with its variety of shapes, is a good progression from the miniature bottles. The rounded curves are a little more demanding than the bottles, but they give you a further insight into dealing with grain. You can add some leaves to the basic shape to create a more interesting piece and add a little realism.

You will need

- Wood for the pear 2 x 2 x 3 in. (5 x 5 x 7.5 cm)
- Wood for the apple 2 x 2 x 2¼ in. (5 x 5 x 5.7 cm)
- Wood for the banana 1¼ x 1¼ x 4½ in. (3 x 3 x 11.5 cm)
- Knife
- Varnish or paints to finish

PEAR

1 *Start by creating templates from the plans and transferring the outline to your block of wood.*

2 *Start carving the pear towards the top end.*

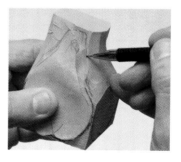

3 *Continue the shaping using your template as a guide. Re-mark the outline as you go to maintain a guide.*

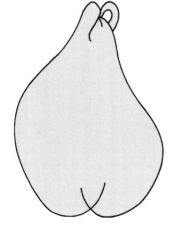

4 *This stage is completed when the required shape of the pear top is achieved.*

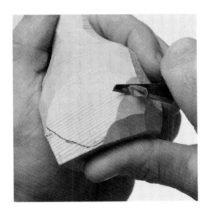

5 *Once you are happy with the top, start shaping the bottom.*

6 *Continue shaping the base checking frequently from all angles.*

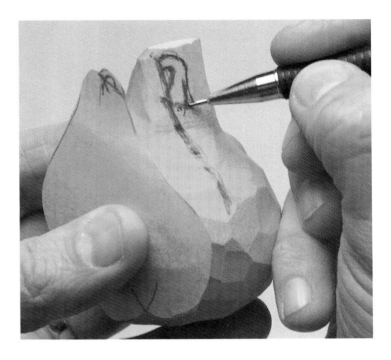

7 *Look at your template and use it to mark the short stem on the top of the pear.*

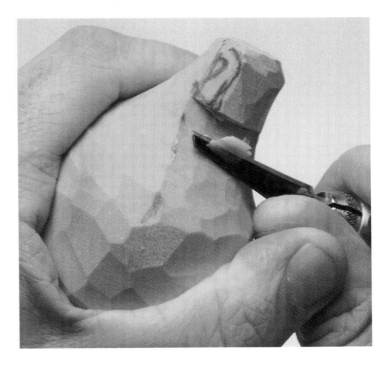

8 *Carve around the shape taking care not to split away the wood.*

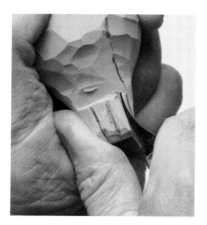

9 *Pare away the wood from both sides of the stalk.*

10 *Insert the base end of the stalk to add more detail. Score a small circle and carve the wood away from the outside.*

11 *Carve three or four shallow grooves into the base and the top to add a little more shape.*

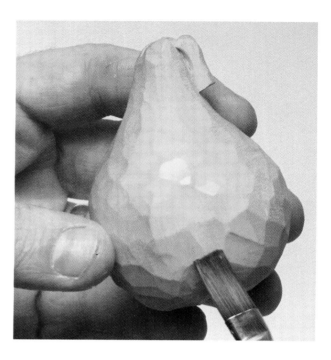

12 *Paint or varnish to finish.*

APPLE

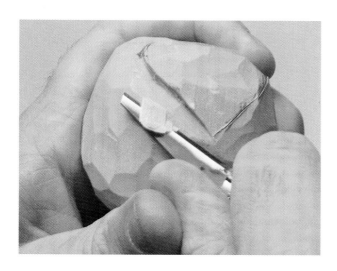

3 *Add a little more detail to the leaf by cutting a narrow channel down the center.*

I *Refer to the early stages of carving the pear. Then mark the leaf on the basic shape of the apple, score the outline, and start removing the wood from around the leaf.*

4 *Carve some narrow channels on either side of the center line. Paint or varnish to finish.*

2 *Repeat the above process to create the stalk.*

BANANA

1 The banana is a fairly straightforward shape, but complements the apple and pear as a group. Refer to the plans and the stages of carving the pear for the basic approach.

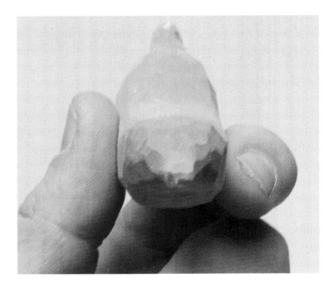

2 Check your carving to ensure you have achieved a rough, four-cornered end view, then paint or varnish to finish.

FISH

While the carvings in this book are ideally suited to using knives, I have used this project to describe the use of a basic set of chisels. Since chisels should be held in both hands, it will be necessary to hold your work tightly in a clamp or vice.

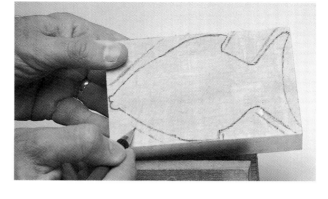

1   *Transfer the plan to a piece of wood. You might find it helpful to put 5 saw cuts in the wood to help remove the excess around the profile.*

You will need

- Block of wood 5¼ x 3½ x 1 in. (13 x 8.9 x 2.5 cm)
- Piece of wood for backplate 7¾ x 6 x ½ in. (19.5 x 15 x 1.3 cm)
- Set of 3 chisels
- Vice
- "G" clamp
- Screws or glue
- Varnish to finish

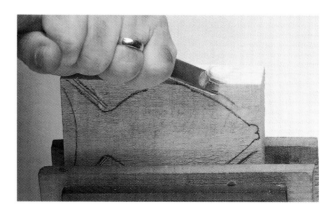

2   *Clamp your work firmly in a vice and remove the wood around the head of the fish with your larger gouge, as shown. You could use a saw cut to help you here.*

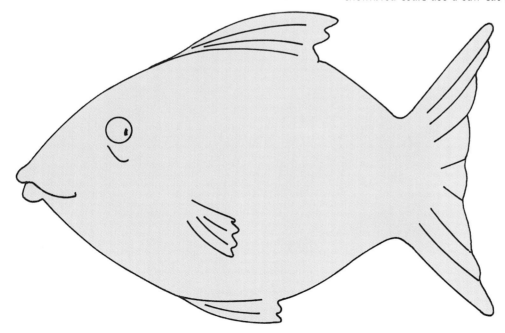

3 Now remove the wood from between the top fin and the tail. You may find it easier to use your smaller gouge here.

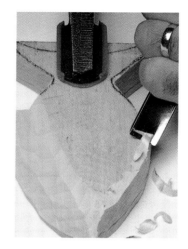

6 Continue the process of shaping the surface down to the marked edge.

4 Having removed all the excess wood from around your plan, draw a line around the fish approximately 6 mm (¼ in.) in from the edge. Finish with a couple of coats of varnish.

7 Take care with the shaping where the body meets the tail. You may need to carve across the grain to achieve a smooth cut.

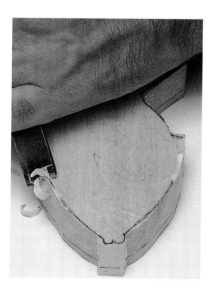

5 Use a "G" clamp to secure your carving to a firm surface and use your large gouge to slope the surface down to your marked line.

8 Refer to your plan and draw a line with your pencil to separate the two fins from the body.

9 Use your "V" tool chisel to carve a line along your pencil mark on the top fin.

10 Repeat the process on the lower fin.

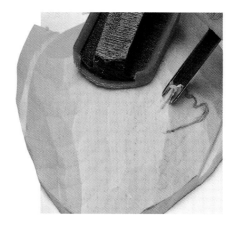

11 Having marked the fin on the body with your pencil, carve around the line with your "V" tool.

12 Take your small gouge and smooth out the sharp edges on your "V" tool cuts around the fins.

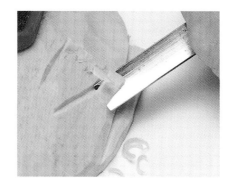

13 Remove the wood from around the "V" tool cuts forming the fin on the body.

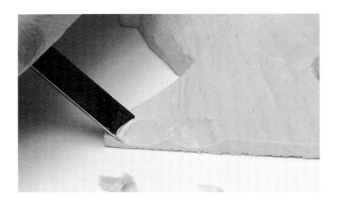

14 Use your small gouge to remove wood from the tail to create a scallop edge.

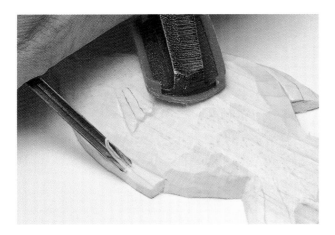

15 Use your "V" tool to put some flowing lines on the fins and tail.

16 The fish has been carved on one side, so you can choose a size of timber to carve a backplate. I have used a piece of South American mahogany. Marking a line about ¾ in. (18 mm) around the border, then use the large gouge to slope down the edge.

17 To complete the backplate, carve over the surface lightly with the large gouge.

18 After screwing or gluing the two pieces together, finish with a couple of coats of varnish.

DOLPHIN

The dolphin is an elegant and attractive creature and your carving should try and capture these features. You could choose a wood with pronounced grain markings and sand the finished piece to create some smooth flowing lines.

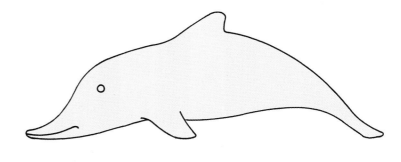

You will need

- Block of wood 5½ x 2 x 1½ in. (13.9 x 5 x 3.8 cm)
- Knife
- Paint or varnish to finish

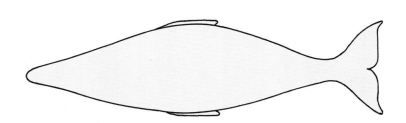

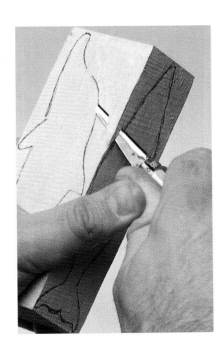

1 *Transfer the plan to a block of wood. Although you will immediately carve away the top view, it is advisable to draw this in so you can get a fair idea of how this looks.*

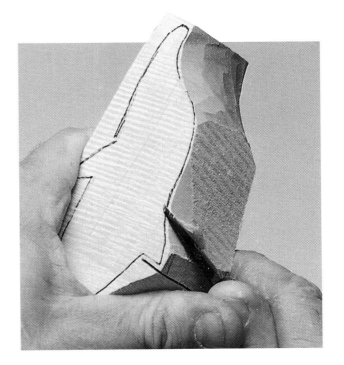

2 *Carve away the wood from the top of the head to the top of the nose. You may like to try a saw cut to assist you here.*

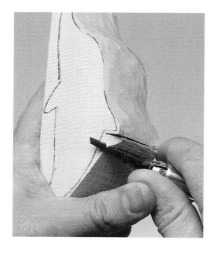

3 Having sawn down the back of the top fin, remove the wood behind the fin.

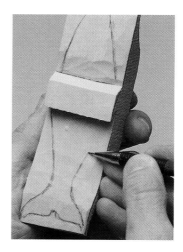

6 Referring to your plan, draw the shape of the dolphin on the bottom of your piece of wood.

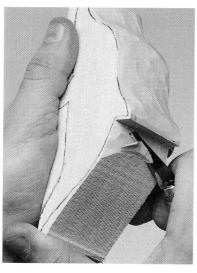

4 Continue to shape away behind the top fin, using a saw cut to assist if you wish.

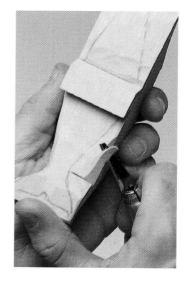

7 Use these guidelines to create the desired shape.

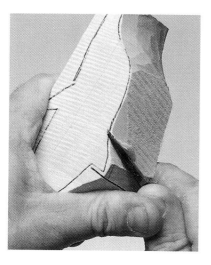

5 Repeat this process for the bottom fins, which you should treat as one for the time being.

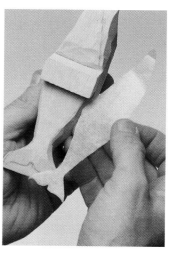

8 Compare your progress with the template.

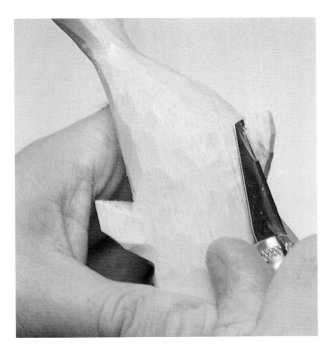

9   *Round off the sharp corners on the whole of the body. You probably have a lot of wood to remove here, so take your time and keep checking the overall shape.*

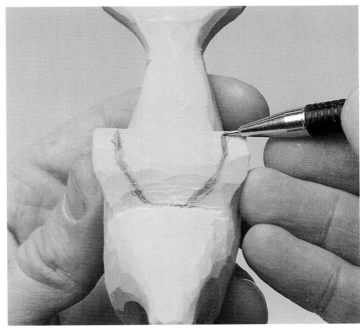

11   *Mark two lines to separate the lower fins.*

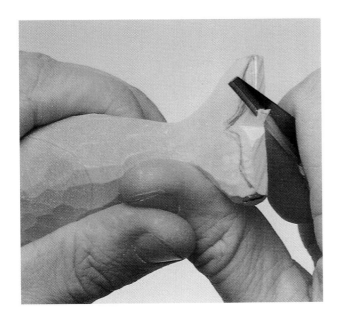

10   *Look at your plan carefully and mark the end of the tail on the wood. Take care to create the desired shape.*

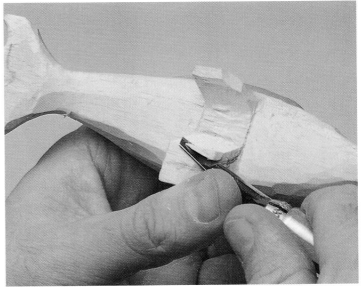

12   *Carve away the wood between the two marked lines. You need to take care, particularly when the fins are approaching completion.*

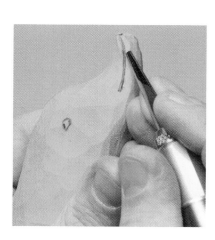

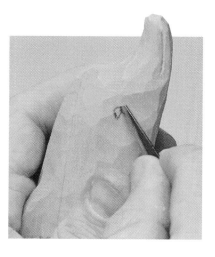

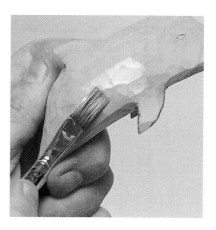

13 *Mark in the mouth and eye with your pencil and lightly score the mouth with the tip of your knife. Open this cut slightly to create the mouth.*

14 *Lightly score the pencil mark forming the eye and carefully remove surrounding wood with the tip of your knife.*

15 *Paint or varnish to finish.*

FLOWER IN BUD

Carving flowers is a rather unusual project. It requires the construction of the final piece from a number of smaller items. It is not really necessary to adhere rigidly to any known species, rather leave it to your imagination. This is an opportunity to create some colorful and attractive items.

You will need

- Wood for the flower head 1½ x 1½ x 2¼ in. (3.8 x 3.8 x 5.7 cm)
- Wood for the stem ½ x ½ x 5 in. (1.2 x 1.2 x 12.7 cm)
- Wood for the leaf 2¾ x 1¾ x ½ in. (7 x 4.5 x 1.2 cm)
- Knife
- Drill
- Glue
- Paint or varnish to complete

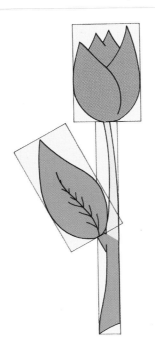

1 *Using the plans mark the outline onto the three different sized blocks.*

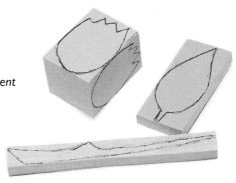

2 *Start by carving the top half of the flower head.*

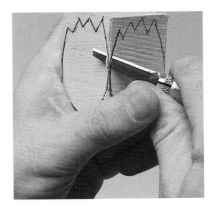

3 *Complete the top part of the flower head.*

4 *Start to work on the base of the flower head.*

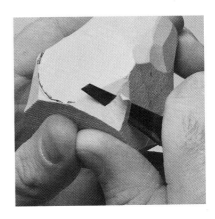

5 *Once you have achieved the correct shape, refer to the plan and mark the petals onto the flower.*

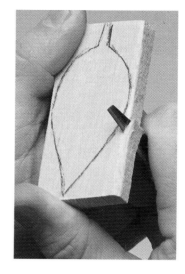

8 *Take the block marked with the leaf and carve the general shape required.*

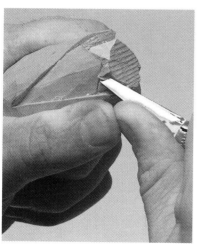

6 *Score in the pencil marks and remove the wood from in-between to create the petals.*

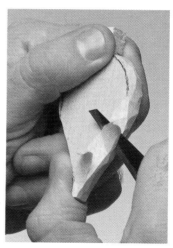

9 *Work on the general shape of the leaf taking care to leave a piece at the base to be inserted in the stem.*

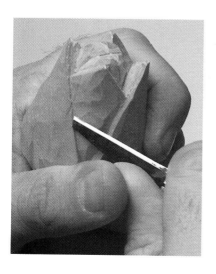

7 *Continue shaping the petals referring to the plan to see how the top of the flower head is formed.*

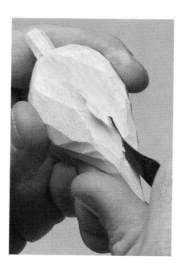

10 *The final process is to carve the edges to produce a smooth rounded edge.*

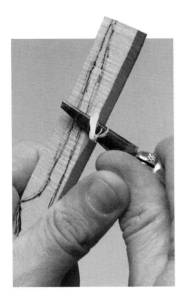

11 Take the stem and start rounding the shape generally.

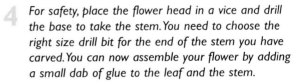

12 Look at the plan to see how to carve the small platform to take the leaf.

14 For safety, place the flower head in a vice and drill the base to take the stem. You need to choose the right size drill bit for the end of the stem you have carved. You can now assemble your flower by adding a small dab of glue to the leaf and the stem.

13 The stem needs a small hole to take the leaf and it is advisable to hold the leaf against the stem to get an idea of the angle required.

15 Paint or varnish to complete.

FLOWER IN BLOOM

This is a version of an open flower, similar to the approach described in "Flower in Bud".

You will need

- Wood for the flower head 2 x 2 x ¾ in. (5 x 5 x 2 cm)
- Wood for the stem ½ x ½ x 5½ in. (1.2 x 1.2 x 14 cm)
- Wood for the leaf 2¾ x 1¾ x ½ in. (7 x 3.8 x 12 cm)
- Knife
- Drill
- Glue
- Paint or varnish to complete

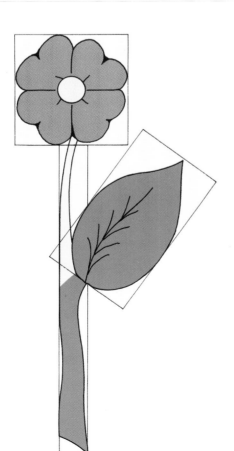

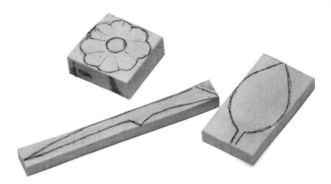

1   *Transfer the plans of the open flower onto the blocks of wood.*

2   *Start by rounding off the shape of the flower.*

3   *Mark the center of the flower with your pencil and score around the line.*

320

4 *Remove the timber from around the center piece of the flower.*

7 *Take your pencil and mark a line along the edge of the flower approximately ¹/4 in. (6 mm) from the face.*

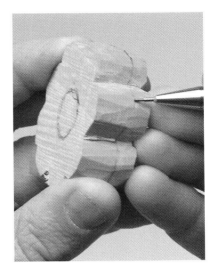

5 *Re-mark the petals on the wood.*

8 *Roughly mark the center piece of the flower on the back and carve up to this feature creating a shape roughly like a hat.*

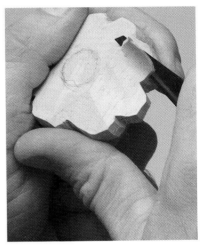

6 *Score along the lines that mark the petals and slightly open the cut with the point of your knife.*

9 *This feature is used to locate the stem into the flower head, so you need to mark the wood accordingly.*

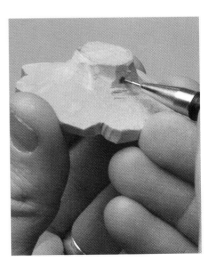

10 *Use your plans to create a leaf similar to the previous project, but add a line down the center and out from the center to create a little more interest. Follow steps in the previous project to complete.*

322

OWL

Sculptures or owls are very collectable items appearing in all shapes, sizes and colors. The main feature of this carving is to create the eyes, which when looking sideways result in a very attractive little creature.

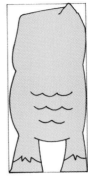
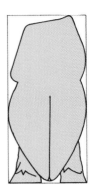

You will need

- Block of wood 2 x 3¼ x 1½ in. (5 x 8.2 x 3.8 cm)
- Knife
- Paint or varnish to finish

2 *Carve away the wood from between the back of the feet and the tail front. You may use a couple of saw cuts.*

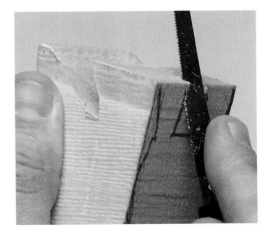

1 *Draw the outline of the owl onto your block of wood. Start by carving in the shape of the ears on the top of the head.*

3 *Take the wood away from between the feet from the front view. Again, a saw cut may assist with this.*

4 *Carve away between the legs until you have a nice sweep from the chest down to the tail.*

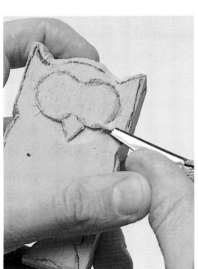

5 *Mark the outline of the eyes and beak with your pencil, score along the lines with the tip of your knife, and remove the wood from around the cuts.*

7 *Shape the ears towards the back of the head. Shape the top of the head towards the front to follow the outline of the eyes.*

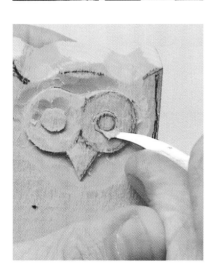

6 *Look at your plan and mark the eye itself in the center of the circle already created. Score along these lines and again remove the wood from the outside.*

8 *Make sure the legs are marked on the block and carve around these to create the front profile.*

9   *Work a little more on the legs creating some feathering above the feet.*

10   *Turn to the back of the owl and create the shape indicated in the rear-view plan.*

11   *Refer to your plan and draw in the feathers on the side of the wings.*

12   *Score in these lines with the tip of your knife and remove wood from just below these cuts.*

13   *Complete the carving by marking in the pupils of the eyes to make your owl look sideways.*

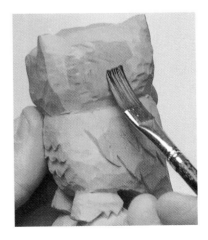

14   *Varnish or paint to finish.*

BOOT

The boot is a popular and attractive item to carve. It can be used purely as an ornament, or, if you carve low enough into the ankle it can be used as a container for small dried flowers or to hold those little items, such as tacks or pins, which you can never find when you want them.

You will need

- Block of wood 3¾ x 2 x 1½ in. (9.5 x 5 x 3.8 cm)
- Knife
- Drill (optional)
- Brown wax boot polish

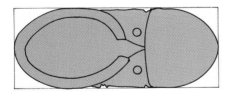

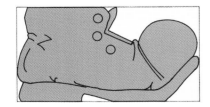

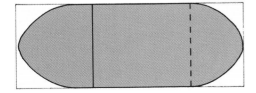

1   Transfer the plan to the block of wood and start carving over the top of the toecap. A saw cut down the front of the ankle part may help.

2   Continue by shaping over the toe.

3 Compare your side plan with the carving to complete the work required here.

4 Mark the bottom view and carve the shape you require.

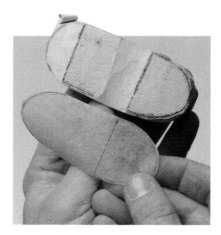

5 Compare your progress with the plan.

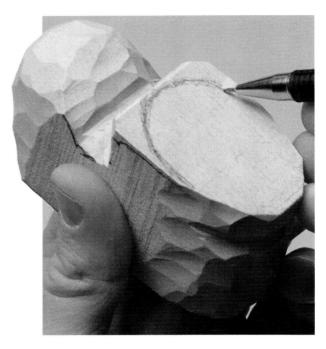

6 Turn now to the ankle and use the top-view plan to mark the shape on the block.

7 Having completed the shape of the ankle, mark the sole all around the bottom of the boot.

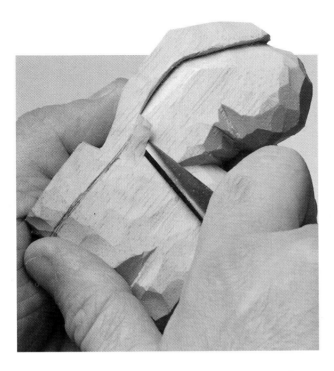

8 Score the line of the sole with the tip of your knife, then remove the wood from above the scored line.

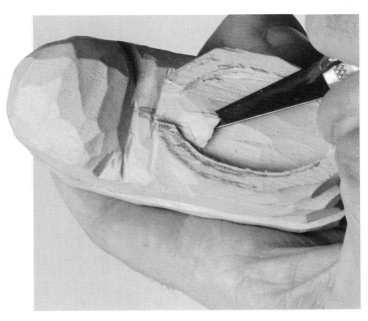

10 Score these lines and remove as much wood from inside the boot as possible.

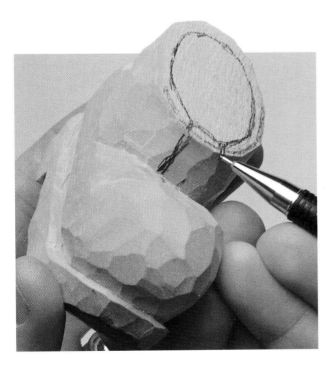

9 Mark on your carving the front of the ankle where the leather separates. In addition, mark the thickness of the leather on the ankle.

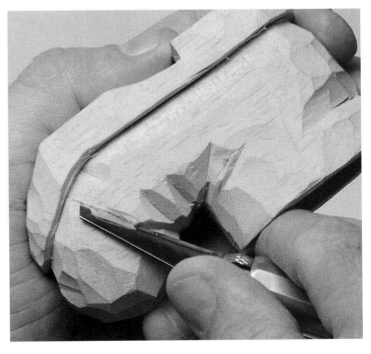

11 Cut in some crease marks over the boot by referring to your plan and carve in the toecap.

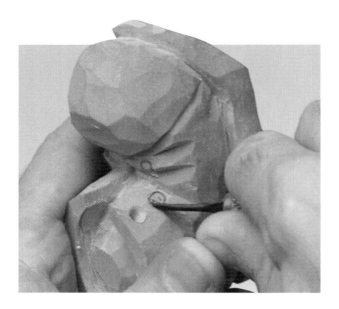

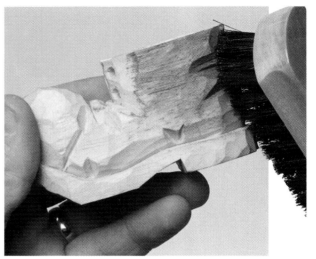

12 Mark in the lace holes from the plan and either drill or carve out with the tip of your knife.

13 An unusual but rather appropriate finish for the boot is to brush with brown wax boot polish, which will darken the wood and also create a nice sheen.

CLOWN'S HEAD

Carving faces is a demanding but very rewarding exercise. Faces and figures hold a fascination for most people and if they are done effectively, can result in very attractive items. However, much practice is required to develop your skills. The clown's features have been simplified to help you complete this character. You can have fun with your paints in the final stages.

You will need

- Block of wood 3 x 2 x 2 in. (7.6 x 5 x 5 cm)
- Knife
- Paint or varnish to finish

2 Score along the line that forms the top of the brim and start carving wood away towards the crown of the hat. Cutting directly across the grain requires care.

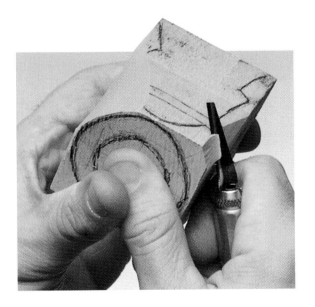

1 Transfer the outline from the plan to a block of wood. Mark the outline of the hat from the top and start shaping the block from the bottom of the hairline to the brim.

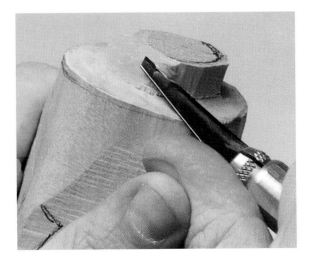

3 Having formed the top of the brim, shape the crown of the hat.

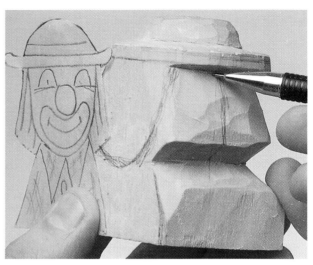

4 Take your plan and re-mark the outline of the front view onto the wood and the lower line of the brim. Score around the line of the brim and shape the hair up to the hat around the whole of the head, repeating the process until you reach the required depth.

6 Refer to the plan and mark in the front view of the face. In addition, mark in the hairline on either side of the head.

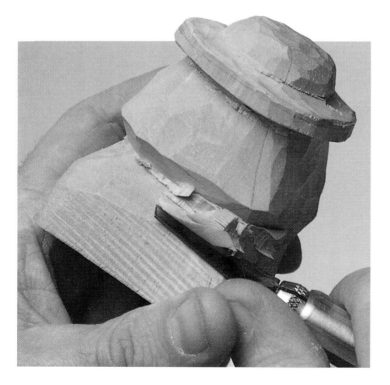

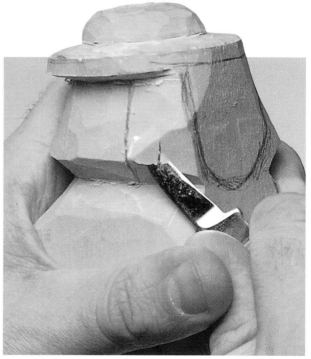

5 Carve the shoulders up to the lower hairline around the back and sides.

7 Score the outline of the hair and remove wood up to the outline of the face on either side.

8 *Shape the chest and shoulders into the hairline and chin by referring to the plan.*

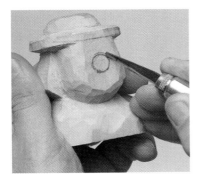

9 *The basic shape of the head should now be formed. Referring to the plan, mark in the nose and score around this feature with the tip of your knife.*

10 *Remove wood from around the nose, repeating the scoring to achieve the right depth. You may have to go through this process several times as there is quite a bit of wood to remove. Take care not to damage the brim of the hat.*

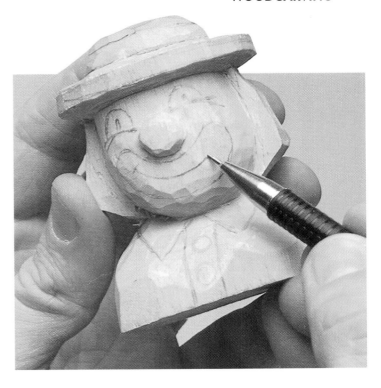

11 *Now, take your pencil and draw in the exaggerated mouth and eyes as shown on the plan.*

12 *Score over the lines you have drawn and slightly widen these lines with the tip of your knife. Raise the mouth by carving the wood from around your cuts. Try and put a little shape into the eyeball and some laughter lines in the corner of the eyes.*

13 *Mark in the details on the shirt and carve around the scored lines.*

14 *Complete by varnishing or painting.*

CLOWN FULL FIGURE

This project enables you to take what you have learnt in the previous project and carve a full figure. The body has been simplified by placing the hands in the pockets and keeping the stance fairly simple. The overall result is a very appealing character.

You will need

- Piece of wood 2 x 2 x 7 in. (5 x 5 x 17.8 cm)
- Knife
- Paint or varnish to finish

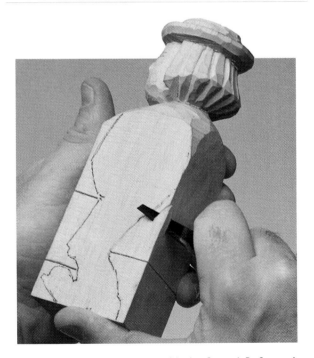

1 *Transfer the outlines to your block of wood. Refer to the previous project for details of how to carve the head and shoulders. Start on the body by putting some saw cuts diagonally into the block, as shown.*

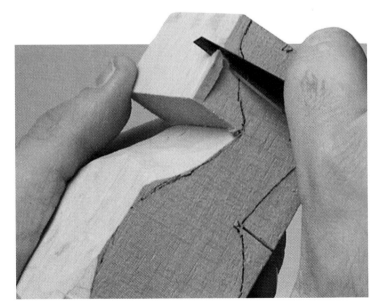

2 *Carve in to the saw cuts using the lines transferred from your plans as a guide.*

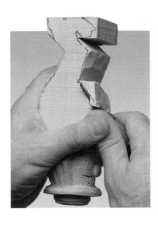

3 Continue this process around all parts of the body.

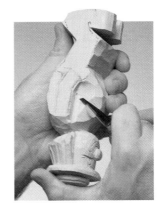

7 Score in the arms and the pockets and carve away the wood from in front of the arm.

4 Use the plans to mark the feet on the base of the carving.

8 Repeat the process behind the arm and then on the other side of the body.

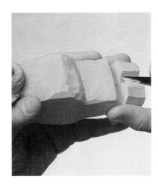

5 Shape the feet referring to the base as required.

9 Use your front-view plan to check how deep you should cut the arms.

6 Use your side-view plan to locate the arms on either side.

10 Return to the legs and separate each leg in line with the feet.

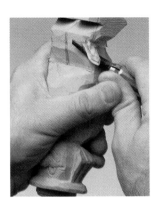

11 Start shaping the legs trying to get a baggy effect in the trousers.

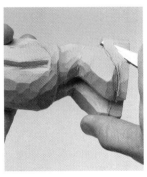

12 Mark in the bottom of the trousers. Score the line and carve wood away from below to form the feet. Refer to your plans to put more shape into the feet.

13 Mark in the soles of the shoes, score the line, and remove wood from above the line and further shape the shoe. You can refer to the Boot project for more detail on this part of the carving.

14 Once you are happy with the general shape of the body, start marking in the detail—that is, waistcoat, collar, buttons, crease marks, etc. Score all these lines and carve away from the outside to complete.

15 Varnish or paint to complete.

MASK MAKING

Masks have been used for dance, theater, carnivals, celebrations, pagan and religious rituals—or sometimes just for fun and disguise. The ancient Greeks first used masks for theatrical performances, and the actors and members of the chorus wore large masks with stylized expressions that could be clearly seen and understood by the audience. Masks were worn by tribal peoples in West Africa to indicate social position, and the Kalahari tribe made ugly masks to drive away demons. Dragon masks are still used to ward off evil spirits in China.

Venetian masks of the kind inspired in the 16th century by the Commedia dell'Arte are still seen today. These masks often take the form of elements such as stars, suns and moons. Half-masks representing characters such as Pierrot and Harlequin are used not only in Italy, where they originated, but all around the world.

Whatever form a mask takes, it acts as a disguise. The wearer can act the fool without being recognized or just simply enjoy being another person. In the 18th century, for example, elegant ladies carried masks so that they could flirt with strangers with impunity. Masks can be used today to conjure up an element of menace, mystery, or fun.

EQUIPMENT AND MATERIALS

PAPER AND CARDBOARD

Paper is a versatile product. It is strong enough to be folded and pleated, but it can be torn and cut and then colored and decorated in dozens of ways.

Paper masks are especially easy for young children to make. Paper plates can be used to make good, strong masks that are light and easy to wear. You can also achieve interesting effects by using colored paper imaginatively to give a fullness and three-dimensional quality to a mask. The mane of the Lion Mask, for instance, is made from thin strips of paper in a variety of shades.

PASTEL AND PAINT

There will be times when you want to decorate the surface of the mask in a particular way. We have used poster paints and pastels for the masks described here.

It is best to experiment with pastels on scrap paper to get a feel for how they work. Try using various colors together, but do not apply them too heavily. Poster paints are ideal for children to use. Colors can be mixed on saucers or in old food containers.

PAPIER-MÂCHÉ

Papier-mâché needs more time because you have to leave the layers to dry out. When finished, papier-mâché is very light but durable, and it will withstand quite a lot of hard wear. It is a very versatile medium and can be adapted to all kinds of styles. The Woodland Half-mask, for example, can perhaps be adapted to look like an animal or even a simple, painted Venetian-style mask.

The layering method

- Tear the paper strips into even-sized pieces.
- Mix a smooth paste from flour and water, or use a commercial wallpaper paste.
- To be sure that you have completely covered the mask with each layer, either use different colors for each layer or lay the strips in different directions each time.
- Make sure that the previous layer is completely dry before you apply the next.
- Leave the papier-mâché in a warm, dry room for 2 hours. Do not put it near a radiator or in front of a fire.

The pulp method

- Tear newspaper into small pieces.
- Mix some paste and immerse the torn paper in it. Do not allow the pieces to become saturated.
- Squeeze the paste out of the paper and mold the pulp into shape.
- It is best to leave the pulp overnight to dry.

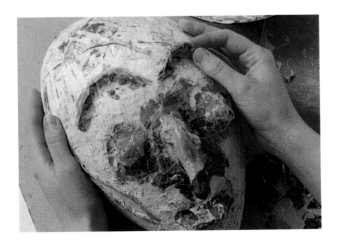

HOLDING THE MASKS

Elastic can be used to hold masks in place, but some of the more complicated masks need strong tape. Outsize masks are best secured with strips of cardboard that run over the top and around the back of the head.

- The simplest method is to attach ties (either plastic or fabric) to the reverse side of the sides of the mask with strong tape.
- Make a small hole at each side and push string or elastic through the holes. Hold the elastic or string in place by tying neat knots on the right side.
- Make a slit at each side of the mask and thread the ties through the slits from the back. Use tape to hold the ends of the ties at the back of the mask. The ties emerge at the front so they can be taken around to the back of the head and tied together.
- Secure a small stick to the back of the mask with tape. This method means that the mask can be raised and lowered easily.
- Cut two strips of lightweight cardboard, one to reach around the back of your head, and the second to reach from the top front of the mask to about halfway down your head so that it reaches the first piece. Check that the mask is comfortable and secure before stapling the strips to the edge of the mask and to each other.

SEASIDE SHADES

We have used the outline of a fish, but you could use a starfish or crabs. You could also design your own glasses, drawing your inspiration from anything on the seashore— shells, for example. We used colored dots and paper for decoration, but you could make it really spectacular with beads or sequins.

You will need

- Medium-weight green cardboard
- Pencil
- Tracing paper
- Scissors
- Hole punch
- Tape
- Colored construction paper
- Colored self-adhesive dots
- Black felt-tip pen
- Clear, all-purpose glue
- Pinking shears

2 *Turn over the shape and use tape to attach the side pieces.*

3 *Decorate the cutout fins with strips of colored paper and self-adhesive dots. Use a felt-tip pen to make some smaller spots in the center of the dots.*

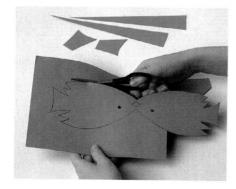

1 *Trace the image of your choice and the side pieces onto medium-weight green cardboard. Punch out the eye holes and cut out the shape and side pieces.*

4 *Score along the narrow edge of each fin and fold them along the score line. Apply glue to the small flap and glue each fin in place on the front of the mask.*

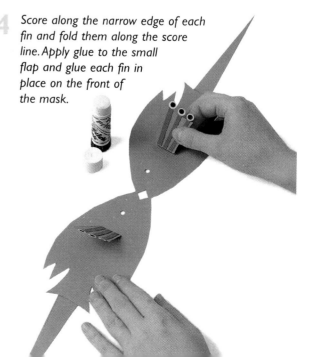

5 *Place a small, black self-adhesive dot in the center of a large white dot and punch a hole through the center.*

8 *Cut some more curved strips in a contrasting color—we used dark-blue—and glue them in place, together with some more colored dots. You may find a wooden toothpick useful for pushing and pressing the small dots into place.*

6 *Place this over one of the eye holes already made. Repeat for the other eye.*

9 *Cut some wedge-shaped pieces of light-blue paper, using pinking shears to give a neatly jagged edge, and glue long triangles of dark-blue paper down the center of each piece.*

10 *Glue these blue pieces to the tails of the fish.*

7 *Cut some curved pieces from a piece of colored paper—we used turquoise—and glue them in position, using the illustration as a guide.*

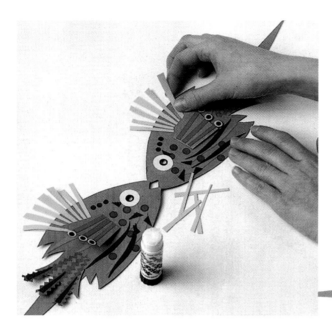

TIP

- You can buy self-adhesive dots—and other shapes—that are already colored, but rather than buy colored ones that you may never use, buy white ones and paint them to match the other colors that you are using on your mask. Apply the paint before you peel the dot away from the backing sheet, so that you can paint right up the edges of the circle. If you try to apply the paint once the dot is in place, you will find it difficult to paint it neatly without getting paint on the background color.

Finish off with some strips of yellow paper, cut into long, narrow wedge shapes, and glue them in position along the top edges of the fish.

HALF-MASK

This striking half-mask is easily made with medium-weight cardboard, and it is colored with pastels. We have included two templates, one for a man and one for a woman. You can use the basic design and method in many different ways, changing the hairstyle and the hat to give a completely different effect. Look through a library book to get ideas from historical costumes, especially uniforms.

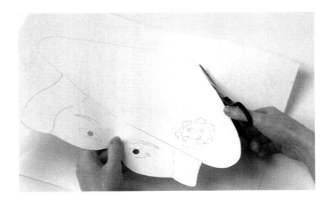

Transfer the outline of the template to white cardboard and cut around the outline.

You will need

- Medium-weight cardboard
- Pencil
- Tracing paper
- Scissors
- Colored pastels
- Fixative
- Black crayon
- Craft knife
- Twill tape
- Tape
- 2 ostrich feathers

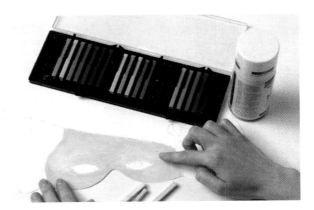

2 *Take a selection of flesh-colored pastels and begin to shade in the face area. Blend the colors by rubbing them gently with a finger.*

TIP
- Half-masks give only a partial disguise because the wearer's mouth and nose are still visible. Try matching the skin color of the mask to the tones of the wearer's skin.

3 *Mark the eyebrows with brown pastel and use darker pink for the areas around the temples. Spray lightly with fixative.*

4 Use several shades of brown to color the hair. Color in the hat, using the illustration as a guide.

5 Cut out the eye holes with a craft knife. Use a piece of paper over the mask to avoid smudging the colors.

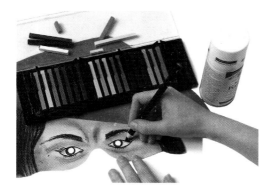

6 Color in the area around the eye holes with black crayon and shade in the darker areas of the face. Finish the hair, lightly smudging the color with your finger, then spray it with fixative.

7 Finish off the hat with random sweeps of orange.

8 Spray the mask with fixative and leave to dry.

9 Use the craft knife to make tiny slits at the side of the mask in the hair area, and push lengths of twill tape through to the back.

TIP
- We used black twill tape to tie on the mask since it is less obvious with dark hair. If you change the hair color, use tape that matches as closely as possible.

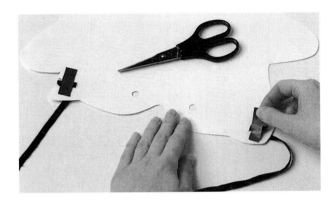

10 Turn over the mask and secure the twill tape with strong tape.

11 Tape two feathers together and put them in position. Attach them to the back of the mask with strong tape.

LION MASK

You will need paper, cardboard and pastels for this mask, which is fairly simple to make, although it does look very impressive. It is quite time-consuming to complete, because the lion's mane is made from individual strips of paper, and although it would be possible to make a less complicated version—a child could easily make the basic mask—the mane really does bring the mask to life.

You will need

- Medium-weight brown cardboard
- Pencil
- Tracing paper
- Scissors
- Hole punch
- Pastels
- Fixative; clear, all-purpose glue
- Black crayon
- Medium-weight paper, four shades from brown to beige
- Lightweight white paper
- Self-adhesive dots, black and yellow
- Twill tape or elastic

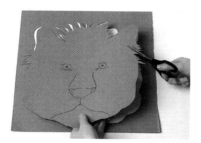

1 *Transfer the outline from the template to the brown cardboard and cut out the shape.*

2 *Cut around the nose area and punch out the eye holes (for you to see through).*

3 *Use brown, yellow, and beige pastels to begin to color in and shade the lion's face.*

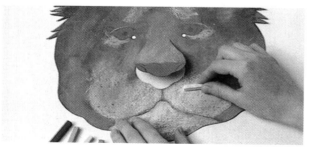

4 *Use white to color in around the mouth, eyes, and eyebrows, and rub the pastels with your finger to blend the colors. Spray with fixative and leave to dry.*

5 *Use the black crayon to draw in the line of the mouth and the nostrils.*

6 *Protect the pastels you have applied by resting your hand on a piece of spare white paper while you work. Draw round the eyes with black crayon.*

9 *Begin to glue the strips to the top of the mask to create the shape of the head, adding strips of paper in different shades of brown and yellow.*

7 *Make a series of small black dots on the cheeks and muzzle area, using the illustration as a guide. Spray again with fixative and leave to dry.*

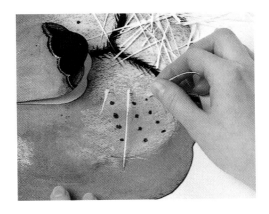

10 *Cut out some strips of white paper for the whiskers on the muzzle and chin, and glue them in place.*

8 *Cut out narrow strips of colored paper for the top of the mane, shaping them into a point at one end.*

11 *Cut some longer strips for the side of the mane.*

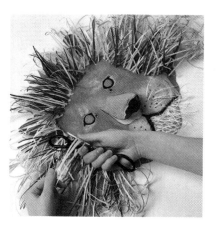

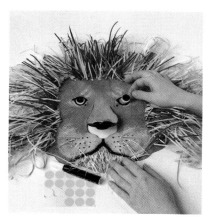

12 *Cut some pieces for the mane from strips about an inch wide. Do not cut all the way along the strips, but roll them up at the uncut end and glue them in place at the sides.*

13 *When the glue is dry, carefully run some of the strips of paper between the edge of the blade of a pair of scissors and your thumb to curl the paper slightly.*

14 *Put a black self-adhesive dot on a larger yellow dot for each eye, and press them into position.*

MEDUSA MASK

This mask is based on the legend of Medusa, a monster in Greek mythology whose hair was a mass of living snakes. This cardboard-and-paper mask requires a little patience to make, and you will also need to exercise your painting skills in decorating the face and applying the hair.

You will need

- Lightweight cardboard
- Pencil
- Tracing paper
- Craft knife
- Scissors
- Clear, all-purpose glue
- Paints, including red, green, and yellow
- Toothbrush
- Large and small paintbrushes
- White paper
- Black paper
- Strong tape
- Self-adhesive dots
- Hole punch

1 Transfer the outlines of the masks from the templates and cut them out carefully from the cardboard.

2 Use a craft knife to cut a slit in the mouth.

3 Cut along the lines indicated on the template and fold the top part into shape by overlapping the cut areas and gluing them to create a three-dimensional effect.

4 Repeat with the lower section. Fold and glue the nose along the lines shown on the template. Do not attach it to the mask yet.

351

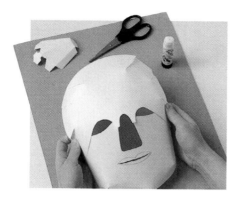

5 Fit the top section of the mask to the lower part and glue the two sections together. Leave to dry.

8 Mix some yellow paint and flick it over the mask and nose until you have built up a good covering of color.

6 Mix some red paint and use an old toothbrush to spatter paint over the surface of the mask and the nose.

9 Make snakes from lightweight white paper. Draw a free-hand circle and mark the snake's outline with a pencil, using the template as a guide. Decorate with patterns and colors to create a variety of textures.

7 Mix green paint and repeat the process, this time using a large, soft paintbrush.

10 Cut out the snakes, using your pencil line as a guide, but do not make them all exactly the same.

11 Glue the snakes to the front of the mask, twining them together to make them seem alive. Leave a few heads and tails visible.

12 Use a fine paintbrush and white paint to add final details to the snakes' heads. Then paint in Medusa's eyebrows and the snakes' eyes in black or brown.

13 Paint in Medusa's mouth with dark red.

14 Cut out some small strips of black paper in the shape of snakes' tongues and glue them to the snakes' heads.

15 Position the nose, securing it at the back of the mask with strong tape.

16 Punch a hole in the center of a self-adhesive dot. Fit the dot into the eye hole. Repeat for the other eye.

WOODLAND HALF-MASK

This is the perfect mask for someone who enjoys walking in the countryside and picking up odd bits and pieces. The base is made of papier-mâché, molded on modeling clay, and it is decorated with leaves and berries. Use good-quality gold, bronze, and silver paints to give it a sumptuous look.

TIP
- If you do not like working with papier-mâché or you do not have the time that is needed to model the mask, try decorating the basic shape of the Feathered Half-mask on page 361—but remember to omit the beak.

You will need
- Pencil
- Tracing paper
- Lightweight cardboard
- Modeling clay
- Newspaper and paste for papier-mâché
- Craft knife
- Scissors
- Elastic
- Gold, silver, and bronze spray paint
- Selection of dry leaves, berries, fruit, and so on
- Clear, all-purpose glue

1 Trace the template and transfer the image to a cardboard.

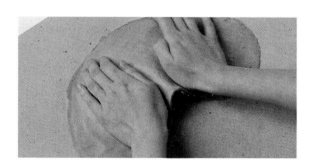

3 Smooth the clay and the edges with your palms.

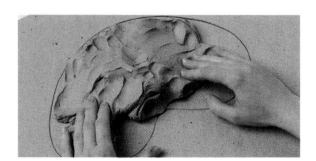

2 Use modeling clay to mold the shape. Build up a three-dimensional shape around the nose area, smoothing and refining the shape out towards the eyes.

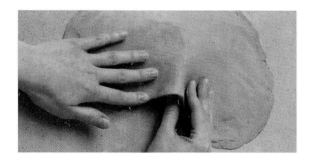

4 Take special care to shape the nose and to smooth the clay around it. Leave the mold to dry for 24 hours.

5 Mix the paste to an even consistency and use torn scraps of newspaper, dipped in the paste, to cover the clay with a layer of papier-mâché. Squeeze the strips with your fingers to remove excess paste from the paper before you press it in place or the papier-mâché will take too long to dry.

6 Leave the mask in a warm place for 2-3 hours to dry. Repeat the process three more times—that is, you will apply four layers of papier-mâché. Let the mask dry completely, before removing the mask from the mold.

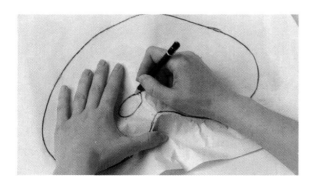

7 Using the template as a guide, draw eye holes on the mask and cut them out carefully with a craft knife.

8 Trim the rough edges of the mask with scissors.

9 Use small pieces of papier-mâché all around the edge to finish it and to make a smooth line.

10 Make a small hole at each side and, from the back, push through the elastic, securing the ends with small knots.

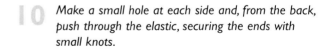

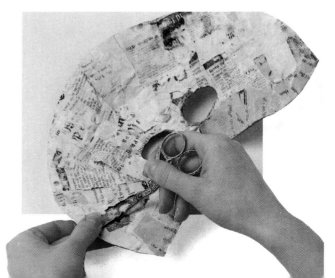

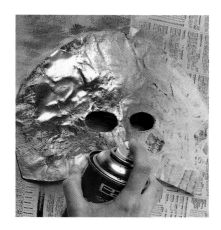

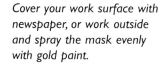

11 *Cover your work surface with newspaper, or work outside and spray the mask evenly with gold paint.*

12 *Spray the leaves, berries, nuts, and fruit with gold, silver, or bronze paint, and leave them to dry.*

13 *Begin to glue the leaves over the mask, using different colors and shapes to build up the overall shape. Finish off by adding the fruits, nuts, and berries.*

TIP

- When you use spray paints, always work in a well-ventilated room—or better still, work outside. You might prefer to use metallic paints that are applied by brush.
- Leaves should be preserved between paper and weighted down with books for one to two weeks before use.

PANDA

Fur fabric is ideal for animal masks—they always look so appealing. You can buy fur fabric in most fabric and craft stores, and it is easy to work with. The panda is very straightforward to make, and you could easily adapt the basic method to make almost any type of animal you want.

You will need

- Pencil
- Tracing paper
- Lightweight white cardboard
- Scissors
- Hole punch
- Fur fabric, white and black
- Clear, all-purpose glue
- White pencil or chalk
- Small, shallow yogurt container
- Buttons for eyes and nostrils

1 Transfer the outline from the template to white cardboard and cut it out.

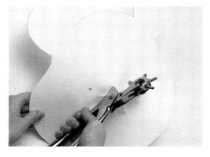

2 Cut out the nose and punch out the eye holes.

3 Trace around the cardboard template onto the reverse side of the white fur fabric. Do not trace around the ears.

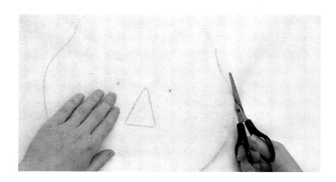

4 Cut out the outline of the head and the nose hole.

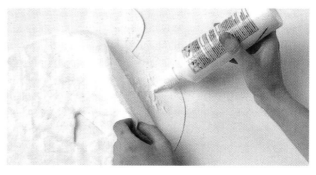

5 Glue white fur fabric onto the cardboard template and leave the glue to dry.

6 Pierce the eye hole with your scissors. Make sure you can see through the holes. You may trim some fur on the right side of the mask to be able to see clearly.

9 Cut out the snout template and cut a piece of white fur fabric to size. Glue it around the yogurt container. Make a triangular shape for the nose patch (see step 11).

7 Cut out the templates for the ears, eye patches, and nose, and draw them on the reverse side of the black fabric.

10 Tuck the extra bits of white fur fabric into the yogurt container and glue them in position.

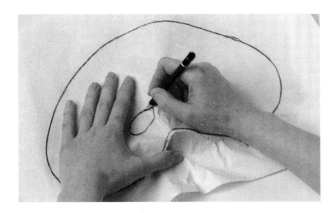

8 Cut the ears, eyes, and nose patch from the black fabric.

11 Glue the black nose piece, reverse-side up, onto the end of the yogurt container.

12 *Glue the eye and ear patches to the main mask. Make sure that you join the edges of the black and white neatly together.*

13 *Glue the nose into the middle of the mask between the black eye patches.*

14 *Glue buttons in position for the eyes and nostrils, and leave until the glue is dry.*

FEATHERED HALF-MASK

This half-mask is quite sophisticated, and it would look great with an evening dress. Feathers always make a mask look elegant and exotic. Although we have used green and black feathers, you can buy dyed ones and, by changing the basic shape of the mask, you could make a parrot or a peacock—or almost anything else you wanted. You can also mount this kind of mask on a stick in case you do not want to wear it all evening.

You will need
- Black cardboard
- Tracing paper
- Pencil
- White pencil or crayon
- Scissors
- Craft knife
- Clear, all-purpose glue
- Wooden toothpick
- Sequins
- Feathers, green and black
- Strong tape
- Black twill tape for tying

TIP
- Sequins can be fiddly to position. Look out for the kind that are sold stitched together in long strings. These are much easier than loose ones to attach in a straight line.

1 Draw the template onto tracing paper and go over the outline with a white pencil. Transfer the image to black cardboard by pressing down on the wrong side of the pencil line. The image should be clearly seen on the board.

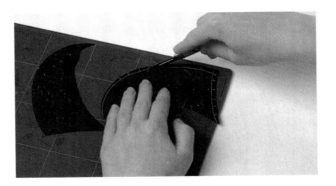

2 Cut out the mask and the two pieces of beak from the cardboard. Score lightly along the length of the upper edge of both beak sections.

3 Cut a series of small incisions along the top edge of the beak, without cutting beyond the score line. Bend along the score line carefully.

4 *Apply a line of glue to the cut edges and press the two pieces together firmly to make the beak.*

5 *Decorate both sides of the edge of the beak with gold, heart-shaped sequins. Use a toothpick to help you position the sequins in an even line.*

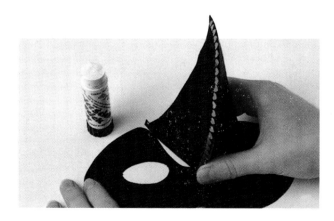

6 *Glue the beak in position between the eye holes. Let the glue dry. You may have to hold the beak in place for a few minutes until it is securely in position.*

7 *Begin to glue the feathers around the mask, starting in the center and working out to the side. Try to make the two sides as symmetrical as possible.*

8 *Turn the mask over and use strong tape to hold black twill tape near the eye holes.*

9 *On the right side, use glue and the toothpick to stick multicolored, heart-shaped sequins onto the feathers.*

10 *Finish the mask by gluing a line of sold sequins around each eye hole.*

SANTA CLAUS

Paper plates make good bases for masks—they are readily available, cheap, and easy to use. You could use the same method to make a pumpkin for a Halloween party or a snowman for Christmas, or even a scarecrow or a soccer ball. Even children can use this method, and you can use all kinds of things to decorate—so save all odd scraps of material, beads, and straw.

You will need

- 4 large paper plates
- Pencil
- Ruler
- Scissors
- Hole punch
- Craft knife
- Paints
- Large and small paintbrushes
- Self-adhesive dots; clear, all-purpose glue

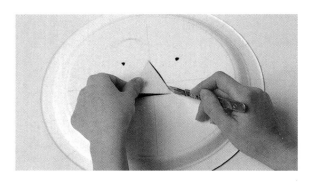

1   *Use the template and and draw the nose and eye holes on a large paper plate. Punch out the eye holes and cut out the nose.*

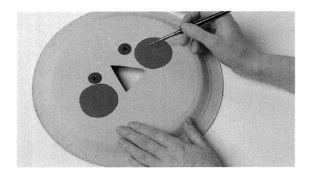

3   *Punch a hole in the middle of the self-adhesive dots and position them over the eye holes. Paint the cheeks red.*

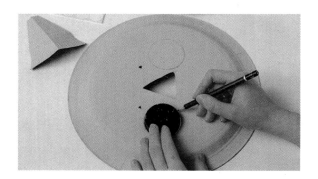

2   *Cut out the separate nose section, fold it in half down the center, and paint it pink. Use the same paint to color the plate. Draw two circles for the cheeks, and color two self-adhesive dots with blue paint for the eyes.*

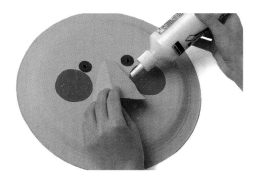

4   *Glue the nose in position between the cheeks.*

5 Using the template and illustrations as reference, cut the hair and moustache from a paper plate.

8 Glue the beard in place.

6 Cut the beard from another plate, making the separate strands as fine and even as you can.

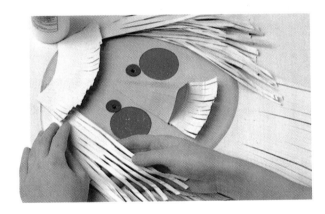

9 Glue on the hair in sections. There are three sections at each side, so begin with the lowest one, making sure they are placed symmetrically.

7 Glue the fringe and moustache into place on the face, holding them until the glue is dry.

10 Cut out the hat and paint it red.

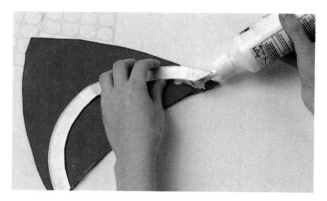

11 Cut out the semicircle for the decorative band on the hat and glue it into place.

12 Glue the hat onto the main mask, holding it in place until the glue is dry.

13 Decorate the hat with self-adhesive white dots.

WITCH

This is a traditional papier-mâché mask, made on a balloon, which is one of the easiest and best ways of making a mask for a complete costume. It is the perfect mask for Halloween or for a costume party. Although it is time-consuming to make, it offers great scope for you to use your imagination, both in making the facial features and in adding decorations to the hat.

You will need

- Balloon; newspaper and paste
- Modeling clay
- Craft knife; scissors
- Black crayon/pencil; white crayon/pencil
- Paints
- Large and small paintbrushes
- Twill tape for ties; length of string
- Thumbtack; strong tape
- Heavy- or medium-weight black cardboard
- Double-sided tape/clear, all-purpose glue
- Black raffia; silver net
- Plastic lizards, newts, spiders, etc.

1 *Blow up the balloon to slightly larger than your head. Tear newspaper into strips and dip the pieces into the paste, squeezing off the excess. Cover about three-quarters of the balloon with pasted paper and leave it to dry.*

2 *Repeat the process twice more and leave to dry. Burst the balloon, remove the pieces, and trim off the edges of the papier mâché.*

3 *Use modeling clay to mold a nose. Add some small round balls to represent warts.*

4 *Tear smaller newspaper strips and cover the nose with papier-mâché. Let dry. Apply one more layer of papier-mâché and leave to dry.*

5 *Cut the nose in half with a craft knife. Carefully peel off the nose from the clay, taking care that it does not tear.*

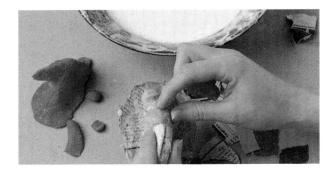

6 Join the two halves of the papier-mâché nose with small pieces of pasted paper.

7 Trim the edges of the nose carefully with scissors so that it will sit securely on the front of the mask.

8 Place the nose in the center of the mask and hold it in place with small pieces of papier-mâché. Leave to dry.

TIP
■ When you make papier-mâché, tear the paper so that you do not have sharp, cut edges, which do not lie smoothly, and always tear the strips in the same direction.

9 Draw on the face, eyebrows, cheeks, and mouth with black pencil.

10 Make a small amount of papier-mâché pulp (see page 341) and build up the eyebrows, cheeks, and chin. Leave to dry overnight.

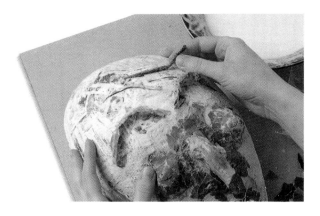

11 Roll small pieces of newspaper and dip them in paste. Glue them on for depicting wrinkles and lines.

12 *Paint the face all over with pale gray, making sure that you cover all the newsprint.*

13 *Use dark-gray paint and a fine brush to paint all the wrinkles and lines.*

14 *Pierce the eye holes with the scissors. Try on the mask to make sure you can see properly.*

15 *Begin painting the cheeks, nose, chin, eyes, and so on, with red and pink paints.*

16 *Use white to paint around the eyes and between the lips, and dark-red for the lips and warts, and to outline the eyes. Make the eyes look bloodshot by painting in fine red lines.*

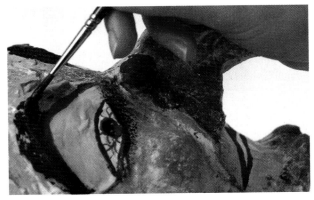

17 *Paint the area below the eyebrows with pale pink. Use black paint for the eyebrows.*

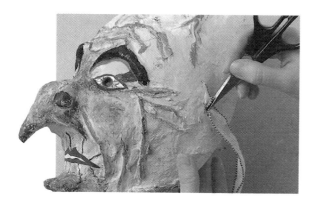

18   Pierce a hole on each side of the face with the scissors. Push lengths of twill tape through the hole and knot it on the inside to hold it secure.

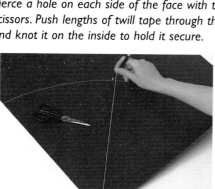

19   To make the hat, attach a piece of string to a pencil. Make a loop at the other end and hold it with a thumbtack in the corner of the cardboard. Draw an arc on the cardboard to make a cone for the hat.

20   Cut out the shape of the hat. Use double-sided tape or glue to hold the long sides of the cone together.

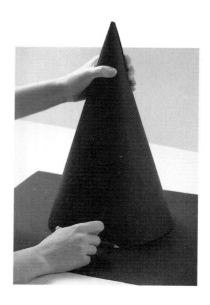

21   Place the cone on a sheet of black cardboard and use a white crayon to draw around the base.

22   Keep the breadth of the brim in proportion with the height of the hat and the features of the mask. Use a piece of paper, compasses, or a large plate to mark the edge of the brim and cut out the ring.

23   Make small cuts around the brim's inside. Folding the cuts upward, apply glue on the sides facing the rim.

24 *Glue the crown of the hat onto the brim, making sure that the brim is firmly stuck to the crown.*

26 *Glue the lizard, net, and spider to the hat, and leave to dry.*

25 *Cut the black raffia to suitable lengths and use small pieces of tape to stick clumps of hair to the inside of the hat.*

PUNK

Papier-mâché masks take a long time to make because you have to wait for the individual layers to dry. However, the results are so impressive that it's worth the effort. We decided to make this punk look fairly restrained and sculptural by applying a single color, but you could use more to make the face look more—or less—sinister.

You will need

- Kitchen foil
- Scissors
- Newspaper and paste for papier-mâché
- White paint
- Paintbrush
- Tracing paper; lightweight white paper
- Pencil
- Clear, all-purpose glue
- Wire for earrings, nose rings, etc.
- Chain, cross, or other decorations
- Twill tape for ties; safety pins

1 *Take three sheets from a wide roll of kitchen foil and press them over your face so that you get a reasonable impression of your features. The mask will eventually fit under your chin and around over the top of your head, so make sure that you have enough foil to cover the whole area. You will need to press quite firmly around your nose, mouth, and eyes.*

2 *Mix the paste to a smooth, even consistency and tear strips of paper. Dip the strips into the paste, removing the excess paste with your fingers. Take care when applying the pasted paper to the foil, so that you do not press it out of shape. Apply one layer of paper and leave to dry for 2-3 hours. When the first layer is dry, apply three more layers—that is, there are four layers of papier-mâché in total—allowing each layer to dry before you apply the next. Leave the final layer to dry overnight. Once completely dry, carefully pull the foil away from the inside.*

3 Make a small amount of papier-mâché pulp and use it to build up the eyebrows and nose. Leave to dry. Roll small balls of papier-mâché pulp and use them for the eyeballs, positioning them carefully on the mask. Leave to dry.

4 Use more papier-mâché pulp for the lips, using the end of your scissors to shape them. Leave to dry.

5 Begin to build up the ears, positioning and shaping them correctly. Leave the mask in a warm, dry place until it is absolutely dry. This can even take 24 hours.

6 Make eye holes with the points of your scissors; then hold the mask to your face to ensure you can see through the holes. Make two holes at the base of the nose so that you can breathe when the mask is over your head. Also make the holes at the sides through which the twill tapes for tying will be attached.

7 Paint the entire mask white. You may need to apply two coats to cover the newsprint completely.

8   *Cut out triangles of white paper and roll them up to make the hair spikes.*

9   *Apply some glue to the inside edge of the paper so that it does not start to uncurl. Do not use stiff paper, which will not roll easily and will also be difficult to keep in shape.*

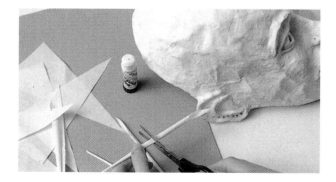

10   *You will need to have smaller spikes for the front of the head, with larger ones toward the back. Cut the spikes so that they decrease in size gradually.*

11   *Snip the ends of the spikes in three places and pull the paper out a little so that there is a larger surface for gluing.*

12   *Apply glue to the cut ends and press each spike firmly down on the top of the mask. You may need to hold each spike until the glue begins to dry.*

13 *Use a sharp pin or needle to pierce holes in the nose as well as the ears.*

14 *Make earrings and nose rings from garden wire and push them through the holes.*

15 *Push a safety pin through one side of the nose, and take the chain and cross from one side of the nose to the ear. Push a length of twill tape through the holes on each side and knot it on the inside to hold it securely.*

Monster mask

This enviro-monster is made from recycled egg boxes—you will need the molded cardboard kind, not the newer, clear plastic containers, and you will need a lot, so begin to collect them now. This mask costs very little to make and it would be a good summer-vacation project. The basic method could be used with all kinds of recycled containers—boxes, cartons, and even bottles—to make some really frightening monsters.

You will need

- Egg cartons; newspaper
- Scissors
- Stapler; pliers
- Large and small styrofoam balls
- Clear, all-purpose glue; paste; strong tape
- Paint, including green, yellow, and red
- Large and small paintbrushes
- Florist's wire
- Self-adhesive dots
- Lightweight white paper; red paper
- Strips of lightweight card

1 *Separate the individual containers from the cartons, then staple them together into the shape of a face.*

3 *Mix a murky green and paint the mask all over. Leave to dry.*

2 *Glue small styrofoam balls between the sections, especially if there are any holes. Leave the eye holes.*

4 *Mix some yellow paint and apply it to parts of the mask to create interesting highlights—or to look like slime.*

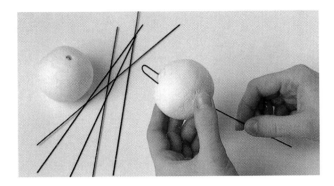

5 Take two large styrofoam balls and push a length of florist's wire into and through each ball. Use pliers to bend over the top of the wire; then pull the wire down so the hook is caught securely in the top of the ball.

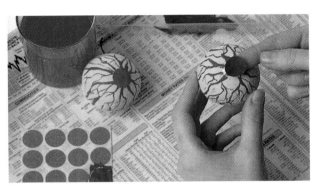

8 Paint two large self-adhesive dots with the same red and place them in the center of the balls, over the end of the wire hook.

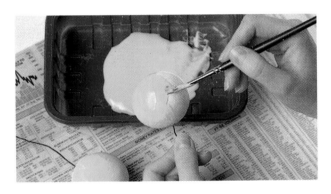

6 Hold the wires while you paint both balls yellow. Leave them to dry.

9 Push the wires through the mask so that the eyes are positioned as designed, then twist the wires around on the inside of the mask to hold the eyes. Cut off any excess wire and cover the cut ends with strong tape. Try on the mask to check that you can see through it.

7 Mix some red paint and use a fine brush to paint red lines representing veins on the balls.

10 Make whiskers by tearing white paper into long strips. Twist the strips and dip them into the paste so that they retain their shape. Leave them to dry.

11 When the paste is dry, paint the whiskers—we chose gray, but you can use any color you wish.

14 Leave the fangs to dry, then paint them, using the red and yellow paints to mix orange for the tips.

12 Use the scissors to make closely spaced, small holes at the sides of the mask. Thread the whiskers through the holes, adding a drop of glue to hold each one in place if you want to.

15 When the paint is dry, glue the fangs to a strip torn from an egg box, curving it slightly so that it fits along the bottom of the mask.

16 Use glue or tape to attach the row of fangs to the bottom inside edge of the mask.

13 Make the fangs from newspaper strips, twisted into shape and dipped into paste. You may find it better to make the fangs when they have been dipped in the paste, curving them slightly while they are still wet.

17 Tear a tongue shape from red paper or color white paper with red paint.

18 Tape the tongue to the mask so that, from the front, it appears to be behind the fangs.

19 Staple strips of cardboard to the back of the mask, trying it on to make sure that the strips hold the mask securely, but not too tightly, over your face.

PUPPET-MAKING

The universal appeal of puppetry is rooted in the ancient traditions of many cultures. The oldest form of theater in the world, it is widely held that the origins of puppetry were in the Far East. In both India and China puppets were used to recount legends and folk tales, and to dramatize religious and moral teachings.

Most famous, perhaps, of the eastern puppets are the Waylang Purwa Shadow Puppets of Indonesia, made from beautifully painted oiled parchment. These were animated in front of a light, thus casting shadows on a translucent screen.

Since puppeteers were itinerant nomadic people, their traditions traveled from land to land. In the Middle Ages the art became more prevalent in Europe, and one of the most known examples is the Commedia del'Arte in Italy in the 15th century.

Puppets have always had the capability of expressing subtle human emotions. Although they are usually made from simple, everyday materials, they seem to come alive when operated and draw the audience into a world of imagination.

Before beginning to make puppets yourself, it will be worth looking at historic examples. Many specimens exist in museums and theatrical collections, and viewing can be most inspiring. You will be adding your ideas to a long historical tradition.

THE PROJECTS

This chapter features projects inspired by traditional culture and the world of folk traditions.

PUPPET TYPES

There are basically four main types of puppet. However, there should be no doctrinaire rules about making them.

1. Stick Puppets

These are the most simple kinds of puppet. They generally don't actually move themselves, but are held by a stick that can be moved to make simple upward and downward or sideways gestures. Examples of stick puppets in this book include the wonderfully simple wooden spoon puppets and the birds on sticks. The inventive variation, the dancing skeleton, is operated with a stick from behind while the arms, legs, and head bounce around independently as they are attached to the body with springs.

2. Glove Puppets

These are usually soft-bodied puppets, which are operated by inserting the hand into the body, the small finger and the thumb operating the arms. This kind of puppet can be very simple, the five-fingered glove puppet and the felt finger puppets being the most easy examples to make. A more traditional puppet of this kind is the Crown Prince—its head is made of papier mâché and a sewn body and legs are stuffed and attached to the front of the tunic. The Marmalade Cat project is an example of the most common form of glove puppet.

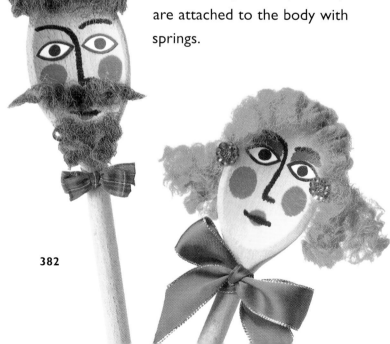

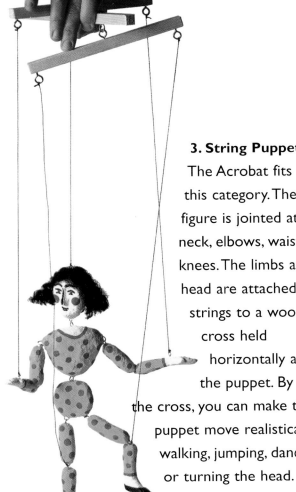

3. String Puppets

The Acrobat fits into this category. The figure is jointed at the neck, elbows, waist, and knees. The limbs and head are attached with strings to a wooden cross held horizontally above the puppet. By tilting the cross, you can make the puppet move realistically—walking, jumping, dancing, or turning the head.

NOTE ON PAPIER MÂCHÉ PULP

- All the materials that are listed for each project are inexpensive and readily available. Proprietory pulp is available from craft or good toy shops. You may like to try making your own using the following method.
- Tear a newspaper into small squares, approximately ¾ x ¾ in. (2 x 2 cm) and put it all in a large saucepan. Cover with water and boil until the paper begins to disintegrate. Turn off the heat and allow to cool. Then mash with a potato masher, strain off the excess water, and squeeze the rest out with your hands.
- Add ½ cup (140 ml) of PVA adhesive, a sprinkling of dry cellulose or starch paste, ½ cup (140 ml) of proprietary wall filler, and a cup of fine sawdust. Knead this mixture as you would bread, on a flat surface, until all the ingredients are well mixed. This mixture will keep for a number of weeks in the fridge.
- The projects on the following pages provide simple, clear instructions for making the puppets. They require no specialist equipment or knowledge—all can be made on the kitchen table.

4. Shadow Puppets

These are usually flat silhouettes of card, the arms or legs being jointed and moved with thin rods. The figure is held upright with another thin stick and operated against a translucent screen. A light is shone from behind the puppet and there should be some degree of darkness in front of the screen for dramatic effect. The Indian on a horse is a good example of a shadow puppet, but can of course be operated without light and screen to good effect.

JUMPING JACK

This traditional puppet is seen in many cultures and something like it was perhaps the first moving toy to be made. We have made a simple version—with a feather in its cap—but the same principle can be used to make quite complicated puppets with many moving parts.

Transfer the template images to the card and carefully cut out the arms, legs, and body.

You will need

- Tracing paper
- Pencil
- Thin, ivory-colored card
- Scissors
- Felt-tipped pens (yellow, black, orange, and pink)
- Hole punch
- 5 paper fasteners
- Strong, black thread
- Feather
- Clear, all-purpose adhesive
- Small, wooden, or glass bead

Jumping Jack Templates

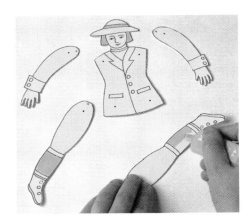

2 Color the hair, hat band, lower legs, and soles of the shoes yellow.

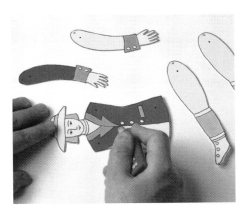

3 Color the jacket and hat in pink and orange, using the illustration of the finished puppet for reference.

4 Color the black areas of the boots and the striped breeches.

5 Pierce the holes shown on the template—one each at the shoulders and hips, and two at the top of both arms and both legs.

6 Attach the arms and the legs to the body with paper fasteners, making sure that the limbs move freely before you turn back the tabs on the fasteners.

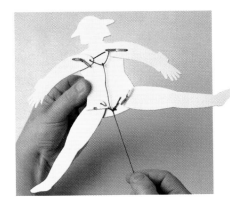

7 Thread the black thread through the other holes in the arms and the legs.

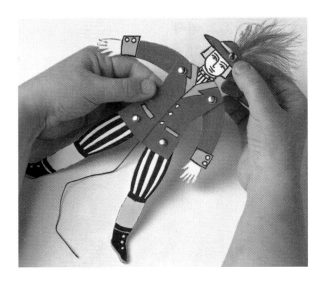

8   *Stick a small, brightly colored feather to the hat and secure it with the last paper fastener.*

9   *Fasten a small bead to the end of the thread.*

INDIAN WARRIOR

This plucky Indian, inspired by American folk art weather-vanes, is easy to make and even easier to operate. You can use the same method to create more characters, so that you can act out a complete drama.

You will need

- Tracing paper
- Pencil
- Thin, black card
- Scissors
- Craft knife
- White wax crayon
- Darning needle
- Hole punch
- Paper fastener
- 2 small split canes
- PVA adhesive
- Strong, black thread

Use a pencil to trace the image from the template. Turn your tracing over and draw over the pencil lines.

Indian Warrior Templates

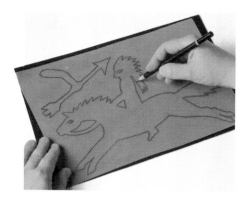

2 *Turn over the tracing paper and carefully draw over the original traced lines with a sharp pencil to transfer the image to the black card. Remove the tracing paper.*

3 *Accurately cut out the image.*

4 *Use a craft knife to cut out the parts that are not accessible with scissors—under the arms, for example.*

5 *Cut out the eyes with the point of your craft knife.*

6 *Highlight the image with a sharp white crayon. Don't forget to add the detail to the arm and arrow.*

7 *Use a darning needle to pierce a hole through the elbow of the arm carrying the arrow.*

8 Position the arrow-carrying arm behind the body and pierce a hole through the two thicknesses at the "shoulder".

10 Glue one piece of split cane to the center of the back of the horse.

11 Make a small hole in the top of the other piece of cane and tie it loosely to the elbow with strong black thread.

9 Push a paper fastener through the holes, making sure that the arm can be moved before you open out the tabs on the back.

DRAGON

Don't throw away your old or odd socks.
You can turn them into a host of colorful
characters—a dragon like this one, monsters,
or whatever takes your imagination—and
watch them metamorphose into a new
existence.

You will need

- Sewing thread
- 2 old socks
- Pins
- Scissors
- Needle
- Felt (orange, black, yellow, and pink)
- Polyester stuffing
- Scrap material (for eyes)
- Fabric glue
- Sequins

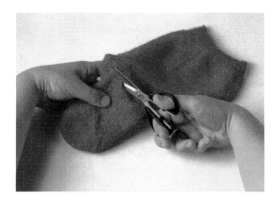

2 *Cut a slit in the same sock on the upper foot and opposite the heel.*

3 *Cut off the toe of the other sock.*

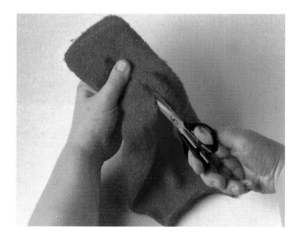

I *Cut a slit down the back of one sock and a little way along the sole.*

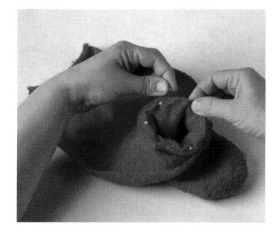

4 *With right sides together, pin the toe section into the slit in the first sock.*

390

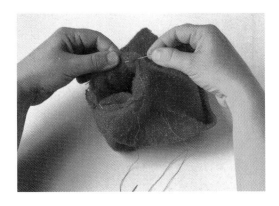

5 Stitch the toe section in place to make the lower jaw.

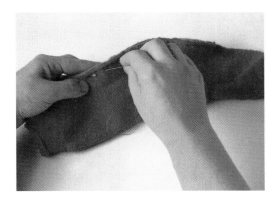

8 Use running stitch to stitch the zigzag in place.

6 Cut out a zigzag from the orange felt. It should be approximately 30 cm/12 in. long.

9 Pull the sock through to the right side, to reveal the fins running down the back.

7 With the sock inside-out, place the zigzag along the slit up the back, pinning it so the straight edge of the zigzag lies along the slit and the points lie inwards.

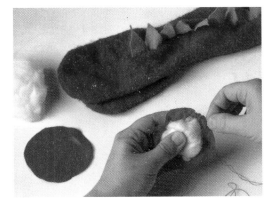

10 Stitch a line of small running stitches about the edge of a circle of pink fabric; do not fasten off the thread. Place a small wad of polyester stuffing in the center.

11 *Pull up the running stitches to form a ball and oversew to hold.*

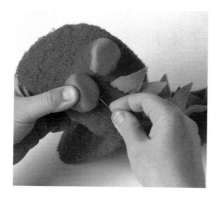

12 *Sew the eyeballs onto the sock head, just in front of the end of the fins.*

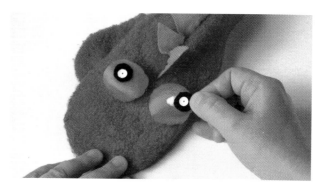

13 *Use fabric glue to stick white sequins onto circles of black felt. Stick the "eyes" onto the eyeballs.*

14 *Stitch on scraps of orange, yellow, and pink felt as whiskers and glue sequins onto the ends at the points they are sewn to the head.*

15 *Cut out a forked tongue from yellow felt and sew it inside the mouth. Slide your arm into the sock, putting your thumb into the lower jaw.*

MR AND MRS WITHERSPOON

Wooden spoons are inexpensive and available in a variety of shapes and sizes. They always seem to impart a slightly prim feeling to the puppet faces. Use the method described here to make a whole cast of characters, or an entire family.

You will need

- White cartridge paper or lightweight card
- Felt-tipped pens (black, pink, and blue)
- Scissors
- 1 wooden spoon
- Clear, all-purpose adhesive
- Stage hair (we used ginger)
- Sequins
- Ribbon

1 Use a black felt-tipped pen to draw two eyes on the white paper. Carefully cut out the eyes with scissors.

3 Use a pink felt-tipped pen to add the cheeks.

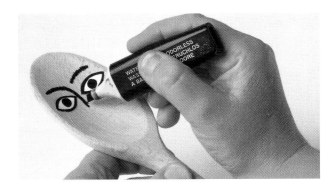

2 Glue the eyes to the wooden spoon, about one-third of the way from the top. Draw in the eyebrows and nose with black felt-tipped pen.

4 Draw in the mouth with pink felt-tipped pen and add a black line. Finish off the face with some blue eye shadow.

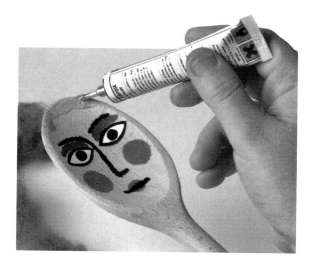

5 *Smear some adhesive along the top edge of the spoon.*

8 *Tie the ribbon in a neat bow around the neck of the puppet and trim to length.*

6 *Stick on the stage hair.*

7 *Stick a large green sequin on either side of the face, partly on the spoon and partly on the hair.*

DANCING SKELETON

This little puppet was inspired by the Day of the Dead Festival, when Mexicans eat sweets shaped like skulls. It's a simple puppet to make, but it dances in a macabre yet entertaining way. Use a proprietary papier-mâché pulp if you do not want to make your own.

You will need

- Papier-mâché pulp
- Knife
- 1 piece of ¼ in. (6 mm) dowel, 12 in. (30 cm) long
- 2 springs, each 5 in.(13 cm) long
- 2 springs, each 3½ in. (9 cm) long
- 1 spring, 1½ in. (3 cm) long
- Acrylic primer (white)
- Paintbrushes (medium and small)
- Acrylic paint (gray)

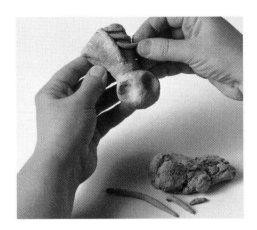

2 Roll out small sausages of pulp and arrange them to form the ribs on the upper body.

3 Use a kitchen knife to model the vertebrae.

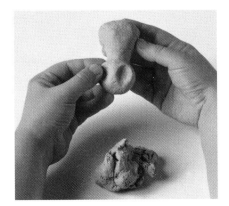

1 Model the body of the skeleton from papier-mâché pulp, narrowing the waist and pinching out the pelvis.

4 Push the pieces of dowel into the back of the skeleton's body to a depth of about 1 cm/½ in.

395

5 *Use pulp to model a skull, keeping it in proportion with the body. Use the end of the dowel to create eye sockets.*

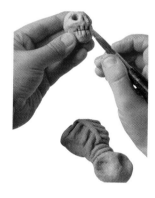

6 *Use a knife to draw in the jaw and to make indentations to represent the teeth.*

7 *Press small bits of pulp onto the ends of the four long springs to form the hands and feet. Insert the small spring into the base of the skull.*

8 *Insert the two longer springs into the hip bones and the two shorter ones at the shoulders. The springs should go in to a depth of about ½ in. (1 cm) Pack the springs with pulp, so they are firmly embedded in the pulp.*

9 *Push the head spring into the top of the skeleton and pack it with pulp. As the pulp dries out, it will help to hold the springs. Leave the skeleton to dry in a warm place—an oven on a very low setting, for instance.*

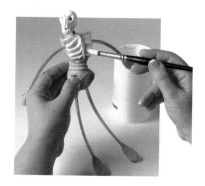

10 *When the skeleton is completely dry give the body, skull, hands, and feet a coat of white primer. Take care that you do not get paint on the springs.*

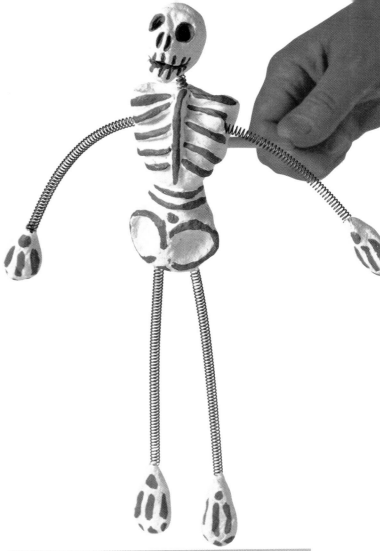

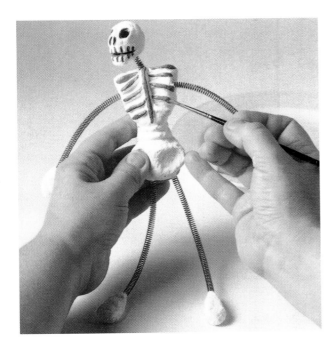

11 Leave the primer to dry, then paint the outlines of the rib bones, eye sockets, jaw, teeth, and pelvis in gray paint.

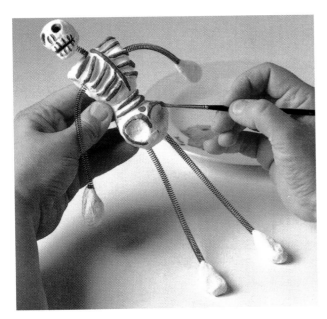

12 Paint in the outlines of the bones in the hands and feet in the same way.

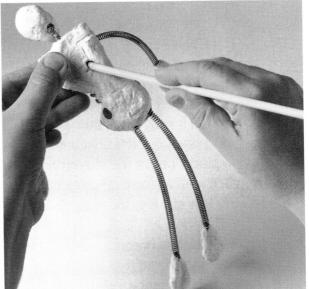

13 Push the dowel into the hole in the back. You can use a spot of glue to hold it, but you may prefer to leave it so that you can take it out.

397

FLIGHT OF FANCY

Have you ever wondered what you can do with all the corks that you find left over after a party? Well, here's one answer—make a flock of birds. This is possibly the easiest of all the projects in the book and one that might lead you to your own flights of fancy. Try adding real feathers or sequins, or use glittery paper.

Transfer the outlines of the template to the white card. Referring to the finished puppet, begin to color in the bird's head and tail with yellow and orange.

You will need

- Tracing paper
- Pencil
- Thin white card
- Felt-tipped pens (yellow, orange, pink, blue, red, and black)
- Scissors
- Craft knife
- Cork
- 1 piece of ¼ in. (6 mm) dowel, approximately 14 in. (35 cm) long

Use red for the crest and comb, and blue to color the face. Outline the beak and eyes with black.

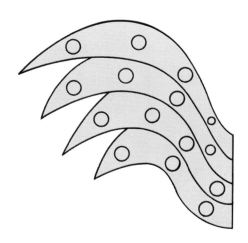

3   *Carefully add the pink spots to the tail.*

6   *Use the point of a pair of closed scissors to make a hole in the bottom of the cork.*

4   *When you have finished coloring, neatly cut out the head and tail.*

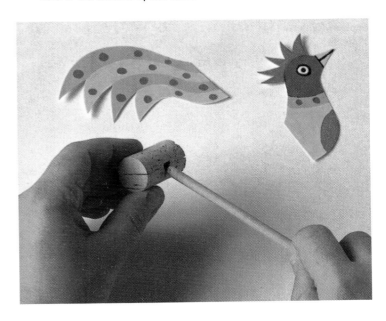

7   *Insert the dowel into the hole in the cork.*

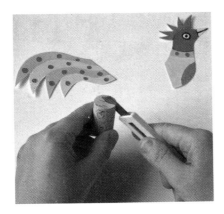

5   *Use a craft knife to cut a slit, about 6 mm/¼ in. deep, across each end of the cork.*

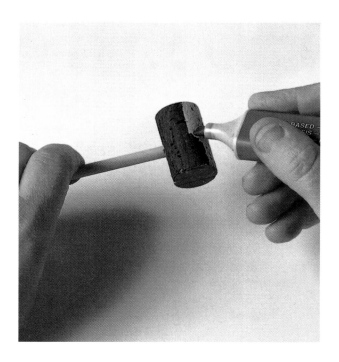

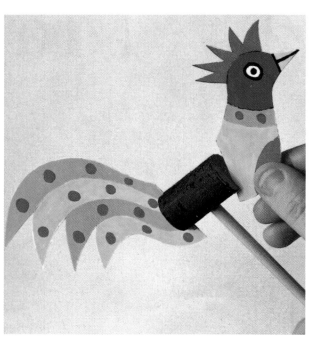

8 *Holding the dowel, color the side of the cork blue and the ends pink.*

9 *Push the head and tail sections into the slits you have cut in the ends of the cork.*

400

Marmalade Cat

This puppet is made using the simple papier-mâché layering technique. Instead of decorating with paint, the cat's face is created using torn scrap paper. In this way, the construction and decoration of the puppet are part of the same process.

You will need

- Plasticine (blue and yellow)
- Petroleum jelly
- Sugar paper (blue and orange; small amounts of yellow and green)
- Colorful wrapping paper (scraps of)
- Paste (cellulose or starch)
- Craft knife
- PVA adhesive
- Masking tape
- Cardboard tube
- Tracing paper
- Pencil
- Scissors
- Pins
- Scrap material, approximately 12 x 12 in. (30 x 30 cm) square x 2
- Pins
- Needle
- Sewing thread
- Orange felt, approximately 12 x 12 in. (30 x 30 cm) square x 2
- Orange embroidery thread

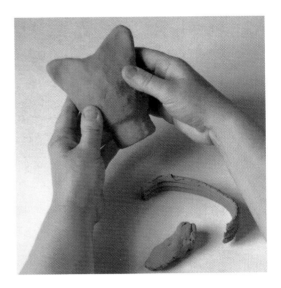

1 *Model the blue plasticine into a cat's head shape.*

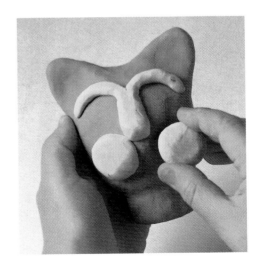

2 *Using the yellow plasticine, make the features—the nose, eyebrows, and two balls for the cheeks.*

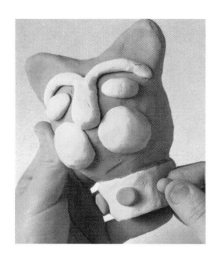

3 *Make a collar out of yellow plasticine and add blue bobbles.*

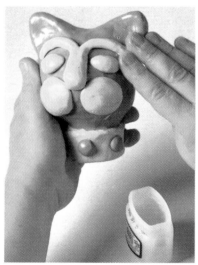

4 *Smear the whole of the cat's head with an even coat of petroleum jelly to stop the paper from sticking to the plasticine.*

5 *Tear some of the orange sugar paper into small pieces and smear with paste, taking care not to make them too wet. Begin to cover the head with the paper, overlapping each piece.*

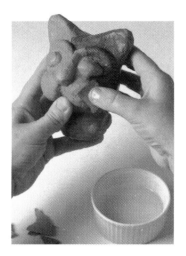

6 *When you have completely covered the head with orange paper, repeat the process with blue paper. Continue in this way, alternating the orange and blue, until you have applied seven layers. You should end with an orange layer.*

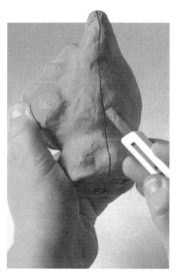

7 *Leave to dry thoroughly. This may take some time, but you can speed things up by putting the head in a warm place—an airing cupboard, for example. When it is dry, use a craft knife to cut cleanly all around the head. Make sure that the blade cuts through the paper and into the plasticine beneath.*

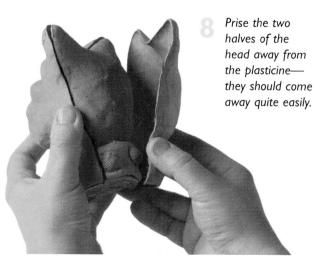

8 *Prise the two halves of the head away from the plasticine— they should come away quite easily.*

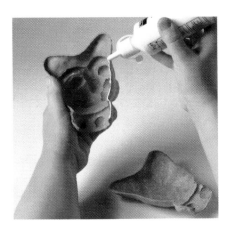

9 Put some PVA adhesive on the rim of one of the halves.

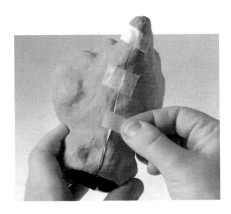

10 Match the two halves and hold them in place with small pieces of masking tape until the adhesive dries.

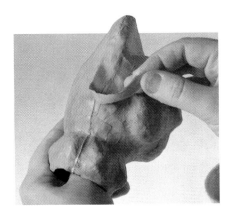

11 Remove the masking tape and disguise the join by pasting pieces of torn orange paper over it so that they blend in with the head.

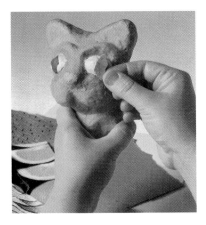

12 Tear some yellow paper and paste it onto the eyeballs. Use some green paper to make the pupils of the eyes.

13 Stick torn pieces of patterned orange paper onto the head. Cover the eyebrows and nose with blue paper and make a small mouth. Cover the collar with blue sugar paper and the raised bobbles with alternate yellow and orange scraps of wrapping paper.

14   *Trace the tunic template, cut it out, and pin it to a double thickness of material.*

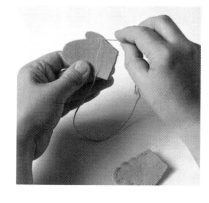

17   *Make the hands by stitching the two layers of felt together with orange embroidery thread.*

15   *Carefully cut out the tunic.*

18   *With the tunic still the wrong way out, turn up the hem and stitch the side, underarm, and shoulder seams together. Leave spaces at the neck and cuffs.*

16   *Trace the hand templates, cut them out, and pin each of them to two pieces of felt. Cut them out.*

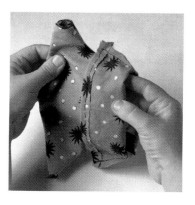

19   *Turn the tunic the right way round.*

20 *Turn down the edge of the cuff to the inside, slot in the hand, and stitch. Repeat with the other hand.*

21 *Push a small section of cardboard tube into the neck of the tunic, sticking it with PVA adhesive.*

23 *Push the head onto the cardboard tube, making sure that the collar covers the join with the tunic. Hold it in place until the adhesive is dry.*

22 *Apply some adhesive to the inside of the cat's head around the collar.*

CROWN PRINCE

This regal-looking character has rather humble origins—paper pulp and scrap material. Although it is a more elaborate puppet to make than some others, each stage is straightforward and requires no specialist technique or knowledge.

You will need

- Newspaper
- Cardboard tube
- Masking tape
- Papier-mâché pulp
- Knife
- Acrylic primer (white)
- Paintbrushes (small and medium)
- Acrylic paints (blue, pink, red, yellow, brown, and black)
- Plate or palette for mixing paints
- Gold paper or gold foil
- Scissors
- Clear, all-purpose adhesive
- Tracing paper
- Pencil
- Pins
- Gold-colored velvet, 2 pieces, 14 x 17 in. (35 x 40 cm)
- Needle
- Sewing thread
- 4 rubber bands
- Polyester stuffing
- PVA adhesive
- Gold-colored braid, 6 ft (2 m)

1 *Scrunch up a ball of newspaper so that it is the size of your fist. Secure the newspaper ball to the top of a cardboard tube with masking tape.*

2 *Evenly cover the newspaper with a layer of pulp. Use a proprietary mix if you don't want to make your own. Smooth down the pulp onto the tube, which will form the neck, and leave to dry overnight.*

3 *Begin to model the nose, pressing the pulp well onto the head and smoothing out any joins. Add the eyes and eyebrows.*

4 *Make the lips and add a moustache and some hair. Model the crown by making even points around the head. Leave the head to dry, ideally for several days.*

7 *Model the hands with pulp, remembering to make a separate thumb. Use a knife to make a dent around the wrists of both hands. Leave to dry.*

5 *Use some more pulp to model the boots.*

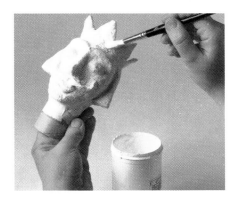

8 *When the boots are dry, give them a coat of white acrylic primer. When the head is dry, give it a coat of white acrylic primer as well.*

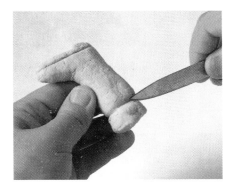

6 *Make a clearly defined dent all around the top of each boot with a knife. The dent will make it easier to attach the trouser legs later on. Leave to dry.*

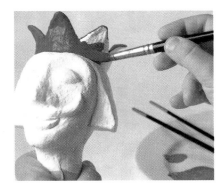

9 *Use the medium paintbrush to paint the crown blue.*

10   *Paint the hair pale-yellow and the face a flesh tone. Make rosy cheeks by mixing red with the flesh color on the face before it dries. Paint the lips bright red. Paint the eyes blue and the moustache and eyebrows dark brown. Add a dark brown line around the eyes.*

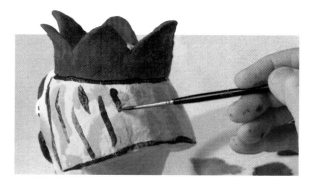

11   *Use a darker shade of yellow to add some rough streaks over the hair. When the paint is dry, add some dark-brown lines.*

12   *Paint some fine, pale-yellow lines on the moustache and eyebrows.*

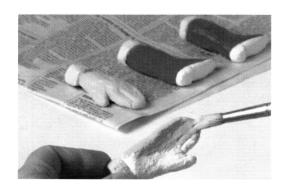

13   *Paint the hands flesh-pink.*

14   *Paint the boots blue, but the soles of the boots in black.*

15   *Cut out pieces of gold paper or foil and stick them to the points of the crown. Cut a long, narrow piece of foil to go around the base of the crown. Glue it in place.*

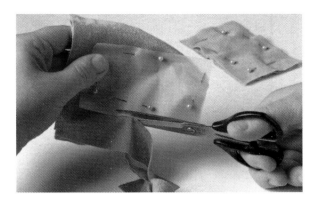

16 Trace and cut out the templates for the tunic and trousers. Pin the templates onto two layers of the fabric, folded with right sides together.

19 Remember not to sew up the cuffs or the top and bottom ends of the trouser legs.

17 Carefully cut out two legs and one tunic.

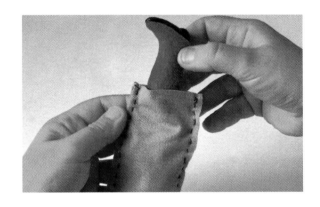

20 Push a boot into a trouser leg so that the boot is completely covered by the trouser leg.

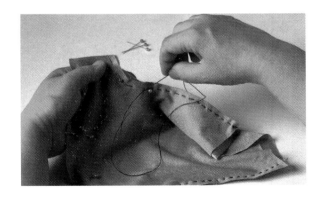

18 Use a neat running stitch to sew together the seams of the body and the trouser legs.

21 Wind a rubber band tightly around the boot where the dent is. Make sure the rubber band is as tight as possible.

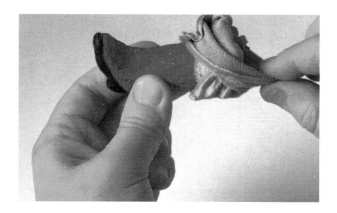

22   Pull the trouser leg the right way round.

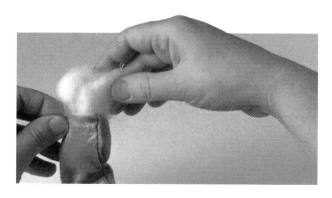

23   Put a little polyester filling in the leg, but do not fill
it too full. Repeat for the other leg.

24   Push a hand, fingers first, into the tunic cuff, which is
still inside-out. Wind a rubber band tightly around the
hand, ensuring it rests in the ridge around the wrist.

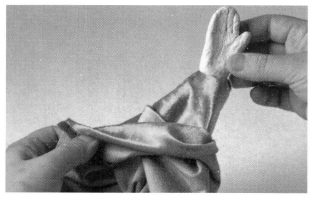

25   Repeat with the other hand, then pull the tunic the
right-way out to reveal the firmly attached hands.

26   Smear PVA adhesive around the neck and push the
tunic onto the neck, over the line of adhesive.

27   Pin, then stitch the legs to the front of the bottom
of the tunic.

410

28   *Stick gold braid around the neck, the cuffs, and down the front of the tunic.*

29   *Finally, stick braid around the hem of the tunic, covering the stitching that attaches the legs.*

The Acrobat

At last—here are simple instructions for making an articulated string puppet. These are usually quite complicated, technical projects, but when you make this acrobat you make the joints at the same time you make the puppet, so all you need is patience. You can use a proprietary papier-mâché pulp if you do not want to make your own.

You will need

- Thin galvanized wire
- Bradawl; wire cutters; pliers; screwdriver
- 2 lengths of wood, each ¾ x ¾ x 8 in. (1.5 x 1.5 x 20 cm)
- Newspaper
- 1 length of wood, ¾ x ¾ x 12 in. (1.5 x 1.5 x 30 cm)
- Wallpaper paste; clear, all-purpose adhesive
- Screw, approximately 1 in. (2.5 cm) long
- Papier-mâché pulp; acrylic primer (white)
- 7 eye hooks
- Paintbrushes (medium and small)
- 2 lengths of strong thread, each approximately 20 in. (50 cm)
- Acrylic paint (black, yellow, blue, and red)
- 2 lengths of strong thread, each approximately 16 in. (40 cm)
- Stage hair
- A length of strong thread, approximately 12 in. (30 cm)

1 *Cut a length of wire approximately 2 ft (60 cm) long. Twist a loop in the middle of this – this will be the loop in the top of the puppet's head – and roughly wind the rest of the wire around itself to make a head shape. Leave a loop of wire at what will be the neck joint.*

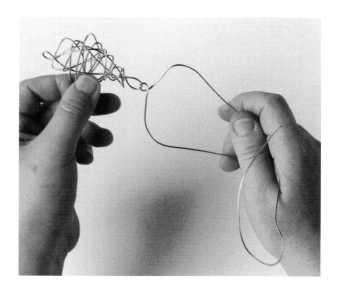

2 *Thread a length of wire, a little longer than the first piece, through the loop at the bottom of the head and twist it to secure it; this will be the neck joint. Continue twisting and bending the wire to form the shape of the upper body. Make wire loops at the shoulders and waist.*

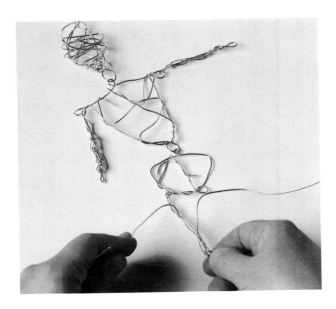

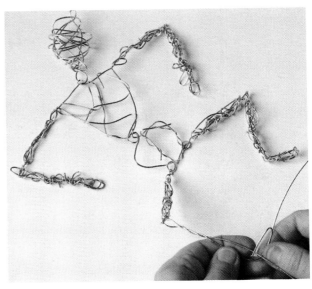

3 Use lengths of wire, approximately 20 in. (50 cm) in length, to make a pelvis, the upper arms, and the upper legs, attaching the limbs and body sections with loops of wire as before.

5 Make the lower legs and feet in the same way, again using 24 in. (60 cm) lengths of wire. No loops are needed here because the leg strings are attached at the knees.

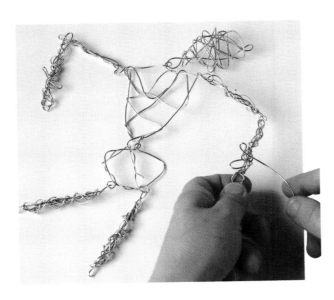

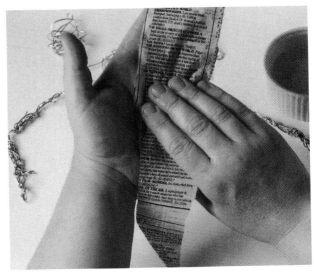

4 Add the lower arms and hands, using approximately 24 in. (60 cm) lengths of wire, leaving an upstanding loop of wire on each wrist, which are not articulated. These loops will be used to attach the arm strings.

6 Tear a length of newspaper so that it is approximately 3 in. (8 cm) wide, and smear it lightly on both sides with paste.

7   *Wind the newspaper around all the sections of the puppet, leaving all the wire loop joins free. Use two layers to build up the shape of the body.*

8   *Add paper pulp to the head and body in an even layer, about ¼ in. (6 mm) deep all over, although you can use more pulp to give the puppet more shape.*

9   *When you add pulp to the lower arm, take care that you keep the wire loop at the wrist free.*

10   *Use extra pulp to model the features on the face. Leave the puppet in a warm place to dry thoroughly.*

11   *Paint the whole puppet with a coat of acrylic primer. Use the small paintbrush to paint blue eyes, black pupils and eyebrows, and the nose and mouth. Paint on red spots for the cheeks.*

12   *Paint the puppet's upper legs, the arms as far as the wrists, and the body as far as the neck, in yellow. Paint a red outline around the neck, wrists and lower legs, then paint red spots on the yellow costume.*

13 *Paint black ballet shoes on the puppet's feet.*

14 *Smear some adhesive over the top of the head. Arrange some stage hair on the adhesive on the head and hold it in place until the adhesive is dry. Make sure the loop of wire at the top of the head is not covered with hair.*

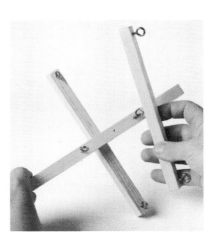

15 *Use a bradawl to make a hole in the center of the longer piece of wood and in the center of one of the shorter pieces of wood.*

16 *Screw these two lengths of wood firmly together.*

17 *Using eye hooks to form a moving joint, attach the other length of wood. Attach the remaining eye hooks.*

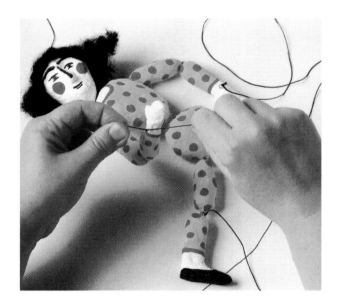

18 *Attach lengths of strong thread to the loops at the knees (approximately 20 in./50 cm), at the wrists (approximately 16 in./40 cm), and at the top of the head (approximately 12 in./30 cm). Fasten the knots tightly.*

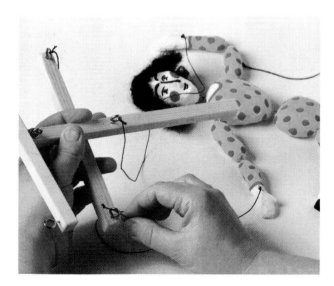

19 *Attach the other ends of the strings to the loops on the lengths of wood. The leg strings are joined to the moving section of wood; the arm strings are attached to the fixed section; and the head string is attached to the eye hook fixed just behind the crosspiece that holds the arm strings.*

SUPERMARKET SHOCKER

Be more creative with your rubbish. You can make some extraordinary characters from the mass of throwaway packaging that finds its way into our rubbish bins every day. You might even find yourself looking along the supermarket shelves, looking out for interesting shapes that you can transform into extraterrestrial puppets.

You will need

- Large plastic bottle (we used a 3½ pint/2 liter milk bottle)
- Craft knife
- Paper or fabric dishcloth (we used J-cloths)
- Thin piece of wood with rounded end (we used a chopstick)
- Plastic squeezy lemon
- Scissors
- 2 bottle tops
- Small block of wood
- Hole punch
- 2 paper fasteners

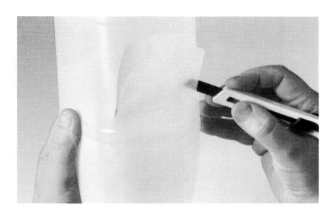

1 *Using a craft knife, carefully cut away the back section (that is, opposite to the handle) of the plastic bottle.*

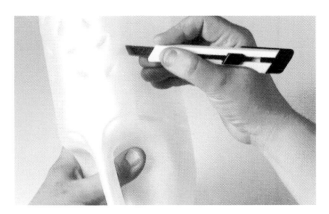

2 *Using the craft knife, make a series of small slits around the top of what will be the puppet's head.*

3 *Cut the paper dishcloth into strips, approximately ½ in. (1 cm) wide.*

4   *Fold a cut strip in two and push it into the slit with the rounded end of a thin piece of wood.*

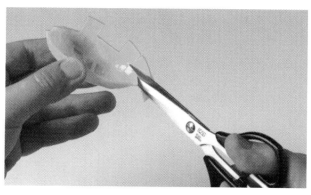

7   *Cut each lemon half into ear shapes, leaving small tabs to fix them to the head.*

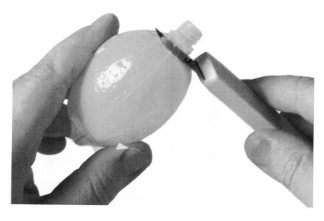

5   *Cut off the screw top from the plastic lemon.*

8   *Cut slots in the sides of the bottle head to correspond with the ears. The bottle handle will be the nose.*

6   *Cut the lemon in half lengthways; there is usually a joining line to follow.*

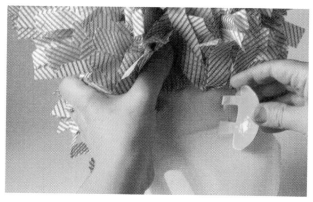

9   *Push the ear tabs into the slots in the head.*

10   *Place a bottle top on the block of wood and pierce a hole through the center with the hole punch.*

11   *Push a paper fastener through the hole in the bottle top.*

12   *Use the hole punch to make holes in the front of the face, one on each side of the handle.*

13   *Place a bottle-top eye over the hole and hold it in place by pushing the tabs of the paper fastener through the hole and, with your hand inside the bottle, pressing open the tabs. Repeat with the other eye.*

FELT FRIENDS

These small finger puppets are an ideal way to use up odd bits of felt that you might have left over from some of the other projects. Make them as bright and jolly as you can. You could add sequins, beads, jewels, or feathers to make them look more elaborate.

You will need

- Tracing paper
- Pencil
- Pins
- Felt (green, pink, red, orange)
- Sequins
- Fabric glue

Cut out two pieces of felt using this template.

Felt Friends Templates

Cut out two pieces of felt using this template.

1 Trace and cut out the templates. Pin the body template to the green felt. Cut out two pieces.

2 Cut out one pink hair shape and one red hair shape.

3 Cut the longer sides of the red and pink felt shapes into a fringe.

4 Stick sequins to the front of one of the green felt body pieces to make eyes, using a large sequin underneath and a smaller one on top for the pupil.

5 Cut small strips of orange felt and stick them to the face as eyebrows and a nose.

6   *Glue the red cheeks in place.*

9   *Stick the green body piece, with the face on it, to the back body piece so that the red and pink hair pieces are sandwiched between, with just the fringe showing.*

7   *Position the pink hair on the inside of the back body piece. Glue it down.*

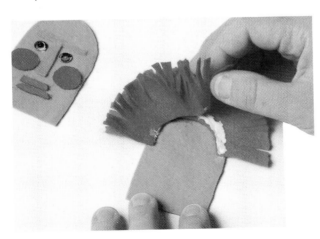

8   *Stick the red hair directly on top of the pink hair.*

FINGER FAMILY

What could be simpler than to convert an old glove into a family of whimsical characters? Each one has its own expression and entertaining hairstyle. You might want to have a happy family on one hand and a miserable family on the other.

You will need

- A woolen glove (we used an orange glove)
- White sequins
- Small, black beads
- Needle
- Sewing thread
- A piece of ¾ in. (1.5 cm) wooden dowel, approximately 12 in. (30 cm) long
- Darning needle
- Tapestry wool (black, yellow, orange, green, pink, and blue)
- Scissors

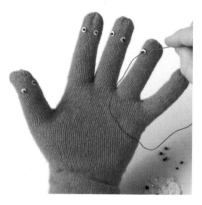

1 *Put the glove on and sew white sequins and black beads onto each finger as eyes. Push the piece of dowel into each finger in turn to support it while you sew.*

3 *Using a different color for each finger, sew loops of tapestry wool to make the hair. Trim the loops of hair evenly around each face.*

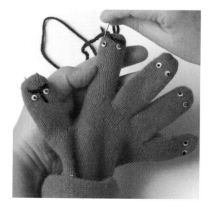

2 *Use black tapestry wool to sew eyebrows and the line of a nose on each face. Stitch the nose straight down between the sequin eyes. Sew on the mouth with yellow wool, changing the expression on each finger.*

TEMPLATES, PATTERNS, AND MOTIFS

TEMPLATES—Decorative Tiling

If you are using a different sized tile from those listed in this book or if you would prefer to create your own designs, you may need to adjust the size. The easiest way to alter the size of an outline is by photocopying.

Alternatively, use the grid method. Use a sharp pencil and ruler to draw a series of evenly spaced, parallel lines horizontally and vertically across the image. On a clean sheet of paper draw a second grid, this time with the lines spaced at a proportionately greater distance—for example, if you wanted to double the size, the lines on your first grid might be 1 in. (2.5 cm) apart on the original and 2 in. (5 cm) apart in your second grid. It is relatively simple to transfer the shapes in one square of the original grid to the corresponding square in the second grid.

CUTTING STENCILS

When you are happy with the size, go over the outlines with a fine felt-tipped pen. Use tracing paper or carbon paper to transfer the outline to stencil card. Working on a special cutting mat or on a piece of thick cardboard, use a craft knife or scalpel to cut through the lines.

Carefully made stencils can be used time and again, especially if you wipe away any paint that is left on them, using water or a solvent, and then allow them to dry flat, away from direct heat.

Sun and Moon Panel

Art Deco Fish

Stenciled Flowers

PATTERN LIBRARY—Stenciling

Magical Mirror

**Pots of Gardener's Delight
(Use the shell template
from Magical Mirrors for the
small pot)
Add pollen dots by hand**

A Framed Masterpiece

Gift Tag

Gift Tags *and*
Merry Mugs

Designer's Delight

Pots of Gardener's Delight

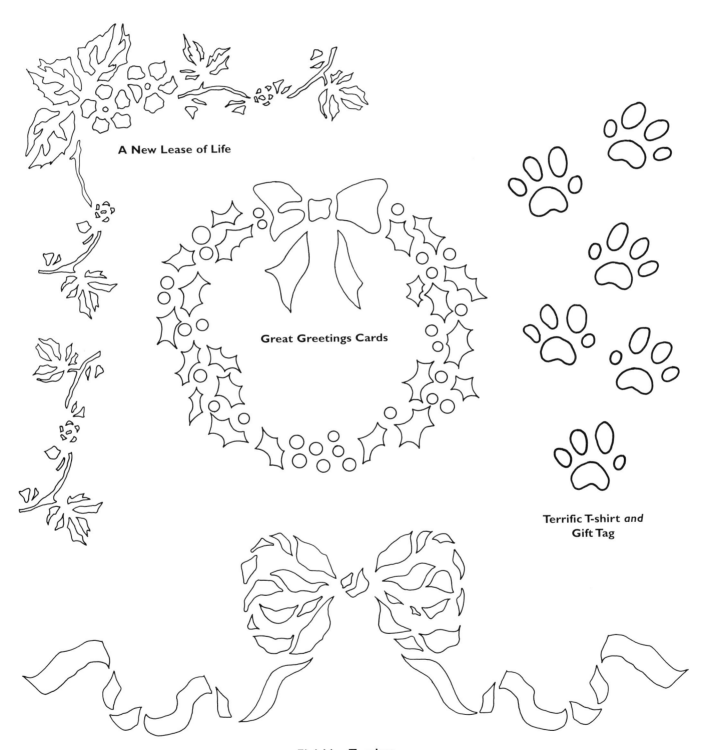

A New Lease of Life

Great Greetings Cards

Terrific T-shirt *and*
Gift Tag

Finishing Touches

Child's Cheerful Chair

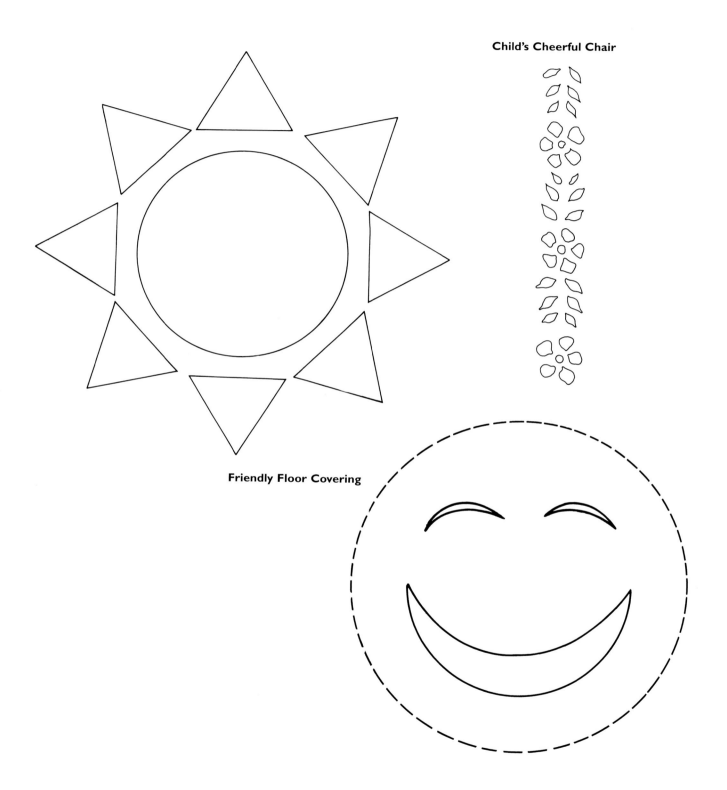

Friendly Floor Covering

MOTIFS—Decoupage

TEMPLATES—Toleware

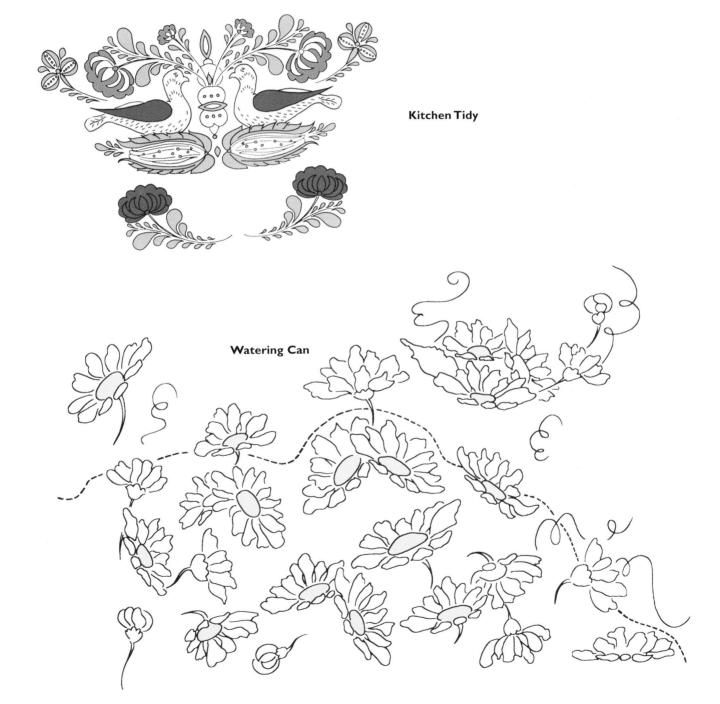

Kitchen Tidy

Watering Can

Umbrella Stand

Umbrella Stand

Lantern

Set of Pitchers

Water Fountain

Gilded Tray

Ladle

Box of Fruit

Flat Iron

TEMPLATES—Fabric Painting

DOLL

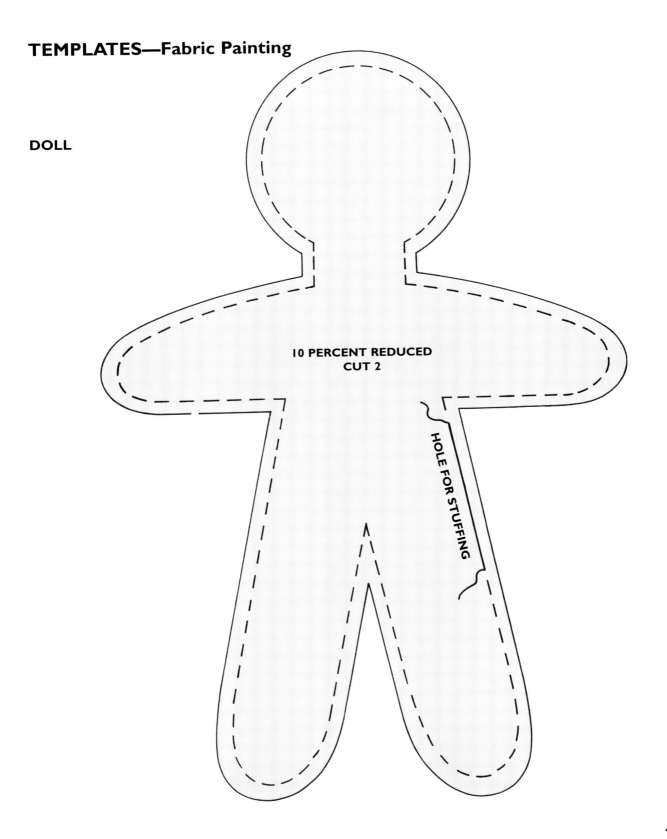

10 PERCENT REDUCED
CUT 2

HOLE FOR STUFFING

ANIMAL CUSHION

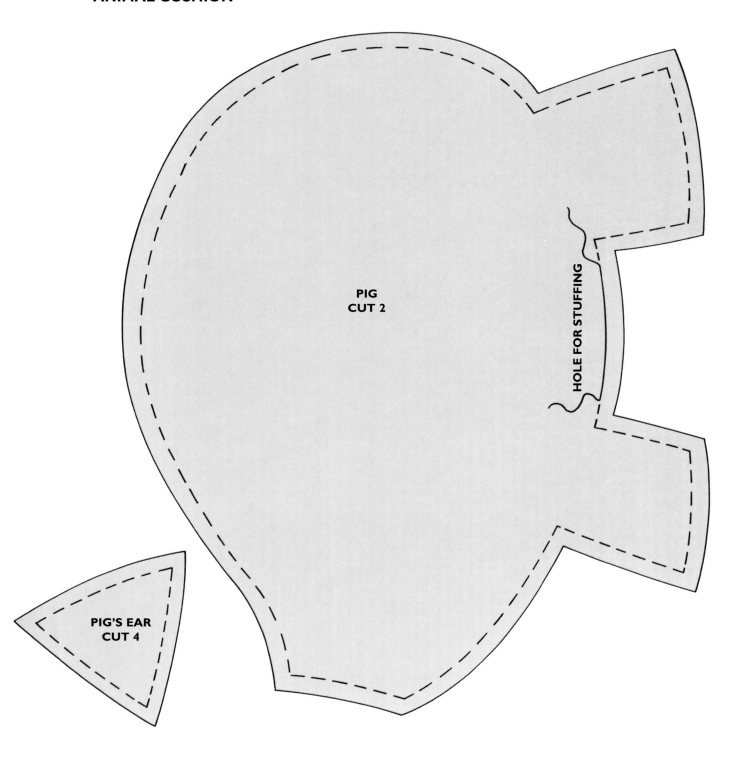

PIG
CUT 2

HOLE FOR STUFFING

PIG'S EAR
CUT 4

ANIMAL WALL HANGING

FOLK ART PICTURE

Templates at 75%

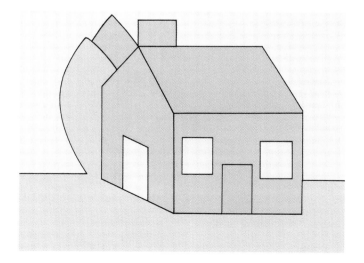

STENCILS IN PLACE

FOLK ART PICTURE

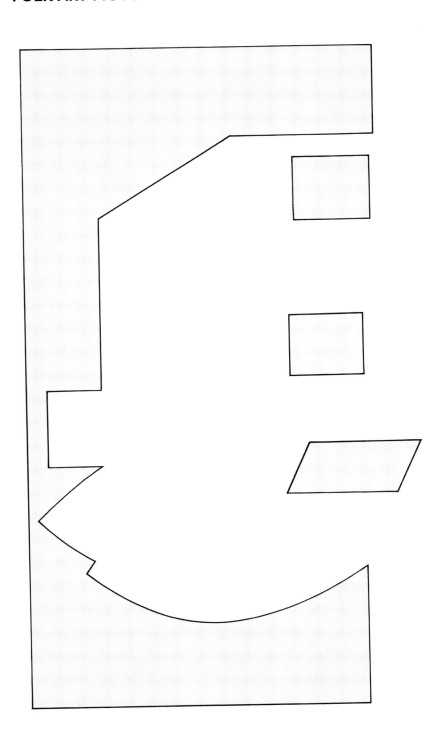

FOLK ART PICTURE

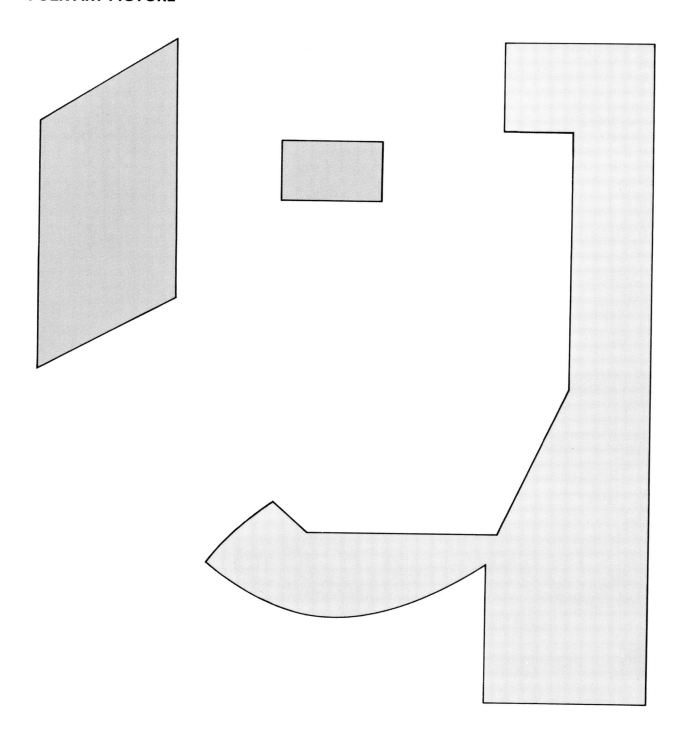

TEMPLATES—Masks

For reasons of space, the templates shown below are reduced in size by 4 times. Before you can begin work, you will need to enlarge the outlines.

The easiest method of enlarging is by photocopying. If you do not have access to a photocopier, use the grid method.

Use a sharp pencil and a ruler to draw a series of equally spaced lines across and down the original template. Surround the curved edges with the edges of a square or rectangle so that the edges of the shape just touch the straight edges. Take a large, clean sheet of paper or cardboard and draw on it a square or rectangle four times as large as the original. Cover this with vertical and horizontal lines that are spaced at twice the distance of your first grid. For example, if the original squares were an inch on the original, your squares would be 2 inches. Transfer the shapes that are visible in each small square to the corresponding larger square on the new grid. You may go over the outlines with a black felt-tip pen.

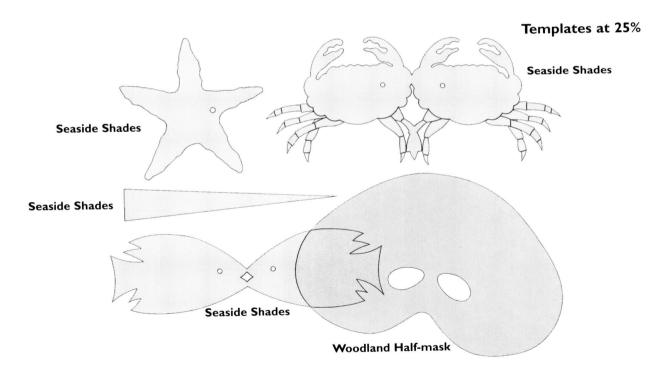

Templates at 25%

Seaside Shades

Seaside Shades

Seaside Shades

Seaside Shades

Woodland Half-mask

Templates at 25%

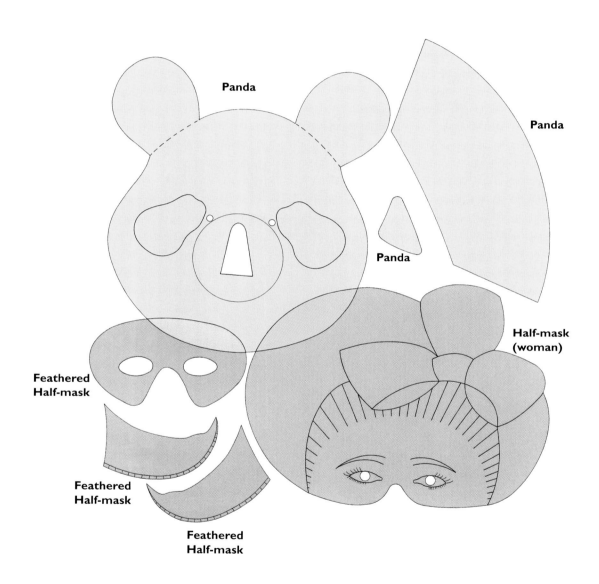

Panda

Panda

Panda

Half-mask
(woman)

Feathered
Half-mask

Feathered
Half-mask

Feathered
Half-mask

Templates at 25%

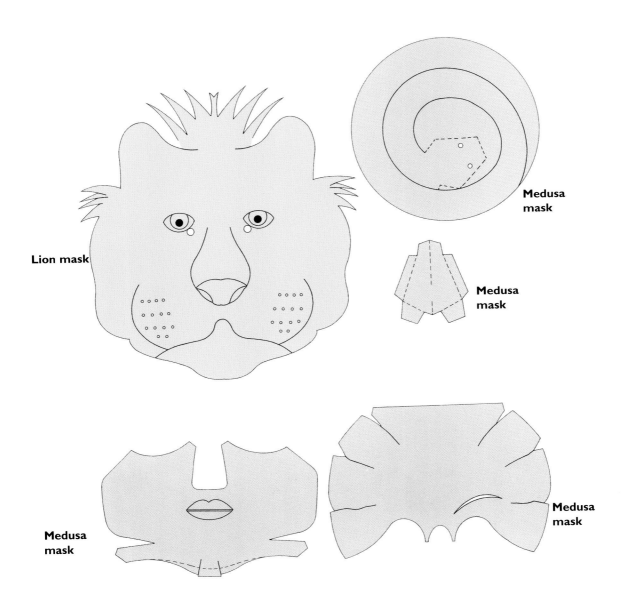

Lion mask

Medusa
mask

Medusa
mask

Medusa
mask

Medusa
mask

443

Templates at 25%

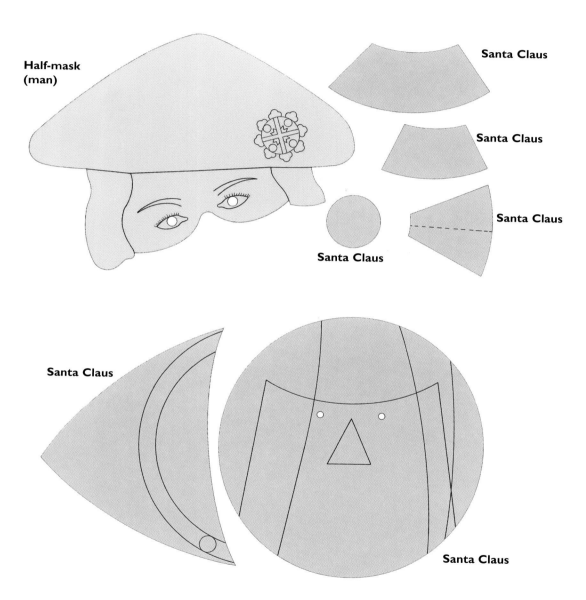

Half-mask
(man)

Santa Claus

Santa Claus

Santa Claus

Santa Claus

Santa Claus

Santa Claus

INDEX